Also By Zohar Love, DD.

PROSPERITY FROM YOUR SOUL: The Metaphysics of co-Creating Your Ideal Life

Seven Stages to co-Creating PROSPERITY FROM YOUR SOUL: A Meditational Manual to Help You Reclaim Your Ideal Lifepath

Coming Soon

Books:

Reiki – The Light of Your Soul: USUI REIKI RYOHO—臼 井 靈 気 療 法 As Originally Taught by Mikao Usui Sensei

Innovative Modalities:

RezoDance: meditative healing movement imbued with reiki energy and Nature elements to affect complete balance, and harness the freedom of spirit to affect freedom of mind and body.

Rezossage: holistic massage modality that treats the whole person, and affects deep changes in a nurturing way. Deep tissue massage without pain!

Retreat Courses:

Level 1 – Prosperity From Your Soul: Combining the metaphysical understandings of the book Prosperity From Your Soul, with reiki training, and RezoDance empowerment, leading you through the Seven Stages of tuning into your Ideal Lifeplan, and devising a specific plan of action to manifest it. A weeklong retreat.

Level 2 – Soul Communications & Soul Mates: Learn to employ True communications in all of your relationships, from the business place to your Soulmates, and by that, magnetize a higher degree of happiness, health, and True abundance into your life. A weeklong retreat course, which includes Second Degree reiki training, as well as a Kindness Massage training.

Level 3 – Reiki Mastership & RezoDance Facilitators Course: Become empowered as a reiki master, and learn the art of hosting and facilitating RezoDance sessions. A weeklong retreat, which empowers and prepares participants to open their own reiki school and RezoDance studio.

Level 4 – Rezossage Course: A yearlong 650-hour course, which teaches the art of Rezossage.

A Lifestyle of
Prosperity
From Your
Soul

A Guide to Living a Prosperity-Magnetizing Lifestyle

Zohar Love

BALBOA.
PRESS

A DIVISION OF HAY HOUSE

Balboa Press books may be ordered through booksellers or by contacting:

Balboa Press
A Division of Hay House
1663 Liberty Drive
Bloomington, IN 47403
www.balboapress.com
1 (877) 407-4847

Because of the dynamic nature of the Internet, any web addresses or links contained in this book may have changed since publication and may no longer be valid. The views expressed in this work are solely those of the author and do not necessarily reflect the views of the publisher, and the publisher hereby disclaims any responsibility for them.

The author of this book does not dispense medical advice or prescribe the use of any technique as a form of treatment for physical, emotional, or medical problems without the advice of a physician, either directly or indirectly. The intent of the author is only to offer information of a general nature to help you in your quest for emotional and spiritual well-being. In the event you use any of the information in this book for yourself, which is your constitutional right, the author and the publisher assume no responsibility for your actions.

Any people depicted in stock imagery provided by Thinkstock are models,
and such images are being used for illustrative purposes only.
Certain stock imagery © Thinkstock.

ISBN: 978-1-5043-3935-3 (sc)
ISBN: 978-1-5043-3936-0 (e)

Print information available on the last page.

Balboa Press rev. date: 09/15/2015

Contents

Introduction

You are the powerful co-Creator of your life. Because your Soul is an integral part of Its Creator, It is always blissful, and blessed with every Abundance available to the Divine, which serves Its highest purpose. Therefore, Infinite prosperity—from the Divine—is already yours, if you listen to the wisdom of your very own Soul, and walk the Ideal Lifepath that It has laid out for you. In *Seven Stages to co-Creating Prosperity From Your Soul,* we've done together some, quite literally, Soul-searching meditations, in which we have each developed intimate relationships with our loving, radiant Souls, and have become privy to the details of our Ideal Lifeplans—the plan that each Soul makes for its person's most auspicious life, in terms of fulfilling our life missions with ease, living our bliss, and harvesting the most abundant, easily flowing prosperity.

This book is about anchoring the metaphysical understandings of *Prosperity From Your Soul,* and the meditational realizations that you've had in *Seven Stages to co-Creating Prosperity From Your Soul,* into reality. For beyond the metaphysical understandings, beyond knowing what your Ideal Lifeplan of prosperity looks like, and even beyond having a specific Plan of Action in terms of steps to take to merge with your Ideal Life, everything that we've talked about so far still needs to stand the test of reality. And the reality that we are talking about here is a reality in which your esoteric understandings, as well as your meditational inner knowings, drive your here-now reality to merge with your Ideal Life—a life in which prosperity, in the fullest sense of the word, is not only co-Created for you ethereally, but also manifests in your physical reality. And the fullest definition of prosperity includes not only an abundance of financial resources, but also health, happiness, and every blessing that you Truly wish for.

To fully merge the current reality of your life with your Ideal Lifepath, two things must happen: You must take some steps to start navigating your current life towards your Ideal Lifeplan, which you've already meditationally seen; and you must stay in a prosperity-magnetizing high vibration on a continuous basis. When taking steps to navigate your life towards your Ideal Lifepath, your actions need to be a balance between doing—taking the steps that you have meditationally decided on as your Plan of Action (see Chapter 7 of *Seven Stages to co-Creating Prosperity From Your Soul),* and receiving—allowing the Universe to meet you halfway and assist you. This is a concept that we've called Setting Your Vision Free. The second requirement— getting into, and staying in a prosperity-magnetizing high vibration on a continuous basis—is achieved by finding the Balance of Grace daily. The Balance of Grace is the balance between the peaceful bliss of your Soul and the vitality of being zestfully alive in your here-now reality, between being optimistic and being realistic. It is a balance that gives you the wonderful feeling of being totally validated just for being you, without having to do anything to justify your existence, but be authentically you. It is the deep feeling within that everything is absolutely going to be more than okay in the greater sense; and it is! It is the combination of taking the steps towards your Ideal Life while setting your vision free, and maintaining the Balance of Grace, that takes you from your 'now' reality into the reality of your Ideal Life, which is naturally endowed with all-inclusive prosperity.

So how can we each find the perfect balance between doing and setting one's vision free, as well as maintain the Balance of Grace – all on a continuous basis? Well, the only version of you for whom the Balance of Grace, and the trust in the Divine Plan that it takes to set your vision free, are natural and effortless, is the Ideal-you (see Chapter 6 of *Seven Stages to co-Creating Prosperity From Your Soul*). In other words, if you can envision yourself maintaining the Balance of Grace on a daily basis, and talking the steps outlined in your Plan of Action while setting your vision free, the 'you' that you are internally seeing is the Ideal-you. This Ideal-you is not quite your Soul Self, yet it is not your current here-now self, but is the way that your Soul has intended your here-now self to be—the best version of your here-now self, which your Soul is still holding space for you to become. In other words, it is a 'you' that is tapped into the wisdom, abundance, and Light-Love of your Soul, yet at the same time grounds all these gifts into your here-now reality in the most graceful way. It is the 'you' that enjoys both your Heavenly and earthly worlds.

Another reason why is this Ideal-you so important to your path as a successful co-Creator is that besides having a natural affinity to maintaining the Balance of Grace, and having the peace of knowing that your most heartfelt wishes are already co-Created, the Ideal-you is also the 'you' that brings forth into this reality your Truest gifts and passions. Therefore becoming this Ideal-you is what's going to lead you to your Ideal Lifework—the Ideal work or endeavor that best capitalizes on your Truest passions and talents, while staying in a joyous, prosperity-magnetizing vibration. Therefore, it is the Ideal-you—as you've meditationally envisioned him or her—that has the best potential for grounding the all-inclusive prosperity of your Soul into manifested reality.

This is where this book comes in. This book is really about giving you some physical tools to merge with the Ideal-you, and your current life with your Ideal Life. There are three bridges that will help that merge happen, and will therefore help pour the ethereal co-Creation of your Ideal Life into physical manifestation in your here-now reality: lifestyle—making room in your life for the new endeavors of prosperity (actions, projects, new careers or investments, and of course gifts from the Universe) that are now going to pour in through your Infinite Funnel of Abundance; physical—getting your physical body to feel vivacious and light; and Vibrational—elevating your body-temple to be a clear and good vessel for bringing forth enhanced Creative energy from your Soul (as One with the Divine Creative energy), through your energetic bodies, and into your physical reality. To truly walk the path of a conscious co-Creator, and to manifest the abundance that comes along with it, your physical life needs to mirror your emotional and spiritual life. And here is how this plays:

Understanding the second bridge is somewhat intuitive: one needs manifest health in one's physical body in order to be able to handle all the tasks of the new auspicious Plan of Action, with ease, lightness, and joy. To understand the first bridge—making room in one's life for new things to come into it, imagine yourself having an all-you-can-eat buffet, where the one rule is that you cannot get a second plate. You can go for more as many times as you want, but you must load your original plate in such a way that when you want more, there is room on it for more. In that case, it would be wise to ensure that the only things that are on your plate are things you actually like, which are nutritious and good for you. In the same way, you need to make sure that everything that is on the plate of your life—lifestyle wise—are things that are good for you from the highest perspective possible: not necessarily the things that you perceive that others, or circumstances, require of you, but things that actually bring you absolute feelings of love and joy. The third bridge is the real ace in the hole: the most important thing that this book will help you achieve is raising the energetic vibration of your body-temple and lifestyle, into a high vibration that resonates with the Infinite Abundance of your Soul, thereby helping you magnetize the prosperous Life that your Soul has chosen for you. Since your body-temple is the vessel through which your Soul has chosen to experience this lifetime, all co-Creations must be anchored within your physical and energetic bodies in order to manifest in your physical reality.

The physical practices given in this book will help you walk the path of a conscious co-Creator in the physical sense—they will help you anchor the potent co-Creative Light of your Soul into your everyday life, physical body, and vibrational self, thus helping you create a good physical foundation for the manifestation of prosperity.

In the last chapter of *Seven Stages to co-Creating Prosperity From Your Soul*, I've mentioned that as marvelous as your meditations were, and as detailed as your notes of your Ideal Life meditations may have been, your Plan to merge your current reality with your Ideal Life was, most likely, not yet complete, and that the more you walk, in your everyday life, the path of a *conscious* co-Creator, the more steps will continue to come to you, both meditationally and synchronistically, to beef up your initial auspicious To Do list into a real Plan of Action that you can follow in your here-now reality. We've talked about the Infinite Funnel of Abundance in the context of your Plan, and have realized that the Infinite Funnel of Abundance does not normally come like lightening on a bright summer day, but instead, finds us each in the "small" moments of our lives, taking us subtly closer to our Ideal Lives with each day that we live as *conscious* co-Creators… until one day, the realization dawns on us that we are walking our Ideal Lifepaths, or are at least at a spot from where we can already see how our lives are about to merge with our Ideal Lives. The physical practices introduced in this book will help you walk the path of your everyday life while connected to the wisdom and Light of your Soul, making it easy to perceive new ideas, and stay in the auspicious synchronistic flow of the Universe.

Of course, on a Soul level, Infinite Abundance has always been yours. Your deepest wishes are co-Created ethereally just as soon as you perceive and desire them. The issue is how to pull them into manifestation in your here-now reality. And actual manifestation of goodies happens at the intersection between the riches of your Soul and your physical reality—where the Infinite Funnel of Abundance actually pours into you and your life, which depends not only on the Free Will of your Soul, but also on the free will of your here-now self (free will is a fundamental law of Creation, which permeates every level). So in this book, we are going to prepare a physical foundation that is open, and capable of accepting and pulling all that abundance into your physical reality.

The relationship between the physical and the spiritual aspects of you could stand some clarification: It isn't that we are physical beings trying to have a spiritual experience. It's the other way around: We are all spiritual beings first and last. It is only at some point in the middle that we come here to have "physical" lives on Earth. And within our multidimensional reality, the notion that changes must happen on a physical level first is a common misconception. The Truth is that physical changes (in both your body and your reality) are but the results of changes that have already occurred on the spiritual-ethereal level of your reality. Therefore physical changes are the last to manifest. All changes in the reality of our lives manifest spiritually-energetically first. Then they filter into the mental and emotional levels (Mental Body and Astral Body), and only lastly, they manifest as changes in our health and in the physical circumstances of our lives.

That being said, the interaction between the spiritual and the physical aspects of reality is a two-way street. The physical arena is also important, because it is the one through which our Souls have each chosen to experience this lifetime. And in order to follow through and reap the rewards that this incarnation affords us, our Souls maintain close interactions with the physical (otherwise you would not be breathing or reading these lines), such that our physical and spiritual realities flow into one another harmoniously. The first direction of flow is from the Heavenly realms of the Soul into manifestation in the physical reality. The second direction of flow, which is also important in the context of this particular lifetime, is from the physical into the ethereal. And in that direction, because of the energetic density and vibrational slowness of this material realm, things or conditions that have already manifested as "physical" seem to take longer to change. I can personally attest to how much longer it takes, for example, to lose weight, once you have manifested the extra pounds in your physical body.

Since the direction of flow that we are most interested in is the integration of co-Creative energies into the physical, let's expand just a little bit on the bridges that facilitate this flow:

On a physical level, it would be very difficult to be vivacious and energetic enough to take the steps towards your Ideal Lifepath, which you have meditationally decided were part of your Plan of Action, if your physical body is deprived, or suffers in any way, especially if you initially have to moonlight some of the activities of your new projects. Unless you are one of those saintly people who are conditioned from a very young age to sit on a mountaintop chanting Om all day, surviving on a few leaves of grass, most of us ordinary humans have needs that behave according to Maslow's Pyramid of Needs: we need to satisfy our basic physical needs before we can thrive mentally and emotionally; and we need to have our mental-emotional needs met before we can proceed to self actualization and manifestation of freedom, joy, love, and abundance.

On an energetic level, the integration of spiritual energy into one's physical existence can also be greatly effected by the physical wellbeing of the body-temple. Because your body is the temple that houses your Soul's energy and facilitates Its experiences in this lifetime, when this vessel is out of balance, the flow of life-giving and Creative energies into it can become restricted, or sometimes even blocked. This can cause you to experience a whole array of medical problems; and it can cause you to harbor emotions, and display actions that are not in line with your

Soul Self. For example, the most angelic woman I know, who is normally a very loving, kind, compassionate, and spiritual person, suffers from severe PMS, during which time she experiences moods swings, depression, and a level of agitation that make her lose her temper with people. So if the most angelic person can be so influenced by the imbalances of her physical body, how do you think the average Joe or Jane would react to imbalances in the physical body? And since health and happiness are both part of your Ideal Lifepath, than from this perspective alone, it becomes evident that you must bring your body-temple into a healthy balance in order to prepare a healthy foundation for all the abundance that you are now going to co-Create into your life.

Metaphysically speaking, if there is energetic density or stuck energy in the physical layers of one's reality (such as ill health, stress, overly hectic schedule, the plate of one's life being too full, lack of sleep and downtime, malnutrition, a physical-emotional heaviness, and the like), than that dense or stuck energy can prevent the Infinite Funnel of Abundance form flowing into one's life and manifesting in the physical. The bottom line is: since you are going to bring such massive amounts of new Creative energy into your life, it would behoove you to prepare your body-vessel and lifestyle (physically and vibrationally) to receive such energies.

In this book, I will touch on lifestyle, sleep, relaxation, exercise and nutrition from the perspective of integrating your Soul's co-Creative energies into your physical body and life. While I have researched and summarized some information from scientific sources for the discussions of this book, the emphasis here is on *energetically-vibrationally* preparing your body-temple and lifestyle to receive the enhanced amount of Creative energy that's coming through your Infinite Funnel of Abundance, to prepare for the prosperity that you are now magnetizing into your life.

We'll start with gentle lifestyle changes, and then proceed to reclaim the multidimensional health of our body-temples:

In Chapter 1, we are going to make room in our lives for both kindness-to-self practices, and for the additional actions, endeavors, and Universal gifts, which are now going to come into our lives as part of our new Plans of Action to merge our lives with our Ideal Lifepaths. In Chapter 2, as part arranging the larger elements of our lives in a way that fosters the upbeat feelings and a prosperity-magnetizing vibration, we'll talk about the importance of getting adequate sleep, as it relates to your Ideal Lifepath, and I'll relate some natural practices that will help you get a good night sleep.

Then, once we've balanced all the bigger elements of our lives, in Chapter 3-5, we are going to shift our body-temples into a state radiant health, so that they can serve us well on our new path, and so that their higher vibratory rates can better facilitate the in-pour of new Creative energy into our co-Creative endeavors. Chapter 3 introduces some physical practices that will help you let go of any stuck energy, and find lightness, freedom, and balance in your body-temple. Chapter 4 discusses nutrition from a holistic perspective—being mindful of what you are becoming one with. And Chapter 5 details **the Zohar Kindness Diet**, which **allows weight loss** (if you need to lose weight) **by adding (not subtracting) things into your diet and lifestyle.** Even if you don't need to lose any weight, the Zohar Kindness Diet puts together all the kindness-to-self practices, in a way that will help you integrate into yourself and your life the Creative resources that the Universe has in store for you.

Finally, in Chapter 6, I'll give you some practices that will help you more fully integrate the vibration of your Soul into your body-temple and reality, for the manifestation of your Ideal Lifepath of prosperity, health and happiness.

So let's start walking the path of conscious co-Creators together.

Chapter 1

A Lifestyle of Joy

We now stand at the threshold of a life that integrates the Infinite Abundance of the Soul into our here-now existence. This is the point at which we each start walking the path of a conscious co-Creator, taking sure steps to merge our 'now' realities with our Ideal Lifepaths, according to our meditational insights, as inspired by our Souls, and as prompted by the synchronistic signs that the Universe is giving us along the way.

Before we can each merge with our Ideal Lifepath of all-inclusive prosperity, we must first look at our current lives from the perspective of a conscious observer, and compare them with the realities that we have each meditationally experienced as our Ideal Lives (Chapter 7 of *Seven Stages to co-Creating Prosperity From Your Soul*). So if you take a step back, and look at the plate of your life from the consciously observant point of view, what do you see? Do you see the clutter of too many tasks, and too many elements that are not in harmony with one another? Or are all the elements harmoniously balanced on your plate? Is your plate full with many tasks and activities that you do not enjoy? Or is everything on that plate positive and enjoyable? Is the plate of your life filled with twelve daily hours of work outside the house, plus four more hours of chores and doing things for others, leaving inadequate time for sleep, and no time at all for joy? Or do you get to reap the rewards of your hard work and actually enjoy your life?

Once you have observed your life consciously, the first physical step that you can take towards the rendezvous point with your Ideal Lifepath is to manage the larger elements of your life in a balanced way that more closely resembles the harmony of your Ideal Life, which as you'll find out through this chapter, is not as hard to do as it may initially seem.

Balancing all the elements of your life will do three things that directly relate to the manifestation of all-inclusive prosperity: First, as it relates to the metaphysics of Abundance, this balance will give you a peaceful-yet-vivacious feeling that will help shift your vibrational energy into likeness and resonance with the prosperity you seek, therefore magnetizing it into your life. From a more mundane point of view, harmony and balance amongst all the elements of your life will affect better physical, mental, and emotional health, as you will no longer have to run around like a crazed rabbit. You could relax, live your life more joyfully, and release a sigh of relief. And health and happiness are certainly parts of all-inclusive prosperity.

1

Secondly, finding this balance is an exercise of free will. To take control of your life as a conscious co-Creator, the free will of your here-now self should now be an extension of your Soul's Free Will. Bringing your meditational realizations into here-now manifested reality starts with exercising control over the arrangement of all the elements of your life in a way that your loving Soul would approve of—a way that incorporates kindness-to-self.

And Thirdly, and perhaps most importantly, let me ask you this: If the Universe were to drop on your doorstep tomorrow morning all the gifts that you wish for, like a stork that's dropping off a baby, would you actually have room for those gifts in your life? Let's say that as part of your Ideal Life, which you have meditational perceived in *Seven Stages to co-Creating Prosperity From Your Soul*, you have a dream endeavor that would bring you much joy, prosperity, and self-fulfillment. If at tomorrow at lunchtime, you were to synchronistically meet the philanthropic investor that wants to make your dream a reality, are you ready? Do you even have time in your schedule to *get* ready for that chance meeting, and to do all the planning involved, such as writing down your idea in a way that is presentable to such an investor?

In this chapter, we are going to talk about arranging your life elements in a way that will make room in it for your new path of prosperity: We are going to discuss taking out of your life elements that do not serve your highest wellbeing, such as <u>over</u>working in a job or occupation that is not part of your Ideal Lifeplan (not yet quitting the old job, but just putting the work that you do in perspective of what's really important in life); bending over backwards to satisfy others instead of your Self; watching too much television, and any other habits that do not serve your highest wellbeing. By the same token, we are going to add onto the plate of your life the things that do serve your highest wellbeing and your new path as a successful co-Creator of your life, such as your Me Time, time to take some of the steps outlined by your auspicious Plan of Action to merge with your Ideal Life, a kindness-to-self attitude, and most importantly, time to do the things that you enjoy—the things that make you authentically you. Then, once we have eradicated from the plate of your life what no longer serves, and added what does serve your new prosperous path, the task is to arrange all the elements of your life in a balance that promotes health, happiness, and the magnetizing of prosperity, which essentially means that you have to have enough time in your day not only for work, but also for sleep, Me Time, meditational downtime, Joyful Physical Activity, the activities of your Plan, and the activities that you enjoy because they are part of who you Truly are.

"To every thing there is a season, and a time to every purpose under heaven." As it relates to manifesting prosperity from your Soul, sure there is time to work, but even the work that you do do should be an enjoyable one, and should leave enough room in your life for enjoyment; there is the time to take steps to bring your Ideal Life into fruition, and a time to *allow* the Universe to step in and help you; there is a time for joyful physical activity (more on that in Chapter 3), and a time to rest and sleep (Chapter 2); there is a time to be meditative and inward, and a time to go out into the world, socialize, and do fun things.

Once you do this major rearranging, and bring all the elements of your life into a harmony that serves your total Self, you become exponentially more ripe for the Universe to meet you halfway and help bring to you the auspicious gifts of your Ideal Life.

What You Should Add to Your Lifestyle

Before we talk about any low-vibrational habits or life-elements that you should (kindly) let go of, let's first talk about the positive things that you should be adding to your life, and how adding them relates to your co-Creating prosperity from your Soul. There are two reasons why, in this case, it's better to start with adding kind things, rather than subtracting the unkind ones: first, in order to motivate yourself to organize your life in a more balanced way, you need to have a taste of the rewards—some of the fabulous things that you are making room for. Sure, once you organize your life, there'll be some synchronistic opportunities that the Universe will flow your way. But at this point, those may not be tangibly palpable yet, whereas the immediate joy that you'll feel from the positive things that you *choose to* add to your life *now* is a more immediate motivator. Secondly, as we shall see later in this chapter, adding positive habits and elements into your life actually gives you the power to change any habit, or let go of any elements that do not serve your highest wellbeing and your Ideal Lifepath of prosperity.

So what is it that we are adding into our new lifestyle of all-inclusive prosperity? Simply stated, things that you should be adding to your new lifepath, because they serve your purpose of becoming a conscious co-Creator and successfully manifesting the blessings of your Ideal Life into reality are: a kindness-to-self attitude, Me Time (more on that in a little bit), time to do the things that you enjoy, which make you authentically you, and also time to take some of the steps that you were meditationally Guided to add to your auspicious To Do list—your Plan of Action to merge your current life with your Ideal Life. And here is why these things, which at first look might seem indulgent, are actually so important to your success:

As you know, the key to co-Creating a healthy, happy, and abundant life is to be authentically you—the Ideal-you that your Soul is holding space for you to be, and to live the Ideal, most auspicious Life that your Soul has planned for you. So as you are now molding your lifestyle into one that is conducive to co-Creating prosperity from your Soul, as you fill the daily schedule of your new life with new things, you need to make sure that you remember to reserve time in it for yourself to do the things that make you happy, healthy, and authentically you. Because the meaning of life isn't to make money or to succeed in your career; it's to experience Love and joy. The funny thing is that as you schedule time for yourself to enjoy life, you are also magnetizing more financial abundance into your life. I know it may initially seem like a paradox. But remember that in order to stay in a vibration that resonates with, and therefore attracts Divine Abundance into manifestation in your life, you must enjoy your life. The pillars of prosperity from your Soul are love, joy, self-validation, and kindness, because those are the feelings-vibrations that resonate with, and therefore magnetize into existence, the abundance of the Divine. Your joyful Me Time, even if it's just one hour that you stake out for yourself each day, also shifts the rest of your day into a joyous vibration, which connects you with Divine prosperity. And scheduling (staking-out) your Me Time becomes easier to do, if it comes out of a deep sense of self-validation, knowing whom you Truly are, and internalizing the feeling that you are worthy of every good thing. You wouldn't consider telling your child that you don't have time to cook dinner for her/him, that you don't have time to play with him/her, or that you don't have the time to love him/her, right?

Why the heck would you consider telling the innocent, radiant child within you that you don't have time to do the things that bring him/her joy?!

Kindness to Self:

Kindness-to-self is a huge concept in the manifestation of prosperity, because it energetically puts you in a mode that is receptive to all the Universal gifts that are now going to fall into your lap. Essentially, you have to feel validated and worthy, to be receptive. Just like in ordinary here-now reality, if someone gives you a gift that you don't feel you deserve, you might turn that gift down, even if the giver's motives are pure. It works the same way with regards to receiving gifts from the Universe—you have to be receptive in order to attract Universal abundance to you.

So from now on, everything you think, feel, and do, and every step that you take, should be with an air of "I'm fabulous," and be dipped in kindness-to-self. Remember, though, the three-faceted nature of kindness: sometimes kindness-to-self would dictate that you push yourself forward to become all that you can be; other times it means that you let yourself off the hook, indulge for a while, and not feel guilty in the least bit about it; and whichever side of the equation you take on any particular day, remember that through every situation and through each difficulty, there is always a softer, gentler, kinder-to-yourself way to do things—the way of grace and Grace.

Staking-Out Your Me Time:

A good place to start introducing into your life an actual practice that would help you affirm kindness-to-self, and thus help you reconnect with joy, is to stake out one hour a day for yourself, in which to do… absolutely nothing! No chores. No screaming kids. No ironing of your spouse's shirts. No changing the oil of your spouse's car. No shopping. No work. In fact, no cellphone. And no thinking of mounting chores either. Before you start your Me Time hour, just jot down everything that still needs to be done in a To Do list, tuck that list somewhere in a drawer and out of your mind, and *just be…* for one hour each day! You can start by saying to yourself – "Today, for this hour, I am free, and I am doing something just for me!" or even, "I'm fabulous. Life is fabulous!"

From that point of proving to yourself that you can have that hour just for you, you can start integrating simple things that make you happy. For example, you can take a little enjoyable walk on the beach (or in park), or even just sit on a bench and stare at the ocean (the mountains, the sunset, or anything beautiful) for a while. You can even just find a quiet place to recline in, close your eyes, and be immersed in music that sends you to the height of joy and Oneness. The point is, just stake out an hour each day to remind yourself of whom you Truly are—a very beloved child of the Divine, who is very worthy of every good thing! Leave guilt out of it for an hour. Take that time to really feel the peace and beauty within and all around you.

As you progress along your path as a conscious co-Creator of your Ideal Lifepath, you can then build on this Me Time practice, by spending some of it on joyful physical activity, such as meditational swimming, Happy Back Walk, Nature Walk (see Chapter 3), or any other activity that brings freedom and relaxation to your body, clears your mind, and makes you feel joy.

This is your daily hour to do something that reminds you that life is not a mundane jumble of dutiful chores, but something worth living—that life is something you must grab by the balls and say, "here I am!" Not to be corny, but if you have the opportunity to spend your Me Time hour making passionate love with your Soulmate, I'd go for it in a heartbeat. But even if you don't yet have that opportunity, or if what's 'calling' you is more alone time, still, this is your hour for making love with life itself, and with your Soul who is facilitating this life for you. It is your time to experience all that is Divine within life—beauty, joy, love, pleasure, peace, and absolute aliveness. And depending on which one of those you actually need at that present moment in your life, you'd pick the appropriate joyful activity that brings that vibration into your life.

Enjoying your Me Time, and not feeling guilty about it, is a first step. At first, this practice may seem forced, trivial, or even irrelevant to your process of co-Creating prosperity. Your mind will likely go to that "efficiency" mode of thinking, "Well, if I'm going to start a new path in life, there must be something productive and efficient I can do." And when this happens, just Stop! Do not allow your mind to go to all the things that are troubling you at that moment in life, or rundown all the things you think you need to be doing at this time. Consciously and actively drive your mind to think positive, pleasant thoughts, and reconnect you with your inner-child, joy, and the feeling of worthiness. Training yourself to stake out your Me Time is the most productive thing you can do right now towards your new prosperity path. Because as trivial as it may seem to stake out an hour a day in which to do nothing, consider that even if you sit for the whole hour and just stare at the ocean, you are not doing nothing. You are reconnecting with beauty and joy, and you are affirming that you love yourself enough to feel worthy of them. So in affect, this simple hour of doing "nothing" is helping you reconnect with joy-Love-beauty—the energetic essence of the Divine, and thus shifting your energetic vibration into resonance with True prosperity.

Ambrosial Time:

Most ancient yogic traditions are adamant about doing their spiritual practices at the ambrosial hours before either sunrise or sunset, generally between four and seven. However, the new information that I have received in my channeling is that the ambrosial time in the day for Me Time practices may actually be different for each of us.

For some people it may very well be the hours just before sunset or sunrise, as those hours do have certain peace about them. But for a full-time mother of three school kids, for example, the most opportune time for personal practices may be the morning hours, after dropping her kids off at school, and before cleaning the house, running errands, and cooking for her family. For a busy executive, the best time may be in the early morning before going to work, but not necessarily at 4 am. You can do just as good a meditation or a walk at 7 or 8 am. For other people, the quietest, most peaceful time for Me Time might be during a long lunch, after leaving the office at 5 pm before dinner, or even late in the evening, under the moon, when the whole world is peaceful.

Your most auspicious time of the day for staking out your Me Time may be non-conventional, as you may have an unconventional schedule. If you really want to find your Me Time, you may have to think outside the box. And what you decide to do may not be what the old yogis recommended, or even what everyone else is doing. What makes your Me Time "ambrosial"— what makes that time sweet in its taste, fragrant in its smell, and divinely auspicious in its feel, is your intent: the fact that you have staked out that time to connect with your True Self, and give yourself all of Its Love, in various ways.

If your Me Time practices include a Nature Walk (Chapter 3), consider that different times of the day bring about different effects, in terms of the healing energies that you derive from nature. Doreen Virtue, a channeler of Angel information and an author whose insight I've come to trust over the years, writes in her book *Angel Medicine* about the effects that natural light, in its various colors spectrum, has on healing. According to Virtue, the red, orange and yellow colors of the sunset have healing effects on our first, second, and third chakras, respectively; moon and starlight heal and activate the third-eye and throat chakras; sunrise light heals the heart chakra; and sunlight in general balances the upper and lower chakras. Doreen emphasizes that when she talks about the healing powers of the sun, moon, and stars, she does not mean standing indoors and observing the sunlight or sunset through your window, but actually being outdoors and bathing in their light.

However, I am a big believer in listening to your internal wisdom. Let your Soul and your inner feelings guide you on what the best time is for you to stake out your Me Time.

Time to Take Steps Towards Your Ideal Life:

In Chapter 8 of *Seven Stages to co-Creating Prosperity From Your Soul,* we've talked about the two balances, which this book will help you find: The Balance of Grace, and the balance between actively taking steps to make your Ideal Life a reality, and Setting Your Vision Free. We've talked about the high level of trust in the Divine plan for you that setting your vision free takes. In Chapter 7 of *Seven Stages to co-Creating Prosperity From Your Soul,* after you tuned into your Ideal Life, we did a Meditation To Devise A Plan Of Action, in which you came up with your initial auspicious To Do list, containing the first steps towards reclaiming your Ideal Life. The integration of these concepts into your lifestyle and schedule is worth reiterating here:

As we've come to understand, the prosperity of your Ideal Lifepath will probably not just land on your doorstep one morning without notice, but will most likely come into your life gradually and subtly, as you take small steps to navigate your life towards your Ideal Life vision, while setting your vision free and maintaining in the Balance of Grace. As we've established, dwelling in the Balance of Grace helps you stay in a prosperity magnetizing vibration on a daily basis. But let's talk about the steps that you take to navigate your life towards your Ideal one. Remember that the reason why your Soul did not reveal to you the whole Plan in the very first meditation was because it didn't want to overwhelm you with lots of tasks and responsibilities weighing on your shoulders, especially since some of the elements of your Ideal Life were not immediately achievable by you, but were to be given to you effortlessly by the Universe, meeting you halfway. This is exactly the purpose of finding the balance of setting your vision free—between doing some tasks joyfully, while leaving other aspects of your Ideal Life for the Universe to bring to you effortlessly. And within this delicate balance, each building block of your Ideal Life, whether that's an action that you are taking or a gift that the Universe synchronistically sends your way, comes into place at its perfect timing, when things are ripe for it.

So the process of navigating your life towards your Ideal Lifepath is a dance with the Universe. The first time you did the Meditation To Devise A Plan Of Action, you came up with your initial auspicious To Do list. Now your initial auspicious To Do list, which you have meditationally derived, did not have to make business sense at that early stage. For example, my initial auspicious To Do included things like "learn Italian," "learn to sail," and doing things that made me feel fabulous about myself. As trivial as those To Do tasks seemed at that stage, they still led me towards my Ideal Lifepath. When you started to walk some of the steps outlined by your meditationally derived auspicious To Do list, you may have noticed the Universe assisting you through little synchronistic events that happen in your everyday life. These synchronistic events might have already brought into your path some likeminded people whose goals intertwine with yours, and who are meant to help you with your plan. And if they haven't yet, they will. Synchronistic events also help bring you more inspired new ideas, and more knowledge about how to make your dream come true. This doesn't even have to be anything major; it could be just bumping into someone in the cafeteria and having a casual conversation, in which someone mentions something that spikes an idea in you about your Ideal Life Plan, or even just overhearing two strangers talking about something related. As synchronistic events keep happening, you'll periodically repeat the Meditation To Devise A Plan Of Action, and each time that you do, you'll add new items to your To Do list… until eventually, it will beef up into a Plan of Action, which you can logically see taking you across the bridge from your 'now' reality into your Ideal Lifepath of prosperity.

As you take the steps of your auspicious To Do list and Plan, the thing to remember is not to overtask yourself. You must keep setting your vision free on a daily basis, both in order to leave room for the Universe to meet you halfway, and in order to keep connecting you with a vibration of joy and Love, which magnetizes prosperity form the Divine realms.

When your auspicious To Do list beefs up into a real Plan of Action to merge with your Ideal Lifepath, the activities required by your new endeavors or projects may require more time out of your day in which to moonlight these activities, just until your project takes off and you start reaping the rewards of your efforts. That's one reason why it is so important to cut out of your schedule all the activities that do not serve your highest wellbeing – to make room for all the activities of your Plan.

By the time you start getting serious about doing all the steps of your Plan, you'll have lots of practice rearranging your schedule to stake out of it your Me Time; and you'll have lots of practice putting things into the bigger perspective of life: joy and love first, chores and work second, and taking care of your body-temple is a given, therefore the time allocated to it is non-negotiable. Your initial practice of staking out your Me Time should prepare you for being able to easily maneuver your schedule in a balanced way—while keeping in mind what's important in life.

One thing to remember, though: Even when the Plan for your Ideal Lifepath is in full speed, never compromise your Me Time! Even if it's only thirty minutes of sitting in a garden, or even just fifteen minutes of meditation, your Me Time is your personal sanity break—your time to remind yourself of the expansiveness of your Soul, and the joy that It wants you to take living this lifetime. It is what allows you to recapture the Balance of Grace, of feeling completely validated and fabulous about just being you, and in that, it allows you to get back into a feeling and a vibration that magnetizes prosperity to you.

What You Should (Kindly) Let Go of

At first glance, it would seem that bringing monetary prosperity into one's life requires hard work, and that having the oomph on top of our ordinary hard work to get up and change one's life, or drive it in any direction, would require a go-go-go achievement mode that doesn't leave much room in it for kindness-to-self. But let us remember that prosperity from your Soul is different than the limited prosperity that may come from working sixteen-hour days at a job that you dislike; it is different than the monetary prosperity that can come from establishing a successful business while stepping on, cheating, or being inconsiderate to other people; and it is even different than being a high paid executive that has a passion for money, but no passion for the actual job he/she does. Sure, prosperity from the Soul does absolutely include financial abundance. But if the prosperity is indeed coming from your Infinite Soul, than it should be effortless, and come as a natural byproduct of capitalizing on your truest talents and deepest passions. Moreover, prosperity from your Soul is all-inclusive—a life that is abundant not only with financial abundance, but also with an abundance of health, happiness, friends, family, beauty, personal enrichment, freedom, Grace, love, joy, and all the things that you really enjoy, which make you feel authentically you. That is why it is also called "living your bliss."

So how do we get busy shifting our lives into our Ideal, and yet have time to feel the joys of life? Well, we must first remember the three-faceted nature of kindness, and realize that having the oomph to change your life, and being kind to yourself are not mutually exclusive concepts. We must remember that when we live solely out of a sense of duty and responsibility, and forget to make room in our lives for joy, than we are not really living in vibrational resonance with the joy and love of the Divine, and therefore we vibrationally disconnect ourselves from the Ultimate Source from Whom all prosperity comes. To manifest money, we must first manifest love and joy within ourselves, as a way of staying vibrationally connected to the Infinite Funnel of Abundance. They come as a package deal.

So one of the first things that we must do to bring our lives into alignment with our Ideal Lifepaths of prosperity is to eliminate out of them the things are not in line with our Ideal Lifeplans, not driving us towards our Ideal Lifepaths, and not supporting who we Truly are. And the first things that must go are stress, <u>over</u>working in a way that does not bring us joy, and doing for others in a way that depletes our personal Ki (life-force).

Most people know that their lives are too hectic. Most of us also know that it would be healthy for us to exercise, meditate, breathe deeper, relax, or just in general have more Me Time. In our society, most people know they need to find more time for fun and enjoyment. But despite all this knowing, most of us don't take time out of our busy lives to take care of ourselves, and do the very basic things that make us healthy and happy. Why? Where is all our "missing time" going? What is it that we need to curve down or eradicate from our lives, in order to have enough time for the things that make us authentically us, and therefore make us conscious co-Creators?

I believe that most of us devote at least some of our "missing time" to our false sense of duty to others in our lives. But to truly shift ourselves into being conscious co-Creators of prosperity in our lives, we must remember that when we forget to be kind to ourselves, than at some point, our inner kindness meters will show empty; we will feel cheated, at which point, we will have dried out our inner wells of joy, and would be unable to continue to do-do-do for ourselves *or* for others. I'm not saying that being selfish is the way to be in life. Quite the contrary: being generous, kind, and loving to others is a wonderful thing that can give you a very euphoric feeling. But as we've discussed in Chapter 4 of *Prosperity From your Soul*, doing for others has to flow out of the endless joy of your heart, which comes out of the Divine Funnel of Abundance that is constantly flowing through and for you.

The biggest thief of our "missing time" is overworking at jobs that do not make us feel gratified, and in which we do not find joy, because they are not part of our Ideal Lifeplans. We feel responsible to finish that project; we perceive that if we push ourselves to work an eighty-hour week, we'll get that much sought after promotion; we know other people are relying on us to do things; or the classic – we want to finish the "must do" chores so that we can really relax and devote time to ourselves. But if we look at the grander scheme of things in life, you and I both know that that's never going to happen! The chaos of life, and the demands it puts on you will never end... not until this game is over anyway (and may you live long and prosper until that transition day). Today's chores may be done, but a new set of chores will be there waiting for you tomorrow; you may do today everything that others are expecting of you, but then tomorrow, a new set of expectations will be in place for you, which of course you would expect of yourself to oblige; you may finish this project, but a new project is waiting for you just beyond the top of this hill; you may get the promotion you want, but then you'll just be putting in more hours at work, with your eyes set on the next promotion... Where does it end? At what point will you be satisfied taking some time to simply enjoy and love your life?!

It's like the fisherman story: one day a rich businessman went out for a refreshing walk by the lake. When he got to the lakeshore, he saw a young man fishing. As he started to chat with the fisherman, he noticed that the young man was very bright and had an openhearted smile. He genuinely liked this fisherman, and so he decided to "rescue" him from his predicament and make him an offer. He offered the young fisherman a secure job in his firm, with a steady pay, and plenty of opportunity for career advancement. The fisherman then asked, "How would this job benefit me?" to which the rich man replied, "well, you'll be putting in long hours at first, but you'll have a steady pay, and benefits. Then after a few years, you could advance to a supervisory position." The fisherman thought about it for a moment, and asked, "And how would this supervisory position benefit me?" The businessman now started to get excited, and replied, "Well, then you'll have employees under you. You'll probably put in more hours than before, but you'll make more money." The fisherman pondered this for a few moments, and then asked, "And then what?" The now excited businessman said, "Well son, then if you work hard, a few years later, you can advance to be a manager…" The fisherman looked at him puzzled and asked, "and what good would that do me?" The businessman went on excitedly, "well, of course you'll have to work even more hours since you'll have more responsibilities, but you'll make much more money." The fisherman, now with a serene smile on his face, then asked, "and what good would that do me?" The enthusiastic businessman replied, "well son, after a few more years, you could start your own branch under our company, and have many more employees under you. You'll still work long hours as you'll now have even more responsibilities, but you'll make lots more money!" The fisherman, still with his serene knowing smile, then asked, "and how will that benefit me?" The businessman then replied, "Well son, after a few years, if you're smart, you can have other people managing your company." The fisherman then asked, "So then, what would I do with my time?" to which the businessman replied in a triumphant voice, "Then you can go fishing!" The fisherman looked at him with the most serene smile and asked, "and what, sir, do you think I'm going now?"

Don't get me wrong; I'm not saying that being lazy is the way to build your empire. When you merge with your Ideal Lifepath, and within it, engage in your Ideal Lifework—the job, business, or endeavor that capitalizes on your Truest gifts and deepest passions, you may or may not work long hours. But you will derive such joy out of your work, and feel so deeply gratified and fulfilled, that it won't seem like work at all. I'm also not, by any means, saying that you should quit your current job tomorrow morning, before something better comes your way, which is more in line with your Ideal Lifework. We all have necessities in life. I too live in the real world. The point here is to remember the higher perspective of things: *work is not who you are; it's what you do* to provide for yourself; i.e., it is a mean, not an end in and of itself. Even if you already work in your Ideal Lifework, the work itself is still just the means to help complete your life mission, not an end or a destination. So work shouldn't be the only element, or even the main element of your life.

Because understand this: Whether you are talking about income-producing work, academic studies, house chores, or your fulltime work of raising your kids, *unless you are doing all of this work with supreme joy, and out of love, the work itself is a wash.* I mean, you drink water, and you pee it all out; you shop, cook, and eat, and then you eliminate it; you clean and do laundry, and it all gets dirty again. In the same way, you earn money, and then you spend it! It's all part of the cycle of life. What I'm saying here is: *It's not the work that you do, or how you pass your time in this life, that matter. The only thing that is of supreme importance is the love and joy that you feel while you are engaged in the activities of your life.* Love and joy change the whole picture into a brighter one. It's like being in love, or having a kundalini opening, when suddenly all colors seem brighter; the air seems more fragrant; and even the weather, rain or shine, seems beautiful to you. That is the way you should live life – as if you are in love with life. Love and joy are not just luxuries. If you're going to live the life of a conscious co-Creator, and manifest prosperity from your Soul, than you need to find joy in all that you do, and in every moment in life. That is the condition of vibrationally magnetizing all-inclusive prosperity to you.

So what is it exactly that we are eradicating from our lives, or at least curving down? To be exact, it is the things that are not part of our Ideal Lifeplans; do not drive us towards our Ideal Lifepaths or the fulfillment of your life missions; and are not in line with our True Selves.

When eradicating, or curving down our time spent on those things, there is also a balance between going forward towards our Ideal Lifepaths, and temporarily keeping status quo with the things that support us in the 'now.' As we have discussed in *Prosperity From Your Soul* and in *Seven Stages to co-Creating Prosperity From Your Soul,* ideally the bridge between your 'now' reality and your Ideal Lifepath should be a smooth and harmonious one.

But we are each unique; our life missions are each unique; and thus our manifested life situations are also unique and specific. So it is not for me to tell you exactly what kinds of limits you should put on the time and efforts that you spend on doing for others, doing for your boss, how much time exactly you should spend in a job you dislike or hate, or how much time you should spend on all the other elements or habits that do not serve your highest wellbeing or your new path as a successful co-Creator of your life. The only one that is truly qualified to guide you on that is, of course, your all-knowing Soul Self.

Changing Non-Serving Habits:

Changing habits that no longer serve our highest Lifepath of prosperity is a huge step towards reclaiming the Ideal-you, and the prosperity that was always meant to be a part of your Ideal Lifeplan. And we all have some habits that do not serve our Ideal Lifepaths. I myself am no different. Despite the fact that I have channeled all the wisdoms for this book series, as of the time of this writing, I still watch some TV; I still lead a lifestyle that is a bit too sedentary; and I still eat way more starchy high-glycemic-index carbs than is healthy for me. We all indulge in habits that do not serve our highest wellbeing, despite knowing that those habits are bad for us. So as the balance of kindness goes, we have to be kind enough to drive ourselves to change for the better, while still honoring and loving who we are at present moment. A dear friend of mine smokes heavily and drinks diet coke instead of water, despite being a brilliant physician who knows that those habits do not serve her wellbeing. So it becomes obvious that to change habits that do not serve our highest wellbeing, two things are needed: a conscious decision to change the habit, and a kind way to let go of the "Ugly Duckling," and mold oneself back into the beautiful swan that we were each meant to become.

Ancient yogis believed that it takes forty days to change a habit, ninety days to confirm the new habit, one hundred and twenty days to assimilate the new habit as the new you, and a thousand days to truly master the new habit.[1] I'll agree that some perseverance certainly does help leave behind the crust of whom you were, and reclaim whom you are becoming and the new Lifepath that goes along with it. But there is more to breaking bad habits than to "just say no."

Step 1 of changing any bad habit is to gain the awareness that the habit no longer serves you, and the motivation to change it. But motivation and perseverance alone are not enough to break a habit.

Step 2: Once you are aware that a particular old habit is not serving your highest wellbeing, and you have the motivation to change it, if you really want to break the habits and step into your Ideal Lifepath of prosperity, you need to get to the core of why you'd gotten into this habit to begin with, and why you've kept it. The idea is to find out what need this old habit has fulfilled for you until now, and replace it with a new habit that fulfills the same need in a healthier way.

After all, bad habits are simply habits in which the price you pay is greater than the benefits you get from them. There is always a certain need that these habits fulfill; otherwise you would not engage in them. Once you find what the original need was/is, you can find a healthier way to fulfill the same need, and substitute a good habit for the bad one.

One way to get to the bottom of it is to deeply meditate on the core reason for this habit, and the need it addresses. You can use any meditational technique that you are comfortable with, to search deep within yourself for this information. Zohar Breath Meditation (see *Seven Stages to co-Creating Prosperity From You Soul* for detailed instructions on how to do this meditation) can help you get the answers from your Soul Self. Once you reach the point in the meditation when you are tuned into the wisdom of your Soul, have your here-now self ask your Soul Self to shed Light on the habit you are trying to change: what need does it fulfill (if any)? What was the core reason you got hooked on this habit to begin with?

Your Soul's wisdom can also give you some wonderful tips on healthy habits that can fulfill the same needs, so as to replace your original need for the habit that you are trying to change. You should do some automatic writing (see Chapter 1 of *Seven Stages to co-Creating Prosperity From You Soul* for an overview of automatic writing) to note the impressions and visions that come to you during the meditation. You can repeat the meditation as many time as needed, until you get a profound insight that feels like it's worth pursuing—an insight that resonates well with the core of who you are.

However, the real purpose of Step 2 is not to dwell on the past (why you started to smoke, for example) and not to beat yourself up over having adopted the non-serving habit to begin with, but to search for higher wisdom on what new habits you could you adopt, which would answer the same needs in a healthier way, therefore negating your need to keep your old habit.

When you come back into here-now consciousness, **Step 3** of this process is to research and ponder how to anchor your meditationally received answers into logical, here-now perspective and implications. So find a convenient time to do some research into the validity and implications of your meditational insight. For example, if the bad habit that you are trying to change is smoking, then maybe you've meditationally tuned into the fact that smoking made you feel cool when you were a teenager; that it made you feel sexy, mature, and accepted by your peers. And perhaps you've even tuned into the fact that none of those original lures still serve a purpose in your life, because you already feel mature, and you can find other things to make yourself feel sexy and accepted by people in your life.

Beyond emotional-mental roots, many non-serving habits also have physical ties or physiological addictive aspects. For example, if smoking was indeed the habit that you are trying to eradicate, than before you'd be ready to throw away the cigarettes for good, you would need to research and understand the physiological and psychological (habit) aspects of this addiction, as well as healthy substitutes that people have successfully used to stop cigarette addictions. I am no expert on quitting smoking, since I myself have never smoked. But people report that nicotine patch or gum works well to substitute the physical nicotine addiction, and that chewing gum or sucking on a straw works well to replace the habit in the first year after they quit smoking. People report that after the first couple of weeks without cigarettes, the toughest thing is drinking coffee without a cigarette. In that case, you'd need to think about how to be able to continue to enjoy coffee without craving a cigarette.

Once you have researched and found some possible substitutes for the non-serving habit, put the results back in your pipe and smoke it. Meditate again and ponder which of these substitutes would work well *for you*. For example, on a deeper level, the first meditation may have shown you that the reason you still smoke is that deep-down, you still feel it makes you feel cool, accepted, and sexy. In that case, once you ponder the things that work for you, you might decide to try taking up a sport that makes you feel cool, sexy and accepted, perhaps playing volleyball on the beach, mountain biking with a group of friends, or any other sport that would make you feel cool, accepted and sexy, and at the same time promote your overall wellbeing. In other words, the good habits that replaces the bad one need to replace the need for it on a multitude of levels: physical, lifestyle, mental and emotional.

Smoking is just one example. Whatever the bad habit you are trying to change, this step of researching and pondering, researching some more, and meditating some more, will help you find out which good habits would work best for you to replace the old habit that no longer serves. For every unhealthy habit, there is a healthy one that can answer the same need and therefore replace it.

Step 4: Now that you have a few ideas of possible healthy substitutes for your old habit, it is time to experiment. The beauty of this process is that at this stage, you don't have to feel committed to any of those new things you are trying. This step is just about experimenting with different new habits, and seeing what works for you. So have fun experimenting with the new hobbies and activities that you are trying, and measure the results according to how they make you feel. The more deeply satisfying they are, and the more you enjoy the new good habit, the easier it would be to quit the old bad one. Be patient with yourself as you go through this process. At this stage, don't judge yourself if your old habit doesn't immediately change. Rome wasn't built in one day.

Step 5: Once you have experimented with a few new things, you will find yourself naturally gravitating towards one, or a few of them that satisfy you and make you feel joy. This is the stage when some perseverance with the new habit may help your quest to wean yourself off of the old one.

If you believe that after a certain amount of time the new habit becomes a part of you, then you may decide to add a regular daily practice of the new habit for an X number of days, in order to help deter you from falling back into the old habit.

Now, changing a habit that no longer serves can be something a lot simpler than quitting smoking. For example, if you have a bad habit of being overly critical on yourself, you may decide to add a daily practice of looking yourself in the mirror for at least three minutes each day, saying to yourself "I'm fabulous" throughout that time, and actively finding at least five things you admire about yourself in those particular moments.

If the substitute habit you've added satisfies the original need; if it is healthy and therefore resonates with your Soul Self; if it is enjoyable to the point that it makes you blissfully happy; and if you persist with it, than the old habit will dissolve naturally, and the new habit will eventually become a permanent part of who you are. Because your True nature is healthy, happy, and abundant. Doctors talk about the amazing healing ability of the human body. And the psyche and habit patterns are no different. Both your self and your Self naturally gravitate towards a state of health and wellbeing, and therefore naturally prefer habits that promote that state. It goes back to what we've talked about at the beginning of *Prosperity From your Soul*: your original Self was designed to be healthy, happy and abundant. You seek health, happiness and prosperity because they are part of who you Truly are. Therefore, once you take away unhealthy habits, and offer yourself a chance to fulfill all of your needs healthily, than perfect balance, harmony, health, and prosperity are inevitable.

TV or Not TV?

One element that is not always supportive the path of a conscious co-Creator, but which most people spend way too much time on, is watching television. If you are one of these individuals who do not even have a TV at home, or who have turned their old television into a planting pot, than I salute you; and you may skip to this subsection about TV, and move on to the section about "The Balance." However, for most of us, TV watching is an activity that takes far too much of our time, and take away from the control that we could be exercising over our psyches and lives. I mean, if you are in the process of changing your life and driving it towards your Ideal, than scheduling the time in it for moonlighting some of the activities required by your new Plan, and for your Me Time, can be a challenge. It can be even more challenging if you're spending three plus hours a day staring at a television screen that has no potential to help you drive your life anywhere near the right direction.

Besides time constraints, let me ask you: If you knew beyond the shadow of doubt that you have the power to co-Create for yourself life adventures that are far more exciting than the ones you watch on TV, would you still want to watch TV? What if you had a fantastic tool for taking all worries off your mind and restoring peace of mind and heart, which far surpasses the temporary relaxation that TV gives you. Would you then still be inclined to watch TV? If you could not only watch fictional stories about people you don't know and don't really care about, but actually hear these interesting stories from people you know first hand—people you care about? Would you prefer to watch those stories on TV or would you rather interact with the people you know and be part of their story? Imagine yourself sitting with your extended spiritual family cuddling around a nice bonfire, sharing dinner, listening to the wise ones tell stories and legends. Would you then rush out of the nurturing togetherness of your tribe and sit in solitude in front of a TV screen? I'm willing to bet the answer to all of those questions is "absolutely not."

If you've read *Prosperity From Your Soul,* you know that the power to co-Create exciting life adventures has always been yours! And the real life adventures that you could potentially have would far surpass just watching other people have those adventures on TV. In terms of relaxation and quieting the mind, in *Seven Stages to co-Creating Prosperity From Your Soul,* you've reawakened your innate abilities to meditate, still your mind, and soothe yourself into a state of peace. And in terms of finding camaraderie, you've also always had the innate ability to deeply connect with others and get involved in the stories of their lives, which far surpasses the fake "camaraderie" that you have with the people on your TV screen.

But despite the fact that all of these abilities are innate to all humans, we all spend far too much time in front of the little screen than is healthy for us, and allow the fake TV "reality" to have too much influence over our lives.

What's Wrong With a Little TV?

To be fair, not all TV is bad. Television watching in moderation could be a wonderful tool for entertainment, as long as it doesn't invade your life or take control of your psyche. If you find TV shows that promote good values, instill hope, remind you of the beauty of the human spirit, and make you feel good, than television could be a great way for mutual entertainment with friends and family, and an inspiration that makes you want to be a better person. TV can also give you a peek into journeys you might consider taking someday, whether that's a journey into the Amazon River in the jungles of Peru, or a deep journey into yourself. It is sometimes possible that your Soul is synchronistically directing you to watch certain shows that are thought provoking, help convey certain messages, remind you of how precious you are, evokes specific feelings that are meant for you to experience, such as romance, youth, or upliftment, or perhaps a show that makes you think deeply about the important questions of your life. All of those could be valuable for your growth, and for your enjoyment of life.

But we have to remember that TV is a tool that conveys an imaginary world. This imaginary world was never meant to replace the real journey of your life with the fake one that someone else took. It was never meant to replace your interaction with people in real life; and it was never meant to replace meditation, which humans have used since the beginning of time to achieve True peace of mind. TV's imaginary world is a poor imitation of reality, since passively watching someone else's experiences, over which you have no control, is far less satisfying than having your own experiences, over which you have a high degree of control. The nature of the television media is such that you are necessarily passive, since you have no possibility of actually interacting with the reality on the screen, and you have no say over what themes are presented in the show.

In his book *Four Arguments For The Elimination Of Television,* Jerry Mander writes, "When you are watching TV, you are not day dreaming, or reading or looking outside the window. You have opened your mind, and someone else's daydreams have entered. The images come from distant places you have never been, depict events you can never experience, and are sent by people you don't know and have never met. Your mind is the screen for their microwave pictures. Once their images are inside you, they imprint upon your memory. They become yours. What's more, the images remain inside you permanently."[2]

What's wrong with experiencing someone else's fantasies for an evening? Nothing, accept the fact that you are allowing *their* stress, *their* fear and *their* paranoia to feed your mind, and alter your vibrational resonance. I cannot even count the number of times I dreamed that the Goa'ulds from *Stargate SG-1* were chasing me, or that I had to help Clark Kent defend Earth from some bad enemy. How many times have you dreamed that the serial killer from some detective show you watched was chasing you all night long? Even if television shows have not yet invaded your dreams, how many times have you caught yourself tossing and turning, unable to fall asleep because you're still mulling over what you've seen on TV?

The influence of TV can even be much subtler than that. I'll never forget the moment I realized that TV was subtly inserting negative themes into my psyche. One evening after watching *Hawaii-5-0*, I had a terrible feeling that something behind the scene of my life was wrong. I felt uneasy, like some injustice or wrongdoing was soon going to be perpetrated on me. Logically there was no apparent reason why I should have felt that way. I was wondering if I was receiving some psychic warning about an upcoming event, or if there was something else at play here, which was tainting my intuition. It was only after I smudged with blessed incense and energetically cleared the room with reiki that I realized: It was not me who suffered the injustice; it was Steve McGarret who was being accused of a murder he didn't commit. I had internalized the negative feelings of this fictional character, because I was identifying him. And while I may be more sensitive than most, because I am a spiritual healer, I am in no way unique in identifying with fictional movie characters and internalizing their feelings. To one degree or another, we all internalize the feelings and experiences we watch on TV. And unfortunately, TV these days have become much less about the greatness of the human spirit, and much more about dark themes. That is one reason why TV is not satisfying.

A study done by researchers Robert Kubey, a professor at Rutgers University and director of the Center for Media Studies, and Mihaly Csikszentmihalyi, Professor of Psychology at Claremont Graduate University, reports that: "As one might expect, people who were watching TV… reported feeling relaxed and passive… What is more surprising is that the sense of relaxation ends when the set is turned off, but the feelings of passivity and lowered alertness continue. Survey participants commonly reflect that television has somehow absorbed or sucked out their energy, leaving them depleted. They say they have more difficulty concentrating after viewing than before. In contrast, they rarely indicate such difficulty after reading. After playing sports or engaging in hobbies, people report improvements in mood. After watching TV, people's moods are about the same or worse than before."[3] So television, especially if you're watching horror or crime dramas can leave you more stressed, anguished, or even in a bad mood. From a metaphysical standpoint, identifying with twisted realities of negative TV shows can put you in a negative vibration that would make it difficult to then dwell in the positive Internal Experience of your Ideal Lifepath. Those negative TV themes are therefore counterproductive to co-Creating prosperity from your Soul.

Now here is what makes things worse: Prehistorically, whenever humans have watched moving images that made sounds, these images were always real, because throughout history (until the last few decades), there has never been a medium capable of creating fake images and sounds that are so realistic. Even today after millions of years of evolution, at the deep subconscious level, the human brain has still not developed the ability to tell the difference between television images and the reality of our lives.[4] So while your conscious mind knows the difference between the reality of your life and the fake TV reality, your deep subconscious does not. That is why thoughts, feelings and impressions from the television get into your subconscious and get categorized in your mind as real. So ask yourself, do you really want to be an incubator for someone else's agenda, fear, danger, stress, and paranoia? Do you want to lock your mind into an illusory reality dictated by someone else? Or do you want to take back control of your mind and life, and co-Create the life that you want?

Part of being in control of you life means that you are in control of how much time you spend in front of the television. If you are glued to your television for more than three hours a day, at a time in which you should be co-Creating your Ideal Lifepath, than something is wrong with the picture here. Because spending too much time in front of TV means you are not spending that time working on the goals of your Ideal Lifepath, or even being kind to yourself as a fundamental co-Creative practice. Remember that you are now on a path of co-Creating a healthier, happier, fuller, more prosperous life for yourself. So there is much to do to get all parts of you aligned to vibrationally resonate with the blessings you wish to co-Create. Time wasted in front of TV is time in which you could have been: meditationally relaxing and connecting to your Soul Self, getting adequate sleep, doing your fun physical activity, or doing some of the activities in the physical reality of your life to start bringing your vision into fruition – all of which would have brought you closer to your Ideal Lifepath. Part of taking control of your life means tearing yourself away from the TV, and mustering the courage to actually take an active part in your life, believing that the adventures that your highest Lifepath can lead you to are much more exhilarating than the ones you view on TV, and that you already have within you the seeds to make your life a success!

Another part of taking control of your life is taking back control of your psyche. You should be the judge of what ideas and themes you allow influence in you. This goes deeper than just feeling bad for an evening after watching a low-vibrational show. As the "reality" of TV is allowed a direct feed into your subconscious, you internalize not just the images and sounds that come from the screen, but the values advocated by the show. You might have been raised to believe that violence is wrong, that a love between a man and a woman is a sacred union, and that honesty is an important pillar on which all relationships are built. But through years of identifying with movie characters that act contrary to those values, as the line in your deep subconscious between TV and reality blurs, you begin to justify their low-vibrational behavior in your mind, almost as if you needed to justify your own behavior. And as you continue to identify with TV "heroes" of substandard values, the original values of your upbringing, as well as the natural high morality of your Soul Self, begin to fade, and you begin to adopt the television's substandard values. Unfortunately, the themes in TV and movies in recent years incorporate so much violence, dishonesty, manipulation of others, sexually taking advantage of others, and other bad values, that it becomes almost impossible to avoid.

For example, kids today watch so much violence even in their cartoons and videogames, that it raises their tolerance for violence, and eventually legitimizes it in their minds. Then as adults, they watch so many crime dramas, in which people die several times per hour and everyone is expected to feel okay with it, that it lowers their value of human life. Human life is precious. So don't let TV persuade you that it's not! In the same way, many people have gotten it into their mind that it's ok to cheat on their significant other, after watching movies that glamorize cheating as a lifestyle. Lovemaking is a communion between two people that is sacred, and brings the Divine spirit of Love into the union. It is the highest form of communication between two human beings. So don't let the television brainwash you into believing that promiscuous sex, or using people through sex are OK. They are not. And deep down within the inner chamber of your heart, which is connected to your Soul, you know it. Other examples are: recreational drugs are bad for you on just about every level of your existence (unless we're talking about medicinal herbs administered and supervised by a well trained shaman). So don't let TV dictate a false belief that drugs are cool. Watching TV shows in which everyone lies and scams one another, and identifying with their "heroes," smudges the lines of what you consider write and wrong, and consequently cheapens the expression of who you Truly are, which in turn lowers your energetic vibration into resonate with all that you wouldn't want to magnetize into your life.

Another negative aspect of watching TV is the solitary way we watch it. Your True Self is a social being Created in the image of his/her Creator, with a natural propensity for love and belonging. Much of our Souls' growth happens through interactions with others. Therefore harmonious interactions with others allow synchronistic events to bring your Ideal Lifepath into manifestation. From this perspective, it becomes obvious that the lone way we watch TV takes us away from interacting with others in the reality of life, and is counterproductive to co-Creating True prosperity.

For many people, television functions as a way to stay in touch with current events. The problem is the way news is usually reported: sensationalized, overdramatized, and reports mostly the negative aspects of every story. And the problem here is twofold: First, it makes you feel bad, like you are surrounded by a world in which there is nothing but misery. This negative vibration takes away hope, and makes you resonate with all that you don't want to co-Create into your life. Secondly, this way of reporting only the bad news usually accentuates our differences as people, and makes the abyss between two sides of any conflict seem unbridgeable. Watching news sends you into a state of mind of seeing only the worst in people. But as you've discussed in *Prosperity From Your Soul*, each person, even the worst criminal, still has the Divine spark within him/her. However hidden or dim that spark may be, it still exists. And therefore, as our brothers and sisters to the human race, even our enemies deserve our compassion. Besides, dwelling on someone's ill intent only perpetuates those ill intents in one's life.

I wish somebody would create a television network called GNN—Good News Network. You could have that network report all the same news, but just look at each story form a more positive and uplifting perspective. It's not that you wouldn't cover an event like 9/11. It's that instead of dwelling on the terror aspect of things, you would report the human stories, and the heroic and compassionate things that people did to save one another. Because after a while of watching, people get tired of the same bad news shown over and over again. They want to watch something uplifting and hopeful. And there is always a positive aspect to every event, because whenever something bad happens, the human spirit is so grand that people always go the extra mile to help one another. It would do so much for the human race if we create a network that constantly remind us of the greatness of our Spirit. I believe that if someone took the initiative to create this Good News Network, it would promote world peace and harmony (not to mention co-Create prosperity for the initiator). But since this network does not yet exist, if you watch news, you need to remind yourself of the positive aspects of each event, of hope, of who you Truly are, and of your natural kindness and compassion towards yourself and others. This will help you keep a positive vibrational resonance with the higher levels of reality, where manifestation of your dreams is possible.

Many people claim that the television helps them relax at the end of the day. The problem with using television, instead of meditation, for relaxation is that it's not a true way of cleansing the subconscious, since the material broadcast on TV inputs more unwanted thoughts into your mind. What TV really does is it stifles your daily worries for a while. Once you finish watching your show, those same worries and stresses are alive and well inside your mind, and they've got company – the worries, stresses and paranoia of the screenwriter and director of the show you were watching. Now after this "relaxing" evening with your television, all of those negative thoughts come out of your now packed subconscious, and start getting all jumbled up inside your mind just as soon as you fall asleep. In comparison, meditation is a tool that has been proven over thousands of years to help relaxation and the clearing of the mind. And as you've found out in *Seven Stages to co-Creating Prosperity From Your Soul*, even the simplest meditation can help cleanse the brainfucking noise out of your mind, and achieve a state of peace.

However, the point of this section is not to take away options from you, and certainly not to replace your inner judgment of what is good for you and what is not. You, and only you, internally know what part of your TV habits feed you with experiences that are important for your growth, and what part feeds you with negative themes that deter you from co-Creating your Ideal Lifepath. So this is another issue on which you need to call upon the wisdom of your Soul to ascertain. If you do decide to indulge in a little TV, *be selective in what you allow into the sanctity of your mind, emotions, and spirit. Remember: you are a radiant child of God. You are of Her-His Light*. So don't let the television cheapen who you Truly are.

Overcoming TV Addiction –

I don't know whether or not TV has taken way too much control over your life and psyche. But let's go through the steps of overcoming a TV addiction together:

Step 1 – Awareness & Motivation: Earlier in this section, we have gone through some of the awareness steps together. However, there is another level of awareness—the awareness of how all this information applies *to you*. Perhaps you watch TV only on occasion, and it does not invade your life? Perhaps you only watch shows that positively inspire you and serve your higher purpose? The point is: don't let me or anyone else dictate which habit does or does not serve *your* higher purpose. You are the best judge of what is right *for you*. So before you could, or even should, have the motivation to change anything in your life, you should search deep within your inner wisdom to what degree TV has negatively impacted your life.

To do that, find a quiet place, center yourself, and connect with the conscious observer within you. From within that highly conscious state of awareness, ask yourself: Do you get into a bad mood occasionally after watching TV and can't explain why? Do you spend such long hours in front of TV that you don't have time to enjoy, or take active part in your life? Are you so attached to your TV "heroes" that you feel unable or unmotivated to go out and make real friends, but at the same time feel lonely? Do you often feel passive and helpless to change anything in your life? Do you yearn for new adventures, but find that for some mysterious reason, you're always stopping yourself from having them? If the answer to any of those is yes, than TV has definitely impacted your life.

Now, if you spend four or more hours a day watching TV, especially if you watch it compulsively with no regard to what's being shown, then you probably already know that you need to change that habit.

Step 2 – Meditation On Core Reason & Possible Solutions: Some of the underlying reasons that people watch TV is that it artificially fulfills some needs that people perceive are out of reach in our modern society: We seek the camaraderie of our "TV heroes" because we perceive it's easier than going out in the world and making new friends; we unwind at the end of the day in front of TV because we perceive that TV will relax us; we seek stimuli and adventures through TV because we perceive that our lives are dull, or that we'd never be able to have as good an adventure in our real lives; and we have an intrinsic need to be told a story, to enrich our human experience.

But as we have discussed, the camaraderie of real friends, which we are all capable of making in real life, is far superior to the illusion of camaraderie of our "TV heroes"; meditation is a far better tool for helping us unwind, relax, and cleanse our minds of all of our day's worries than TV ever could be; the best stimuli and adventures are the ones we could absolutely have in our real lives, which have the potential of being much more exhilarating than what we watch on TV, because we'd be experiencing them first hand; and the best stories are not the ones we passively watch on TV, towards which we have been told by someone else (the screenwriter, producer, director) how we must feel, but the ones in which we participate, know the heart of the person telling the story. Even when we read a book, even though the story has been thought out by someone else, we still exercise control over how we imagine the scenes and characters.

Now that you have been made aware of some of the needs that television usually attempts to fulfill, meditating on the reasons you watch TV has been made easy. It is still beneficial for you to meditate, though, and ask your Soul what needs the TV tries to fulfill *specifically for you*. Is it more about social needs for you? Is it more about the need for stimuli and adventure for you? Is it mostly about relaxation and getting your mind off of your daily worries? Or is it about the need for a story for you? Doing the meditation, and searching deep inside yourself will help you decide which substitute habits are best suited *for you*.

Step 3 – Research Into Healthy Substitutes: After the meditation, you should have some clue as to which need is most urgent for you to fulfill. And since television attempts to answer a few needs, there may be many possible substitute habits that you may adopt, to answer the same needs in a healthier way. The research that you should do depends of your level of self-awareness. If you are as clueless as I was when I first started to wean myself off of TV, you'd probably need to start with some simple online search on "activities that can answer XYZ need." If, on the other hand, you already know yourself a little better (kudos if you do), you may only need to research where and when you may engage in your chosen activities.

If your need to have adventures in life is not being met, think of the adventures you want to have as part of your Ideal Life, which you've internally experienced during your Ideal Life Meditation (in *Seven Stages to co-Creating Prosperity From Your Soul*). An Internal Experience Meditation, envisioning and internally experiencing all the exhilarating adventures that you wish to have, may be a good temporary substitute for TV, until you get a chance to manifest some of those adventures in real life. And really and truly, if hang-gliding in the Alps, or diving with whales is a deep passion of yours, go do it! Never mind about how this experience will bring you financial prosperity. You never know what gifts the Universe would precipitate upon you when you do. For example, some years ago, midway through climbing the Huayna Picchu (the big mountain that rises over the Machu Picchu in Peru), I met an older man who was climbing down the mountain, and the insight that he gave me in a casual conversation not only stuck with me as important insight into life, but also made us friends for years to come. Gifts from the Universe can come in many forms, especially along adventures that you feel magnetized to take part in.

In a very real way, every day should be a mini little adventure. Sure, some days can be big adventures. But it doesn't have to be a big adventure that satisfies your need to be stimulated and feel alive! Start with little adventures, such as friendly interactions with people that you meet along your way, and fun experiences throughout your day. Make it a point to engage in some pleasurable activities each day. Revive some of your old hobbies, or take on new hobbies. There are so many things that can satisfy your need to feel the adventure of life, such as horseback riding, sailing, or playing sports, just to name a few.

Pay special attention to activities that make your heart sing a song that resonates favorably throughout your entire being, as those are probably related, in one way or another, to your Ideal Lifepath, even if the connection is not yet obvious. Trust that in the coming weeks and months, the connection to co-Creating prosperity will become apparent. Incidentally, going out and experiencing life adventures also helps you get into the harmonious flow through which the Universe precipitates synchronistic gifts on you.

If for you, the TV mostly answers your social needs, you may want to research into activities you can do, which involve social interactions, through which you can meet new friends and companions. Some ideas are: volunteer activities (which might give you a high degree of satisfaction), and attending social events, or attending gatherings that people organize for meeting likeminded people (for example, meetup.com is a good website to find some social gatherings in your area). It is true that creating a close network of friends is not always easy, as it depends not only on you, but also on the free will of others, which cannot be controlled by you. But while you cannot control other people's openness to friendship, you can start simply by being open to creating friends wherever you go, even in the market. Opening up your heart, looking for the good in each person that crosses your path, and not being afraid of starting friendly conversations with strangers, are first steps towards making friends, who might eventually become your close supportive network. I met my best friend and Soul-sister one morning many years ago, making a casual remark while standing in line to clear Immigration in Nassau (Bahamas). Another friend told me today that she had met her husband one day while standing in line to use a public restroom. So you never know which casual conversation you start will end up in a lifelong friendship. Just keep being friendly and open, and give friendship a chance. Intimacy, in both friendships and romantic relations, is one of the greatest joys of life. Don't give up on the possibility of having this joy in your life—don't settle for the fake camaraderie you feel with your TV "heroes."

If your TV needs is more about your need to enrich your human experience with a story, it's true that we no longer sit around bonfires and listen the elders of our tribes tell their stories. But you can quench that thirst for story by reading a good book, attending opera, a play, book clubs, storytelling groups, or even a social gathering. The ultimate satisfaction comes from a story that you yourself experience, or from hearing the story from someone who animates the story well, say someone who has experienced the story first hand. So talk to people, and find out their stories. I used to be timid asking people about themselves, as I was afraid of intruding. But in recent years, I find that once a basic level of trust and friendship have been established, people love knowing that someone is interested in their stories. And the stories and adventures that people share with you first hand have much more depth and reveal many more layers than the stories on TV. Whenever a film comes out of a book, people almost always say they've enjoyed the book better than the movie. That's because a book is much better suited for giving you all the layers of the story, not just the facts, but the thoughts, and emotions of the story too. Well, when you talk to people and get their stories first hand, you get not only the facts, thoughts and emotions of events, but the energy and spirit of the story. When someone tells you the story, you can tell their level of sincerity, and the aim of the story—whether it aims to give you wisdom, entertain you, or uplift you. You can also tell if the person telling the story has made peace with the events, or if they are still seeking resolution for something unresolved. That is why Native Americans say that when a story is being told (as opposed to reading it in a book), you know the heart and spirit of the storyteller.

If relaxation is the need that the television attempts to fulfill for you, try and add a meditation to your evening, even if it's a short one, listen to relaxing music, read a good book, do some relaxing yoga or RezoDance, watch a beautiful sunset, and see if that answers your needs better than TV.

Step 4 – Experiment & Choose: This is the fun step. Until now you've meditated, you've researched activities, and thought deeply about things. Now it's time to start filling your life with activities from the list of possible activities that you feel are best suited for you.

And here is where this starts to plug back into your Plan to merge with your Ideal Life: when you experiment with the possible activities to replace your TV needs, pay close attention to ones that resonate with you deeply and make your heart sing with joy. Even if these items have not yet made their way into your auspicious To Do Plan, if they make your heart sing with joy, they resonate well with whom you Truly are, and therefore become auspicious activities to engage in to magnetize prosperity from your Soul into your here-now existence.

Start trying all the items on your list of activities that could replace your TV needs, and then evaluate which one of these activities fulfilled you the most, to the point that you didn't even think of opening the TV afterwards. Is this an activity that you can do almost every day? Say you decide to go see a play once a month. You still need to experiment with activities that fulfill you, which you can do almost daily. So have fun with this. Go out and enjoy yourself, and don't forget to make a mental note of activities that resonated musically throughout your entire being—the ones that not only dissolved your need to watch TV, but also made your heart sing.

Step 5 – Choose & Persevere: As explained above, once you allow yourself a period of experimentation, you will naturally gravitate towards the activities that suit you best. The ones that you decide to adopt as the habits that replaces the TV should be ones in which you can engage on a semi-regular basis, and that answer all of the needs. But most importantly, they need to be healthy habits that support your highest wellbeing and your Ideal Lifepath to prosperity.

However, don't stress out over choosing one. Everything can be a work in progress. Let yourself naturally gravitate towards the activities that fulfill you and give you joy. Now, when I say persevere, I don't mean cutting yourself off TV cold turkey. Don't think of this perseverance as depriving yourself of your old TV time. Just persevere in the sense of adding these new healthy activities that bring you joy daily. Keep reminding yourself that your first responsibility is to yourself, and concentrate on enjoying the activities. Let your TV habit wind down on its own, as your need for it subsides when you fill your days with the adventure of life.

Now, if you think about the activities that you add in terms of time management of your busy day, than you can do a perfectly blissful Nature Walk (see Chapter 3) in a half-hour. And if that negates your need for TV, than you actually saved time by doing the Nature Walk, since you would have otherwise spent three to five hours watching television. In the same way, if a particular meditation helps cleanse your mind of your daily worries, and you find that that activity helps you turn off the TV, than instead of spending four idle hours in front of TV, you did a twenty-minute meditation, which vacated more than three-and-a-half hours for... grabbing life by the balls, and saying, "Here I am." Even social activities are less time consuming than TV. So don't think about how time consuming the activity you add is, especially since the aim is to add into your life activities that help awaken the Ideal-you and give you experiences related to your Ideal Lifework, all of which help propel you into your most prosperous Lifepath.

Finding the Balance

Despite the fact that metaphysically speaking, time does not really exist, I know how challenging it can be to find time in your life for all the activities that you want to do. As you struggle to fit all the elements of your life into a healthy balance, of course work is important, especially if it is your Ideal Lifework—the work or endeavor that capitalizes on, and brings forth prosperity from, your Truest gifts and passions, while helping you fulfill your life mission. But in the life of a Truly successful co-Creator, other elements of your life are just as important: Sleep (see Chapter 2), your joyful physical activity (see Chapter 3), and time to prepare and leisurely eat holistically nutritious meals (see Chapters 4 and 5) are important to the health of your body-temple, as the vessel that anchors all the co-Creations of your Soul into manifestation in your physical reality. Having some extra time in your day, in which to continue to contemplate the rest of your steps towards your Ideal Lifepath (repeat Meditation To Devise A Plan Of Action, from Chapter 7 of *Seven Stages to co-Creating Prosperity From Your Soul*), and in which to joyfully take some of those steps that you've meditationally decided on, are also integral parts of driving your life towards your Ideal Lifepath. And of course, in terms of vibrationally attracting Divine prosperity into your life, time spent in meditation, relaxation, and especially time spent actually enjoying the fruits of your labor—doing things that you love and enjoy—the things that make you authentically you, is the most important time of all, since it helps you connect to your True Self, and bring forth Its Infinite Abundance into this physical reality.

Arranging your life in a balanced way that serve your new path as a conscious co-Creator requires that you take a moment to step aside your hectic daily reality, and with a cool, collected, and Soul-centered mind, put conceptual order amongst all the elements of your life. First, you need to decide: What are your non-negotiables, and how much time do you *need* to devote to your non-negotiables? What elements in your current life are temporary necessities? And if they are an unpleasant necessity, than realistically – how much daily/weekly time *are you willing* to allocate to them? What are the things that you *want* to do, because you feel strongly drawn to them, and feel that they would make you feel fulfilled and happy? Those, by the way, are monumentally important. Even if they do not yet seem directly related to prosperity, and you cannot yet see their obvious connection with the Ideal Life that you've meditationally perceived, they may be steps or elements that are leading up to your Ideal Life, and their connection to it will reveal itself in due time. What are the things that give you joy—hobbies, meeting with friends, social events, and the things that you are passionate about because they help you connect with who you Truly are?

To start taking control of your life in the most harmonious way, you need to realize that you actually have the power to arrange your life the way you want to. Even in the here-now sense, everything in life is about choices, and there is always an alternative way to do things. For example, a number of years ago, I was extremely busy with my career, and was gaining ten extra pounds per year. A few years later, I visited an old friend whom I haven't seen in a few years. He was in awe of how heavy I'd become and how out of shape I was, and I was in awe of how much weight he had lost, and how good he looked. When I asked him what his secret was, he answered that he never misses a day of enjoying a walk in the hills around his neighborhood, listening to his favorite music. My first reaction was: "Who's got that kind of time?!" His answer was simple, but so profound that it stuck with me all these years. He asked me, "When you get up each morning, do you always eat breakfast, brush your teeth, and do your morning bathroom routine?" I said, "Yes." So he continued, "You wouldn't consider going through a day without brushing your teeth and doing your morning bathroom routine, would you?" to which I replied, "No. Of course not." And here comes his final question, which drove my profound realization: he asked, *"Then why would you consider going through a day without doing the things that make you healthy and happy?"* The implication here, of course, is that you don't just have the time to do the things that keep you healthy and happy, you <u>make</u> that time.

The Math of Scheduling Time for Yourself:

As you go through your daily life, it can seem like a never-ending sequence of events that you have no control over; and it seems to never stop for long enough for you to have any momentum to change things, especially if some things, such as your work hours and your chores, seem constant within it. So now, remember the cool-collected place that we said you needed to be in when you arrange all the elements of your life? Well, when you step aside of your life and into the consciousness of an objective observer, you could approach the scheduling issue like a math problem. And as simplistic as it might seem, the first question that you need to ask yourself is: where is all my time going?

I know that most people tend to think of work as the main event in their lives, and of chores and the things that they do for others as the second most important events in their lives. Therefore they figure that those should be the biggest time consumers of their schedule. But as I'm sure you're beginning to realize, your health, your energetic vibration, your joy, and your path towards your Ideal Lifepath are the most important. Your health, for example, should be one of your non-negotiable. So the time related to sustaining it—sleep, joyful physical activity, and mealtimes—should never be compromised. Likewise, we each have other things that are non-negotiables. For me, for example, having some daily time to do reiki self-healing is one of a non-negotiable. Therefore, even if I have to be late for an event, take on one less task during the day, or even sleep less, I always find the time to reiki myself. You too must have some things in your life that you won't compromise, and shouldn't have to. So after you figure out where your time is currently going, then, still in that same cool, collected place that is connected to your Soul's wisdom, you need to make inspired yet realistic decisions about how to re-arrange your schedule, so that you have ample time for the most important things, yet you still have enough time to do the things that sustain your living (such as life chores, and your current job, which you probably shouldn't quit until something better comes along that is more in line with your Ideal Lifework).

Okay, so since you first need to figure out where your time is currently going, it would be helpful to write down as a list how you usually spend your day. Let's go through an example together. Let's say that in our example, the person's current daily schedule looks like this:

> Wake up at: 6:30am
> Drive/commute to work: 7:00am – 8:00am
> Work: 8:00am–7:00pm (with an hour lunch, but most days working through lunch)
> Commute home: 7:00pm–7:45pm
> Eat microwaved dinner: 7:45pm–8:00pm
> Spend time with your kids: 8:00pm–9:30pm
> Do life chores: 9:30pm–10:30pm
> Read files & work materials: 10:30pm–12:30am
> Sleep: 12:30am–6:30am

So now let's total how many hours a day the person in this example devotes to each element of his/her life (activities that should be negotiable and variable are in gray; non-negotiables are in bold typeface; and below it in normal typeface are activities that are somewhat negotiable):

> Work: 12:45 hours
> Commute to and from work: 1:45 hour
> Life chores: 1 hour
> **Sleep: 6 hours**
> **Wakeup & breakfast: 30 minutes**

Mealtime: 30 minutes
Me Time: 0 hours
Joyful physical activity: 0 hours
Leisure & fun time: 0 hours
Spending time with kids: 1.5 hour

In light of what we've talked about regarding the important things in life, do you see anything wrong with this schedule? Leaving aside the person's commute-time to and from work (which may be a necessary evil), this person spends almost thirteen hours a day working, if we consider that the person in this example grabs a quick sandwich and eats it quickly on the side of his/her desk, while continuing to work through lunch, and if we include the two late night hours that he/she devotes to work from home. On the other hand if we look at the elements of life that should be non-negotiable, this person is continuously sleep-deprived, and devote inadequate time to enjoying nutritious meals, and no time at all for Me Time or Joyful Physical Activity. And on top of that, this person devotes very little time to his/her kids (and devoting time to one's kids is something that brings us love and joy, which are great vibrational co-Creators), and no time at all for enjoying life.

Next, if the person in this example wanted to shift their life to co-Create their Ideal Lifepath, than he or she would have to meditatively, and from a deep place of connecting with their Soul (see Zohar Breath Meditation in *Seven Stages to co-Creating Prosperity From Your Soul),* ask themselves some hard questions, such as:

- ☯ Am I blissfully happy and supremely fulfilled in my life, the way it is now?
- ☯ Do I derive pleasure, satisfaction, and the highest self-actualization from this job that I spend so many daily hours working at? Is this my Ideal Lifework? Does it make me feel more authentically me (the Ideal-me)?
- ☯ Is there a way for me to spend less daily hours at my current job, so I can devote more time to the non-negotiables, and to the joyful side of life, and still sustain myself financially without rocking the boat too much?

Once this person figures out all the practical aspects of shifting his/her schedule to working less hours, it's time to construct his/her dream schedule. The way to do that is to first write down the non-negotiables, than work and other necessities, and then plug these into an actual schedule that could become practical with enough creative flair. So let's say that the person in our example writes down his/her non-negotiables this way:

Sleep: 8 hours
Wakeup, get dressed, etc.: 30 minutes
Breakfast with the family: 30 minutes
Lunch & dinner times: 1.5 hours
Me Time, Joyful physical activity: 1 hour

Well, these non-negotiables amount to eleven-and-a-half hour a day. And since there are twenty-four hours in a day, this leaves about twelve-and-a-half hours for both necessities (work, chores) and the somewhat negotiable things. So, our example person plugs into his/her calculation his/her negotiable tasks:

> Work: 8 hours
> Commute to and from work: 1 hour
> (Let's say he/she figured out a way to shorten the commute)
> Life chores (paying bills, laundry, shopping, cleaning, cooking...) not done during the week but only on part of Saturday

So in this new calculation, our example person meditatively and creatively figured out a way to work less hours and still provide for him/herself and his/her family well; he/she has figured out a creative way to shorten the commute to and from work; and most importantly, he/she has written down first the non-negotiables first, and plugged into the schedule work and chores second.

Now, if we total the non-negotiable and negotiable times, we'll see that the non-negotiables total eleven-and-a-half hours, and the negotiables total nine hours, which together totals twenty-and-a-half hours. This leaves this person with three-and-a-half hours a day that are negotiable and maneuverable.

In conclusion of this mathematic Soul-searching, our example person concludes that he/she wants to spend his three extra hours a day as such:

> Fun/leisure time, family, kids time: 2 hours
> Tasks to merge with Ideal Life: 1 hour
> Additional time with kids/family: half hour

Now, it is one thing to figure all this out hypothetically, and another thing to actually live by this calculation. Aside from, in this case, this person's figuring out how to reduce his/her commute time to and from work, and negotiating reduced hours at work while still being a good candidate for the job and being able to support him/herself well (which this person world have to creatively do), there is the matter of following through. So this person would actually have to reconstruct his/her daily schedule, based on his/her new decisions, creative negotiations, and other maneuverings of the schedule. So let's say that this person now writes his/her new schedule as such:

> Wake, get dressed, etc.: 6:30am – 7:00am
> Breakfast with loved ones: 7:00am – 7:30am
> Work on Ideal Life goals: 7:30am – 8:30am
> Drive/commute to work: 8:30am – 9:00am
> Work: 9:00am – 5:30pm (with a solid half-hour for lunch)
> Commute from work: 5:30pm – 6:00pm
> Me Time*: 6:00pm – 7:00pm
> (*includes joyful physical activities on some days of the week)

Dinner with loved ones: 7:00pm – 8:00pm
Leisure, fun & family time: 8:00pm – 10:30pm
Sleep: 0:30am – 6:30am

You see from this example that everything is possible, even from a here-now perspective—even before the Universe meets you halfway and helps you fulfill your dreams and your Ideal Lifepath. It's true that there may be a few here-now things that you would have to either negotiate, or find creative solutions for, just as our example person had to negotiate working less hours for higher hourly pay, and cutting down his/her commute times (perhaps by driving to/from work at different hours or different routes). But when you think of all the wonderful things that the Universe is bringing to the rendezvous point, such as synchronistic opportunities, abundance, and important Soul brothers and sisters to help you along your path, just to name a few, than the things that you'd have to negotiate or think creatively about do not seem like such a big deal. And the joy that you'll derive from your new, more leisurely schedule will far surpass the lifestyle you were leading before. Who knows, maybe in this initial effort to balance your schedule more harmoniously, you'd "accidentally" stumble across a better job, with better pay, which is more inline with your Ideal Lifework. And even if not, you won't have to moonlight the activities of merging your current life with your Ideal one for too long, since synchronistic gifts from the Universe will bring opportunities into your lap, which will drive you towards your Ideal Lifework and your Ideal Lifepath—the path through life in which your Truest wishes just manifest themselves naturally, and your level of bliss skyrockets.

Now keep in mind that the calculations above were only an example. Your life circumstances may be totally different from the person in our example, and of course we each have our own unique talents and passions. So the elements that you are struggling to fit into your life may be completely different from this example. You may have some very particular hobbies or activities that you are passionate about, which you would like to fit into your life. Even your method of calculating and thinking about your schedule may be different. And that's okay. What is the same is the process of allowing yourself to step outside the mundane, connecting with the conscious observer within you (or better yet, your Soul Self, if you've read *Seven Stages to co-Creating Prosperity From Your Soul* and are proficient at doing Zohar Breath Meditation), and from a cool, collected place, figuring out creative ways to maneuver your schedule to fit into it all the things that are important to you, in a kind and leisurely way that will help you interject more joy into all the small moments of your life.

You are in total control of your life. Sure, the bigger circumstances of your life are controlled by the Free Will of your Soul as part of the Divine, which is beyond the control of your here-now self. But even your here-now self was given a free will, and thus has power to control your decisions of how you want to spend your life. And that starts with how you choose to construct your daily schedule. When you construct your daily schedule, you need to set up your non-negotiables as such, and leave enough room in it for doing the joyful things that reawaken within you the real You, and also for taking some of the steps of your auspicious Plan to merge your current reality with your Ideal Lifepath of prosperity.

Of course, beyond the contemplative time to do this deep thinking, calculation, and planning of how to arrange your life more Ideally, as you walk through the everyday of your life, you need to keep interjecting joy into every moment, reminding yourself of whom You (Soul) Truly are, and taking the time to breathe and connect with your Soul Self.

One of the wisest metaphors that are attributed to the Gautama Buddha is: "a guitar string – if it's wound too tight, it snaps, and if it's too loose, it won't play right." Happiness, health, and prosperity can only come through your Infinite Funnel of Abundance, when you *allow* them to flow in, and when you align your life path with the Ideal Lifeplan that your Soul has laid out for you. Allowing the Infinite Funnel of Abundance to flow freely into your life starts with, and depends on finding the Balance of Grace—the perfect balance between the Heavenly energy of your Soul Self, and the earthly energy of your physical existence, in each of the small moments of your life. A human being is the bridge between the Heaven and the earth. And when we balance both the Heavenly and the earthly energies within us, besides magnetizing the prosperity to actually manifest in our lives, we also harmonize the entire universe.

Aligning your current life with your Soul's Ideal Lifeplan is a process that first took cognition—understanding the metaphysical process of co-Creation (*Prosperity From Your Soul*); then took communications—developing an intimate relationship with your Soul and tuning into the details of your Ideal Lifeplan (*Seven Stages to co-Creating Prosperity From Your Soul);* and finally necessitates driving the physical reality of your life towards your Ideal Lifepath, while consciously setting your vision free, and finding the Balance of Grace.

The first steps towards driving the reality of your life towards your Ideal Lifepath and bringing your co-Creations into physical manifestation is to creatively find the harmonious balance amongst all the elements of your life: the non-negotiables—sleep, rest, mealtime, joyful physical activities, and Me Time; the negotiables—work, commute, and life's chores; and the things that you wish to add—time to spend with loved ones, time to complete some of the tasks on your auspicious Plan, and most importantly, time to just have fun with life. It is the harmonious balance amongst all these elements that not only leaves room in your life for the auspicious inflow of Universal gifts, but also makes your life so joyful and vibrationally light, that it vibrationally resonates with the prosperity, health, and happiness that you seek, and therefore attracts it into your life. For only by maintaining a healthy and harmonious balance among all the elements of your life can the vibration of your life sustain the flow of Divine life-force and Creative energy into and life.

In this chapter, I've given you just some food for thought, in order to drive you to deeply think about, and hopefully find, the balance of life that is best suited *for you*. Ultimately, I hope that your own inner wisdom would guide you to find the beautiful balance that will make your life resonate with the Universe like a beautiful symphony, so that It can help you co-Create all the blessings that you wish for and more.

In chapters 3 to 5, we'll prepare your body-vessel both in terms of being receptive to the enhanced Creative energy that is now going to flow through your Infinite Funnel of Abundance, and in terms of prepping your physical body for the activities of your new path.

In the next chapter, we'll discuss an important element, which plays an important role in both finding balance amongst all the elements of your life, and in the multidimensional health of your body-temple—sleep and relaxation.

Chapter 2

Sleep & Relaxation

Contrary to most people's conception of a lifepath of prosperity as a continuous go-go-go mode, sleep is actually a very important element of your new Lifepath, which contributes a great deal to the achievement of True prosperity—from your Soul. And there are several layers to how sleep helps bring about prosperity:

The first, most obvious one is kindness-to-self, which is an integral part of prosperity from your Soul. Since you now adjusting your lifestyle to accommodate the new Abundance energy that is coming into your life, it is time for you to bring kindness-to-self into every nook and cranny, and into each small moment in your life. Getting enough Me Time, relaxation time, and adequate sleep is not just an indulgence. It is monumentally important for all levels of your multidimensional existence of health, happiness, and prosperity.

On a purely physical level, sleep gives your body a chance repairs and heals itself. According to Harvard School Of Medicine[1], research shows that "many of the body's restorative functions, muscle growth, tissue repair, protein synthesis, and growth hormone occur mostly, or in some cases only during sleep." Doctors tell us that sleep also plays an important role in immune function, metabolism, memory, learning, stress reduction, mood improvement, and in boosting our energy level during the day. So the first relationship between getting a good night sleep and your highest path to prosperity is maintaining good health, which is an integral part of all-inclusive prosperity.

The second relationship is: if sleep can reduce stress, improve your moods, and boost up your energy level, than in terms of prosperity from your Soul, getting a good night sleep can help you on two levels: it can help you wake up calm and centered, yet refreshed, vivacious and upbeat enough to tackle all that you've set up for yourself to do that day as part of your Plan to merge with your Ideal Lifepath; and it is also that peaceful yet upbeat vibration that resonates with, and therefore attracts into your life the prosperity that you seek. This scientific data can be backed up experientially: Think of how many times you've felt sad, tired of life's challenges, sometimes even hopeless, at night after a stressful day; but then after a good night sleep woke up in the morning refreshed, hopeful, jazzed about life, and ready to tackle any challenge. Indeed, a good night sleep has a multidimensional healing effect on us.

The third relationship between sleep and your Ideal Lifepath is spiritual. There are extensive spiritual benefits to getting good quality sleep, some of which we have discussed in our discussion about dreams in *Seven Stages to co-Creating Prosperity From Your Soul*. The possibilities of doing spiritual work during dreamtime, when our "logical" here-now mind is switched off, and therefore cannot interfere, are endless. During dreamtime, we go through life experiences that would be difficult for us to experience during our wakeful hours; learn lessons that yield Soul growth in a short time; and easily receive messages and inspired ideas from our Souls and from our Spirit Guides and Angeles (or any other deity that you believe in). And receiving more inspired ideas from our Soul Selves regarding our Ideal Lifepaths is directly related to co-Creating prosperity in our lives. In dream reality, your Soul may also give you a more complete experience of your Ideal Life, which also serves to vibrationally attract that Ideal Life into your reality. Why does all this have to take place during sleep? It doesn't have to. But during sleep, the "logical" part of your mind—the part that during wakeful hours tells you "You can't do that," "you don't have enough money," and other self-defeating dialogue—is turned off. So it is a perfect time for your Soul to communicate clear messages to you. Remember that messages that are Truly coming from your Soul will always be very clear (as opposed to the jumble of thought of your here-now subconscious), peaceful, high-vibrational, empowering, and support your highest wellbeing and Ideal Lifepath.

What is important for you to know is that sleep is more important to your overall wellbeing (physical, emotional, mental, and spiritual) than you may have realized before; and that getting adequate sleep is what enables you to wake up wide eyed and bushy tale – ready to reclaim your Ideal Lifepath of prosperity.

How much sleep is enough is a much-debated question, on which medical opinions vary. Studies show that most adults do best with eight hours of sleep per night. Some medical conditions, however, such as migraines for example, dictate that its sufferers get at least nine or ten hours of sleep per night. There are also some medical conditions that require a specific sleep schedule. Children and teens need more sleep, while older people often need less sleep than they used to. The consensus seems to be that if you fall asleep within five minutes of hitting your pillow, or if you need to take naps during the day, you aren't getting enough sleep.[2]

In this chapter, I will relate some practices that can help you fall asleep easier, and get better quality sleep, so you can wake up refreshed, energized, and ready to reclaim your Ideal Lifepath with joy.

Prepare for a Great Night Sleep

The practices listed here are a compilation of yogic wisdom[3] that has proven itself over thousands of years, naturopathic[4], and modern medical[2] knowledge. As with anything else, I encourage you to choose from them only the ones that resonate well with your internal wisdom.

Bed Position:

Yogic as well as Kabbalah recommend having your bed facing East-West, so it is not aligned with the Earth's magnetic field. Kabbalah recommends the head facing east especially during child conception (particularly if you want to have boys, combine this bed orientation with missionary position), so as to align well with the intent of the Divine's creative energy. On the other hand, according to most New Age thinkers, the bed actually *should* be aligned with the magnetic poles of the earth—north to south—with the head on the north side, and the feet on the south side. So this is another issue on which you should listen to your higher intuition. You can try one way and give it a week to check the results, then try the other way, and see how you sleep.

Most Feng Shui books and sleep experts will also tell you that your bedroom should be a place designated just for sleeping (and hopefully also for making love with your Soulmate). Your office—the space in which you are used to engaging your active logical mind—should be separate from your bedroom, even if these are just separate areas within your tiny studio apartment. In your bedroom or sleep area, you should have no distractions, and no associations that could stimulate you. You should set up your bedroom or sleep area in a way that allows you to make the room dark, quiet, peaceful and nurturing. The point is that your bedroom/sleep area would allow you to disconnect from the external world, reach the ultimate peace, and connect with your Soul Self. So to facilitate that, your inner guidance may guide you to design your own unique bedroom décor, with a unique bed orientation, such as for examples a bedroom that is adjacent your garden, an oval, dark, and nurturing cave-like room with water fountains and crystals, or any other unique décor that you feel guided to create for yourself, which will facilitate a peaceful night sleep.

Letting Go:

Before you go into your final stages of preparation for sleep, write a To Do list in which you include all the things that you didn't complete today. Include in it all the things that are on your mind, troubling you, or which need resolving. But don't get too preoccupied with this list. Just spit it out on paper quickly, almost like you do when you engage in automatic writing. The purpose is that once you've put it down on paper (or electronic notepad), you can clear your mind of those thoughts and move on to the relaxation part of the evening. Keep this list out and away from your bedroom, preferably hidden in a drawer in your desk, where you do creative work, so that tomorrow you can think of creative and inspired ways to easily and smoothly accomplish these tasks or resolve all these issues.

Once you have put down your issues, and tucked the list away, put them out of your mind and completely let them go. This is a conscious decision to put a stop to the go-go-go mode, and begin the relaxation part of the evening, knowing that tomorrow, with a fresh and clear mind, your ability to deal with the issues of your life will increase exponentially.

You may want to ask your Angels for help with any issues that need resolving—completely surrender the issue into the hands of the Angels (or other deity) that you invoked. Ask Archangel Raphael (or any other deity that you believe in) to assist you in the relaxation and healing of your body and mind. Finish this little letting go ceremony by envisioning all unresolved issues on a silver platter inside a bubble of Divine white Light, seeing them all (in the eyes of your mind) perfectly resolved by the Universe on your behalf. Even if you are a complete atheist, this visualization will help put your mind in peace, and help you psychologically detach from your troubling issues in a healthy way.

It is also important to feel comfortable and fulfilled with your achievements of the day, and with the lessons that life has afforded you that day. So take a few moments to reflect on your day. Give yourself kudos for all the things that you achieved today—it doesn't have to be in the business arena; it could be a certain feeling-vibration that you maintained, a certain personality characteristics that you brought to its higher-vibrational expression, or anything else that you feel you deserve credit for.

Now find at least a few things you feel grateful for today—at present moment. This will help finalize your transition to relaxation and sleep mode.

Slow the Rhythms:

Two to four hours before going to sleep, start slowing your biorhythms into a mode of unwinding and relaxation, so that your transition to sleep time will be a smoother one. This is probably why we all find the need to veg or do something relaxing in the evening, because it helps our respiration and heart rate to slow down, helps the mind start detaching from the worries of the day, and start getting us into the peaceful, graceful part of the day.

So two to four hours before going to sleep (depending on how much spare Me Time you have), slow down. Be conscious of slowing down: walk slower, move slower, and stop any heavy mental activity. During this time, don't do any complicated math problems, and don't start strategizing your next life-move.

This unwinding can be in a variety of ways: watching a nice sunset, cuddling with your Soulmate, listening to relaxing music, reading a book, meditating, crocheting, having a beer with your buddies, creative writing, or just contemplating the moon… The point is: unwinding before going to sleep is a basic human need. It is not just an indulgence. So allow yourself to unwind in the most nurturing, kind ways you can think of.

Food for ZZZ's:

In the last eight hours before sleep, avoid stimulants such as coffee, black tea, or chocolate.

Avoiding or minimizing the consumption alcoholic beverages will not only promote a restful sleep, but also support the general good health of your mind, body and spirit. If you choose to have an occasional glass of wine or beer, finish your drinking at least two hours before bedtime. Medical studies have shown that alcohol dehydrates us, as well as disrupts deep REM sleep.

Sugar will send you into a sugar hyperactive mode that will keep you up all night. I used to be a sugar addict, so I can vouch that this is true. I was fidgety for at least four hours after the sugar boost, tossing and turning in bed with an overactive mind. So avoid sugary sweet foods for several hours before sleep.

Heavy meals are hard on the liver and on digestion. Yogic recommendation is to eat your last meal two hours before bedtime. On the other hand, I believe that you should not go to sleep hungry. So if you need to eat late in the evening, eat lightly. It is said that heavy animal proteins (such as steak) are especially hard on digestion. So eating a steak just before bedtime does not promote a good night sleep. On the other hand, complex carbohydrates are very relaxing. So a meal consisting of a hot vegetable soups, steamed vegetables, and plenty of whole grains will help sleep. However, if you depend on animal proteins (like I do), you can have a heavier meal for dinner at about 5 or 6pm, and have a lighter meal of milk, cereal, yogurt, and/or fruit later in the evening just before bedtime. A glass of warm milk or yogurt before bedtime is a time-honored sleep aid.

Natural Sleep Remedies:

There are a number of herbal remedies that have proven themselves over hundreds of years effectively promote sleep and relaxation.

Herbal Teas ~

A cup of tea, brewed with chamomile, lavender, or mint tea helps soothe the entire nervous system. I'll never forget the first time I tried this combination of herbs in a tea. I was strolling through a mall, and was for some reason agitated that day. So I stopped by at a specialized tea store, and sat at their tea bar sipping slowly a cup of hot chamomile, lavender, and mint tea. By the time I was halfway through the cup, I felt drowsy and ready to either sleep or meditate.

Skullcap can also be brewed into a tea: use about five grams of skullcap, and steep it in eight ounces of boiling water for about twenty minutes. Than drink it before bedtime.

Naturopathic Recommendations ~

If you have trouble falling asleep, here are some herbs that have been well known for hundreds of years to be effective sleep aids, without causing grogginess or other side effects that pharmaceutical sleep aids produce: valerian root (300-500mg), melatonin (3-24mg), hops (60mg), skullcap, calcium, vitamin B6, passionflower (200-300mg), and/or corydalis. These can be bought at your local health food store, and taken in pill form (tablets or capsules) about one hour before bedtime. Herbalists normally recommend taking skullcap as a tincture—10-30 drops of the tincture in a glass of water about thirty minutes before bedtime, and another 10-30 drops right at bedtime. Although I have seen skullcap often used in capsule form together with hops, valerian root, and melatonin, in different dosages and combination. Check the recommended dosage for the tablets you are buying.

Passionflower, valerian, hops, skullcap and corydalis can also be brewed as a tea, although I'm not sure what quantities you'd need to make them effective as teas, and I'm also not sure how it would taste. I know that valerian root tastes very bitter.

I encourage you to do your own research to verify the dosages and get the perfect herb combination that works well for you, and your unique body issues. Then meditate and connect with your inner wisdom to decide if, when, and how much of these herbs to take.

A word of caution: if you've taken valerian, skullcap, hop, or corydalis, you should not drive or operate machinery. Melatonin also gets you into a deep fatigue mode, although the fatigue that melatonin gets you into is more similar to the natural fatigue that you feel when you are deeply tired. So depending on how much melatonin you've taken, you probably shouldn't drive after taking it either. Also, you should consult with your physician before ingesting any naturopathic medicine or herbs that you think may be adversely effect any specific health condition that you suffer from.

Bach Flower Remedies Include –

Bach Flower Remedies are tinctures (extracted with alcohol 27%) of different flowers, which are believed to have certain subtle energetic healing effects. There are a few flower remedies that indirectly promote a good night sleep: Rescue Remedy reduces reduce stress; White Chestnut helps quiet a noisy mind; and Red Chestnut reduces worries. All of those can be found at your local health food store. Rescue Remedy also comes in candy form, which is non alcoholic, and convenient to carry in your purse or briefcase, in case a stressful situation comes up at work.

To use Bach Flower Remedies, drop about four drops of the tincture into a glass of water. But the effects of Bach Flower Remedies are so very subtle—much subtler than the effects of the herbs discussed above. Bach Flower Remedies will not make you drowsy or sleepy. So I recommend that if you use them, do so several times a day, to promote an overall reduction in stress, worry, and the brainfucking noise.

Again, make sure you read labels, check for contraindications, and consult with your physician before ingesting any naturopathic medications that you think may be adversely effect any specific health condition that you suffer from.

Set the Stage for Peace...

Protection Before Sleep:

I know this may seem a little out there, but on a spiritual level, many people can't sleep because their Souls are keeping them grounded in this reality, in an effort to protect them from interactions of the wrong kind. So I recommend adopting a habit of energetically clearing and blessing your space (as we've discussed in *Seven Stages to co-Creating Prosperity From Your Soul*) each night before going to sleep!

If in a particular period of time, you are having very active dreams, from which you wake up still tired, you are probably doing some spiritual work and learning some important lessons that serve your growth. If you prefer to postpone the spiritual work to a later time, and just have a restful and replenishing night sleep, you can set that intent prayerfully before going to sleep. In that case, the prayer is a quick and easy way to affirm your free will, and communicate it to your Soul, your Spirit Guides, and your Angels.

Aromatherapy:

If you are in tune with scent, putting a few drops of essential oil in a diffuser, or anointing a candle with essential oils, may tremendously help set the atmosphere for your evening meditation and relaxation, as well as promote a good night sleep. Essential oils that are known for their relaxation effects are: roman chamomile, lavender, lemon verbena, neroli, spikenard, and ylang-ylang. Other essential oils that are can assist in relaxation to sleep are: sandalwood, because of its grounding, centering effect, as well as frankincense, myrrh and patchouli, which can drive you into a deeply meditative mode.

Music:

Music is the most distilled energy that can be used as a medium for healing, stilling our minds, evoking certain feelings, and tuning into long forgotten parts of oneself. There are many genres of music that are totally relaxing and appropriate for sleep. And that choice usually depends on your taste and the personal experiences that certain music arouses.

There are some types of music that are universally thought of as relaxing. Mellow classical music of Beethoven and Chopin can evoke not only relaxation, but also elevate your spirit. Mozart's music has been especially researched and found to sharpen your mind while relaxing and instilling peace. Also, earth tone music and music that has Brain-Sync or Hemi-Sync technologies are scientifically proven to promote relaxation, and balance the brainwaves. I find that a CD called "Shamanic Dream" by Anugama puts me to sleep every time – no exceptions. In fact, this CD is so effective for me that I do not listen to it while driving. Sometimes, if you are noise fatigued, you may prefer absolute quiet, and listening only to the vibration of the Divine within. Again, your inner wisdom will guide you on this issue.

Hair:

Yogic lifestyle recommends combing your hair with a wooden comb before going to sleep. Yogis explain that the wooden comb stabilizes the magnetic field to maintain one's youth, and the act of brushing also stimulates circulation in the scalp.

Even if you don't ascribe to every yogic recommendation out there, you may still find the habit of slowly and softly combing your hair for a few minutes before bed to be very soothing. I personally don't know if I believe it stabilizes my magnetic field, but I know that I've become addicted to the scalp massage of brushing my hair at night with the wooden brush. And I know some yoga teachers who are bald, but who like to use the wooden brush to massage their scalp before bedtime. I also find that energizing my reiki hands, and softly using them to caress my hair and scalp is extremely soothing, and lulls me into a peaceful sleep.

Feet:

Yogis recommend washing your feet with warm water before bedtime. They profess that it relaxes all seventy two thousand nerve-endings in your feet and entire body. And what is being referenced here is not physical neuron endings, but spiritual nerves—the seventy two thousand nadis, which are the energy channels distributing the life-force energy coming through the Etheric Body, from each chakra into the physical body.

I find it very soothing to wash my feet with in warm water before going to sleep, softly massaging them while envisioning that I am washing away all the worries of the day, and nurturing myself with good things.

Zohar Hydro-Therapy

Different temperature of water can produce different effects on our entire nervous system and thus our circadian rhythms. The yogic way recommends an ice-cold shower in the morning, to stimulate the blood into all the capillaries and get us going. And in Western tradition, it is well known that a very hot shower or bath is relaxing.

So if you are truly having a problem falling asleep, instead of just washing your feet with warm water, have a relaxing hot bath just before going to sleep. Consider a flower bath to fully bless yourself before going to bed. Roses are symbolic of Divine love, and also have soothing, cooling, and uplifting aphrodisiac affects. And since most of us are in dire need of nurturing and love, I recommend including rose tea in your evening ceremony, with the intention of giving yourself all the love and nurturing that you deserve. Lavender, Chamomile, and Rose buds are great for relaxation and can be made into a tea. So consider the following ceremony:

While you are still engaged in the unwinding activity of your evening, be it watching a movie, reading, having a conversation with a friend, or meditating, gather a fistful of the flowers that 'speak' to you that evening. Hold the flowers between your hands and pray over them, intently imbuing them with perfect peace, relaxation and nurturing. Then boil a large pot of water with the blessed flowers. Let it steep for a while, so that the water fully absorbs the taste, aroma, and blessings you have imbued the flowers with. Then, start filling the bathtub with hot water (as hot as you can bear, checking with your elbow). Add to it a few drops of essential oils of lavender, chamomile, lemon verbena, neroli, spikenard, or ylang-ylang, or you may have other essential oils that are very relaxing to you personally, because they have a particular association in your mind. Pour yourself a cup of the blessed flower tea you've brewed, so you can drink it during the bath. Add the rest of the tea and loose flowers in it into your blessed flower bath. (Make sure, though, that your bathtub drain has some kind of a net, so that when you drain the tub, the dried flowers would not clog it.) Dim your bathroom lights, or turn them off and light some vanilla candles so that the light is soft and kind.

As you undress yourself, envision that you are shedding off all your worries and troubles of the day... Now bathe in the blessed flower water, and envision that you are bathing in pure Divine Love, Light, and blessings... Close your eyes, take some relaxing deep breaths, fully relax, contemplate your own fabulousness, and just and enjoy. This should get you not only fully relaxed and ready for a great night sleep, but also feeling like a blessed child of the Divine. You'll probably wake up in the morning feeling blessed, and find some aspects in your life healed.

Reading a Book:

If you like reading a book to relax before sleep, do so now, before the next steps. Make sure it's not a suspense thriller, as that would stimulate you and keep you up all night worrying about what happened to the hero in the story. Also, avoid reading technical manuals or anything that gets your left-brain too active figuring out logical things. I like reading something spiritual and relaxing before I fall asleep. But I find the practice of Meditate to Sleep (next paragraph) much more effective in promoting peace, and tuning into the highest Divine realm during sleep.

Meditate to Sleep:

Sit for a few moments on your bed. Close your eyes, and start a Zohar Breath Meditation—just breath deeply, envisioning that as you inhale, Divine white Light coming into the back of your heart chakra and flooding your whole body, and as you exhale, the Divine white Light expands and engulfs your entire aura and room… After a few minutes of Zohar Breath Meditation, your breath-visualization will become a pure exchange of Light between you and the Divine. Envision that you are completely bathed in the peace, Love, and nurturing of the Divine, nourishing every cell and organ… Whatever thoughts come up, release them into the God Bubble of Light. (See Chapter 2 of *Seven Stages to co-Creating Prosperity From Your Soul* for discussion of The God Bubble, and for a more detailed description of Zohar Breath meditation, including how to bless your space and set the intent for the meditation.) Come to the point in which your mind's brainfucking chatter has stopped, and you are in a state of supreme peace. Know that when you feel that supremely nurturing peace, you are bathed in Divine Love-Light and peace.

In *Seven Stages to co-Creating Prosperity From Your Soul*, we used Zohar Breath Meditation to actively tune into specific answers from your Soul. In this meditation, the intent is simply to dwell in the peace of your Soul, and in Its deep feeling that everything is going to be ok. So sit and be healed in this Light for a few moments…

Then, lie down, shut the light, cover yourself comfortably, kiss good night whomever you need to kiss goodnight, and drift off into a restful, enjoyable, and blissful sleep…

Ancient yogis thought advocates laying on the right side first, so that your left nostril is up and active, which essentially puts you into Moon Breath (again, see *Seven Stages to co-Creating Prosperity From Your Soul*)—the breath pattern that activates the spiritual right brain hemisphere and facilitates relaxation. I advocate lying in whatever position makes you feel peaceful and nurtured—whichever position helps you reconnect with the feeling of being the beloved child of God that you are.

In this chapter, we looked at sleep as a tool replenishing your life-force energy, a time of introspection and rebirth, so you can wake up refreshed, upbeat yet centered, and excited to walk the path of your life in each day anew. I've also given you a few natural remedies to promote a good night sleep.

Enjoying a good night sleep is an integral component of living your Ideal Lifepath, as kindness-to-self is an integral aspect of all-inclusive prosperity. As we have discussed, sleep also has some very important co-Creative powers: It facilitates a state of joyful alertness during the day—a state that helps you walk the steps of your Plan to merge with your Ideal Life, while joyfully dwelling in a prosperity-magnetizing high vibration. Your dreams at this stage also have a tremendous co-Creative benefits: during dreamtime, you may receive additional insights and ideas from your Soul and your Spirit Guides, to beef up the Plan of Action that you started to make at the end of *Seven Stages to co-Creating Prosperity From Your Soul* into a real-life plan that you can start following in your here-now reality, which will lead you towards your Ideal Lifepath. In other words, in dreams, your Soul may choose to give you advice, and show you how the humble steps that you take in your current reality can tie into your Ideal Lifeplan, and how they are expected to fit in the overall picture of your Ideal Life.

In the next chapter, we will discuss joyful physical activity as one of the most potent movers and balancers of Ki (life-force energy) – a balance which helps bring our energetic vibration into resonance with the high-vibrational reality of prosperity from your Soul.

Chapter 3

Lightness in Your Body Temple

Up to now, we have been dealing with the first bridge between the ethereal co-Creation of your Soul and your here-now reality – balancing your lifestyle and making room in it for all the elements of your Ideal Lifepath to come through your Infinite Funnel of Abundance. The second and third bridges, which we began in the last chapter's discussion of sleep and will continue to build on in this chapter, are the preparation of your body-vessel, both physically and vibrationally, for your new life as a successful co-Creator.

It is true that we are all spiritual beings (even if you are currently an atheist). But we are spiritual beings who have chosen to have a physical life on Earth. It is also True that our Souls were blessed with Infinite Divine resources. But it is the integration of these Heavenly energies into the physical, which facilitates the pouring of health, happiness, and prosperity in our physical reality. And since our bodies (physical and energetic) are the vessels through which Soul has chosen to experience this incarnation, they are also the anchors that bring forth all the co-Creative energies of the Soul into manifestation in our physical reality.

The physical body is an anchor for Soul Abundance on several levels: On a here-now physiological level, a healthy and in shape body can help you move with ease, and be better able to complete the tasks of your new prosperous path. Vibrationally, this ease of movement, and the comfort that you feel in your body-temple can help you experience more joy as you go through your day, thus keeping you in a high vibration that magnetizes prosperity into manifestation in your life. Metaphysically speaking, to make room for fresh Creative energy to come in through your Infinite Funnel of Abundance, you need to regularly engage in some type of practice that can help move your Ki (Divine life-force and Creative energy) around—getting rid of any energetic debris and blocks, getting stagnant energy healthily moving again, bringing new Ki in, and balancing your physical and energetic bodies apparatus. And nothing moves Ki better than joyful physical activity.

Joyful Physical Activity

Physical exercise has benefits on many different levels. Firstly, health is one of the major components of all-inclusive prosperity—a prerequisite if you will, of experiencing the True joy that is part of prosperity from your Soul. And from the pure health perspective, exercise not only helps maintain a healthy diet by burning calories and boosting the metabolism (which we will talk about in more detail in Chapter 5), but also has some important physiological[1] benefits:

- Boosts HDL (good) cholesterol
- Reduces LDL (bad) cholesterol & triglycerides
- Improves circulation
- Reduces risk of heart disease
- Boosts metabolism
- Helps prevent – strokes, type-2 diabetes, arthritis, certain types of cancer, and cognitive decline
- Boost brain power and sharpen memory
- Improve muscles strength, pliability & endurance
- Helps maintain good bone density and bone health
- Helps increase your energy level

On a physical level, as I mentioned, being in shape prepares your body for the demands of the new prosperous path you are now starting to walk. Whether that's opening your own business, a promotion in a career that brings you much joy, marrying your Soulmate, or manifesting prosperity through any other unique idea that grounds the Light of your Soul, being in a reasonably good physical shape helps you feel joyful and light about fulfilling your daily tasks with ease.

Psychologically speaking[2], there are also commonly known mental-emotional benefits to being physically active, some of which are: stress reduction, improved self-esteem, an overall feeling of accomplishment (despite the fact that your Truest accomplishment is simply being you), and the stimulation of brain chemicals that improve mood and leave you feeling happy and relaxed. And these psychological benefits certainly do relate to co-Creating prosperity, since peace, joy, a healthy self-esteem, and a trust in one's ability to accomplish things are all emotions that shift your energetic vibration into resonance with the Infinite Funnel of Abundance.

On a spiritual-energetic level, exercise helps move Ki (life-force energy) within your energetic and physical bodies, and thus helps let go of any stuck or blocked energy, making room within your expanded auric field for new Creative energy to enter through your Infinite Funnel of Abundance. To illustrate, if your hose of abundance were dry-stiff and full of dried dirt, then that might limit or even block fresh living water (energy) from flowing through your hose. Exercise is like flexing the hose every which way in order to break loose the dried dirt and restore the hose's elasticity and its ability to conduct water. And if your hose were always connected to an Infinite Source of water (and you certainly are permanently connected to an Infinite Source of Ki) than the movement would restore the hose's ability to conduct enhanced amounts of clear water. In the same way, joyful movement of your body helps move your Ki around, thereby cleansing your body-vessel as the funnel through which Infinite prosperity and life-force energy flow into your reality. Of course, as you exercise, your breathing rate (prana energy) also increases, and you are inviting more of the Infinite's energy to flow through you.

It is true that some of the freshness and lightness you feel after exercising are partially due to the release of endorphins, dopamine, serotonin (the body's pleasure hormones) and adrenaline into your bloodstream. And it is also true that as you condition your body to exercise, part of why it becomes easier for you to move is the adjustment of your nervous system, followed by the conditioning of your muscles. But since any manifested physical state is the result of energetic changes in the ethereal reality, the main reason you feel so light and lighthearted after exercising is that your life-force energy is cleansed, balanced, and renewed.

However, there is a reason why I named this section "Joyful Physical Activity" and not "Frontal Attack On The Gym." Even on a purely physiological level, overly strenuous physical exercise have been linked to heart disease, bulimia, headaches, immune damage, and permanent scaring of muscle tissue, including the heart muscle[3, 4, 5], whereas activities that are joyful (not just exercise, but also orgasms, dance, and anything else that is pleasurable) cause our brain, blood, blood vessels, and lungs to produce a signaling molecule called nitric oxide, which triggers an increase and balance all the pleasure chemicals of the body—endorphins, dopamine, serotonin, oxytocin, and DMT. So physiologically speaking, pleasure is not only relaxing and uplifting, but also brings tremendous health benefits, such as preventing strokes, assisting the fighting of infections and tumors, balancing neurotransmitters, and reducing cellular inflammation, just to name a few. Those are only the physiological reasons why physical exercise should be pleasurable. But physiological health is not the only reason why we are adding a physical activity into our lifestyle. In her book *Goddesses Never Age*, Christiane Northrup (despite being a medical doctor) says that she "find[s] it helpful to think of nitric oxide as the physical manifestation of the vital life force... that animates the body."[6]

Indeed, on a spiritual level, if physical activity is something you do during your Me Time, than it had better be something that is deeply pleasurable for you—something that helps you reclaim your joy, and gives you deep inner peace. Because if you think of physical activity as something that functions to energetically move your Ki around and facilitates the in-pour additional life-force (Creative energy), than *it must be something joyful*, because the purest Source for all Creative energy is Divine Love, which is synonymous with joy. Therefore in order for this activity to help you tap into the Infinite Funnel of Abundance, it must resonate with the vibration of Divine joy.

What I propose is simple: Each one of us has an array of activities that he/she loves to do, some of which are physical. It could be dancing, skiing, window-shopping in the mall, playing basketball with friends, meditational walks in your neighborhood, mountain biking, or even jumping jacks—anything else that is physical and gives you pleasure. If you think about it, you'll surely find that you already have at least one physical activity that is pleasurable for you. Happy Back Walk and Nature Walk (discussed later this chapter) are two excellent Joyful Physical Activities that will give you all the health benefits of regular exercise, but are also deeply enjoyable, and have the added benefits of balancing your energies, and restoring your peace of mind. But as wonderful as these practices are, they are just some suggestions for Joyful Physical Activities. Whatever your most enjoyable physical activity is, make it a point to engage it for about thirty minutes a day.

For example, one of my most pleasurable physical activities is swimming. When I was working for the airlines, I used to swim long distances in beautiful places where we overnighted in the Caribbean. But for many years after having moved to California, I stayed away from swimming because of the cold temperatures of the Pacific Ocean water. Then, I found out that the city where I lived had a beautiful public swimming pool that was indoors, heated, and semi-Olympic in size. I decided to try it. To make up for the fact that I no longer had the outdoors beauty of the Caribbean's turquoise water, I found a meditational mental activity (I mentally project reiki healing to myself and my life, or sometimes silently sing yogic mantras) to keep me from getting bored while I swim. I have come to really enjoy swimming in the local pool. The point is that the swimming pool was always there. So was my innate ability to avoid getting bored while swimming in a pool. It took readiness, on my part, to do something kind for myself. I hope that for you it wouldn't take years to find a way to engage in your favorite physical activity.

Maybe you love horseback riding, but you think that you couldn't afford to ride all the time. But if you truly connect with the synchronistic flow of life, it is very possible that you'll find someone who has a horse that he/she doesn't have time to ride, who will let you exercise the horse (by riding it) in exchange for some simple brushing and feeding chores. Or maybe you don't go on your favorite nature hike because you don't want to pay seven dollars for parking each time, and after a little research you find out there is cheap meter parking just a few steps from that spot.

The point is simple: exercise doesn't have to be painful. Whoever invented that slogan "no pain no gain," excuse me but, is an idiot! Exercising shouldn't be painful, and it doesn't have to be a frontal attack on the gym. That would not even be beneficial on a physiological level, since overexerting yourself will prevent the body from releasing any fat tissue, will not build up muscle, and it may cause a variety of health problems.

Moreover, if exercise is a chore, you'll never do it. You'll find every excuse in the book not to do it. Believe me, I've done it. And from a metaphysical standpoint, if it is a chore, it would *not* help you purge out any energetic blocks, as necessary to renew your Ki, since you'd be accumulating new negative energy just from your resentment of "having to do it." The bottom line is: if you are not doing it with joy, than it's not helping you reconnect with your Infinite Funnel of Abundance. In order for your physical activity to also help you reconnect with the Infinite Funnel of Abundance, it needs to be something that you enjoy doing, which connects you with True joy!

Now, to be perfectly honest, we all have some level of natural affinity to the couch. Most of us have a feeling of "I just don't want to move right now," which usually dissolves as soon as we start the physical activity, especially if it a joyful one. Here is another place where the three-faceted balance of kindness needs to be honored: As mentioned in *Prosperity From Your Soul*, if the origin of your fatigue is physical—if on a particular day you are legitimately tired, sleep deprived, hungry, or sick, than you should not be exercising on that day. On those days, you should catch up on sleep, eat nutritiously, and nurture yourself, so that you *can* go back to your joyful physical activity the next day. If, on the other hand, your limitation is mental-emotional (laziness is usually mentally-emotionally based), than you should push yourself through, because on those days, getting out and doing your fun physical activity is exactly what you need to burn (purge) out the heavy feelings and troubling thoughts, and consequently get yourself back into a happy balance. And the third facet of kindness is: whichever side of the balance you chose on a particular day—even on the days that you do push yourself to exercise because you know you'd feel better afterwards, there is always a kinder, softer way to any physical movement. For example, your lunges or sit-ups don't have to be emphatic to work out your muscles. They could be graceful ones that brings softness into all the tight places in your body, brings the energy of kindness into your physical body, and affects new flexibility and freedom. For beyond joy, even on a physical level, tuning into softness and kindness within actually helps you achieve more out of the exercise – it helps you build endurance and a different kind of strength.

Physical activity can and should be fun. I find that even if I woke up tired and upset, if I do a Nature Walk, a meditative swim, or RezoDance (more on RezoDance in a little bit), not only does my mood improve, but also my vitality increases, the rest of my day becomes more productive, and I sleep better at night. As lazy as I used to be with regards to exercise, I have actually gotten to the point that I crave my Nature Walks and my RezoDance sessions as medicine for my body and Soul.

Three Joyful Physical Activities that were communicated to me while channeling the information in this book are Kindness Movement, Happy Back Walk, and Nature Walk. While practicing these activities and teaching them to others, I've found that they bring a tremendous amount of freedom to the body, while uplifting the Spirit, and bringing people into the perfect balance between peace and vitality, bliss and a groundedness—the Balance of Grace, which is a state that helps naturally bring about the all-inclusive prosperity that you were meant for. I find that even if I have to pay bills on a particular day, if I've done a Nature Walk first, or at least some Kindness Movement, than the bill payment activity that follows goes quickly and is not nearly as annoying as it would otherwise be—it becomes like a monopoly game from which I am emotionally detached, because my consciousness is still in the perfect balance after the Nature Walk. And when I'm in that kind of a Balance of Grace, auspicious synchronicities always find me.

Another activity that helps people find the Balance of Grace (see Chapter 8 of *Seven Stages to co-Creating Prosperity From Your Soul*), which attracts prosperity even more profoundly, is RezoDance. RezoDance is a meditative, healing movement modality that is based on Kindness Movement, and imbued with reiki energy, in which the individual's manifestation intents are empowered by group consciousness and by the sacred reiki symbols projected to the participants by a facilitator who is a reiki master. It is an incredibly potent and powerful manifestation tool, as well as a tool to heal the body, mind, and spirit, and bring them into a perfect balance of health, radiance, happiness, and abundance. However, at the time of this writing, I am still in the stages of planning how to offer this new modality to the public, and training facilitators.

So for now, Kindness Movement, Happy Back Walk, Nature Walk are also incredibly effective tools for finding freedom in your body, uplifting your spirit, and getting yourself into a state that is grounded, centered, balanced, and joyful. Give them a try, and you'll experientially find out how wonderful these tools are in helping you ground more Creative energy through your Infinite Funnel of Abundance into your physical reality.

Kindness Movement will help you find again the perfect postural alignment that you had when you were a young child, and feel true freedom within your body. Once you get comfortable with Kindness Movement, you can move onto Happy Back Walk, which will teach you continue to find freedom in your body throughout your Joyful Physical Activity and daily activity. The idea is that if you can carry the freedom that you found within your body and spirit during Kindness Movement throughout a walk, than you've achieved a high degree of attunement with the freedoms of your Soul Self, and can therefore carry that freedom into your other daily activities. Body freedom in and of itself is an opening/clearing of your energetic apparatus, which allows the energy of your Infinite Funnel of Abundance to flow into your life. When you get to the point that Kindness Movement and Happy Back Walk become natural for you, you'll naturally want to move onto Nature Walk, which introduces a meditational aspect to Happy Back Walk, and makes it into the ultimate activity (short of RezoDance) for bringing you into the perfect balance that is in vibrational resonance with prosperity.

Kindness Movement

Kindness Movement is a meditative movement that can restore your body's perfect posture, relax deep muscles, realign joints, and put you into a relaxed yet alert state of mind. It was Given to me as part of the information that I channeled for this book. Kindness Movement can be practiced on its own, whenever you feel tense in your body and want to relax, when you feel stressed and want to actively bring relaxation into your mind and spirit, or as a way of establishing freedom in the body before a Happy Back Walk.

A Word (or two) About Holding Patterns:

We are each born with wonderful flexibility and a perfect postural alignment of the body, which enables our wonderful spirits to flow freely within our body-temples, and manifest as vitality, peace, and perfect balance. As we learn to do certain things with our bodies, we develop holding patterns. Positive holding patterns are the muscle-memory that teaches us everyday tasks such as tying our shoes, sitting up, or walking. Our muscles do not have to relearn all those tasks every time anew because we have a muscle-memory, or a holding pattern.

However, as we go through life's challenges, our bodies adjust and form negative holding patterns. Negative holding patterns are muscle memory patterns developed after an injury or a surgery, to prevent use of the injured muscles in order to allow that area of the body to heal. For example, if you've had an injury in your supraspinatus muscle (the rotator cuff muscle on top of your shoulder blade), your body will automatically teach itself to bypass using the injured muscle and use alternate muscles in its stead, such as the upper trapezius in this case, to lift your arm. Your body will also automatically limit a certain part of your arm lifting range in order to immobilize the injured muscle, and give it time to heal. These holding patterns have an important role while the area is healing. But what often happens is that the new protective muscle-memory pattern stays active for years after we have finished healing from the injury or surgery. That is why it is advisable to go through a course of physical therapy after surgery for example—to retrain the muscles and restore our original healthy body mechanics.

The surprising fact is that we all have holding patterns that no longer serve us. Even if you haven't had surgery, and don't remember being injured, we all stumble and fall from very early on in our childhood. And it doesn't always take a massive injury to form a holding pattern that doesn't serve us. Some muscular holding patterns originate from emotional and psychological issues. For example, some holding patterns of the neck and shoulders could originate from shrinking your shoulders and turning your neck when your father used to slap you as a child. Other negative holding patterns originate from particular postures that the person has adopted. For example, most people have unhealthy holding patterns in their shoulders from either side sleeping with improper pillows, or from carrying a heavy shoulder bag. Many people suffer muscular tightness in their lower back, resulting from postural holding patters, walking, sitting, lifting, and carrying themselves with tight muscles as a result of stress.

Unhealthy holding patterns are nothing to be ashamed of. Most adults and adolescents have them. The good news is that you can re-educate your body. If you have indeed had an acute injury or have undergone surgery, than you should see a physical therapist to rehabilitate and retrain the specific muscles involved with your injury/surgery. If you haven't—if your holding pattern are simply the result of… life, than Kindness Movement can help you restore the perfect posture that you were born with.

Removing Unhealthy Holding Patterns:

There are many healing modalities that proclaim to "fix" your posture and restore it to its perfect alignment. Among them, Rolfing (Named after Ida Rolf PhD) is the most painful and invasive. Rolfers usually perform a series of extremely painful deep tissue manipulations, which render the clients' muscles and connective tissue a bit more pliable for a certain period of time after the series. However, as in all of the therapies that proclaim to "fix" posture, the holding patterns that made the muscles tight in the first place still remain in the body, and continue to restrict movement, which after a short period of time causes new muscle tightness to re-form.

Receiving regular Rezossage from a skilled therapist is of course always recommended, as this healing modality is the only one that can restore the ideal workings of your muscles without pain, and while nurturing your whole self. However, at the time of this writing, I am still in the process of patenting Rezossage, and writing an approved curriculum for teaching it. So it may take some time before there are Rezossage therapists in your area.

Like Rezossage, the approach of Kindness Movement is completely opposite to all invasive Rolfing-style approaches. Firstly, during Kindness Movement, you are the one doing the movement, so you are not letting anyone do anything *to* you. Secondly, the concept here is the opposite of invasive. Kindness Movement reminds us that underneath all the unhealthy holding patterns that we may carry, at some subconscious level, we all still have the memory of the perfect posture, and the freedom we felt in our bodies when we were children. The idea is to use your mind to first tune into tune into feelings of softness, kindness and freedom within. Then from this meditative place of kindness, delve into the subconscious place where the memory of the perfect posture resides, and let that direct our movements. It is as if you are getting your conscious mind out of the way, and letting your subconscious—your body's innate intelligence—direct your movement. And this is not as complicated as it sounds—we're not talking hypnotherapy here.

While I have listed some specific suggested movements, which have the potential of freeing up particular muscles (if you do them softly enough), the real Kindness Movement is a very gentle, continuous wave-like movement, envisioning that you are moving like the waves of the ocean. The reason that ocean waves provide a good inspiration here is that our bodies consist of nearly 70% water. So at a subtle level, all that water in our bodies does have a certain natural wave to it. Moving your body in accordance with its natural wave helps greatly in directing your movement from that subconscious place that remembers perfect postural alignment. Also, our spirits move as energy – in waves, which is why we talk about a spiritual "vibration." And all these waves (both physical and spiritual) are individual. Your particular wave might have a tendency to be wide (amplitude) and slow (frequency), while your spouse's wave, for example, may tend to be quicker (frequency) and smaller (amplitude). Also, in different moments and different stages of Kindness Movement, even your own wave may vary from quick to slow, wide to small, forceful to gentle. It all depends on what your body and inner child needs at that moment. Once you fully get into this mode of listening to your body and indulging in the softest wavy motion that it naturally wants to be in, then you'll be able to carry that soft wave into a walk, or any other routine activity. And you'll find that this Kindness Movement mode will always induce an overall feeling of kindness and joy.

Suggested Kindness Movements:

First of, let me just say that no one can really teach Kindness Movement to another person, since the kindest movements that best serve your particular body and spirit are unique to you. Your own body, and its innate intelligence is the only one that can truly teach you Kindness Movement. All that an outside person could do is show you a few suggestions for Kindness Movement, and guide you to keep finding softness and kindness in each move, so that once you can get the gist of it, your inner intelligence can guide you into the real Kindness Movement. And that is what I'm doing in this section.

Before you begin your Kindness Movement, you should put on some music that will help you get into a wavy flow of kindness, or music that you know tunes you into the most tender part of you—your inner child. In the beginning, this should be very soothing music that is not too rhythmic. I like, for this purpose, shamanic music that incorporates tones of the womb of the Earth for this purpose, such as Anugama's *Shamanic Dream*, *Healing*, or *Tanra* (all names of CDs by an artist named Anugama) for example. That seems to drive people into Kindness Movement almost automatically.

As the music starts, close your eyes and take a few deep breaths to signal your body that it is time to let go and relax. Just stand still with your eyes closed, spread your legs about shoulder width apart, maintain soft (unlocked) knees, and breathe deeply for a moment… Start by tuning into subtle softness within you. Envision yourself as your inner child, who has perfect posture, is feeling very free, light, and joyful within his/her body. Or you could envision that the softness of a feather is coming into all the tight spaces of the body. When I teach Kindness Movement, I usually go around the room with my little teddy bear that has the softest feel to it, lightly touch the bear's soft hair to people's neck, and I tell them, "Imagine this kind of softness touching your insides," which helps people immediately tune into the feeling of softness. You can certainly do that for yourself: find something very soft, and lightly caress yourself with it, to help you tune into the softness and tenderness within you. Or just let your inner child and your breath guide you into more softness within…

The following movements are suggestions to help you get the idea of Kindness Movement. At first, you may feel slightly ridiculous doing these moves. For this reason, you should do your first few Kindness Movement practices on your own, so that you are not too self-conscious.

Important things to make sure of are that your movements are not forced, and that they feel good. As you do each suggested move, you'll start with the specific move as I've described it. But after a few seconds, you should consciously introduce more softness, freedom and kindness into each move. After you've read this list once or twice, and have tried each of these moves for a few moments, you should aim to let go of the consciousness that's directing each move, and get lost in a trans-like indulgent wave of all the moves that feel best for you at each moment. Once you know a few Kindness Movements, it becomes like automatic writing – uncensored and unfiltered by your logical brain, driven entirely by Spirit.

- Start with some soft rolls of the neck… Make each neck roll more and more indulgent… When you are fully into the indulgence of the move, ask yourself: "can this movement of the neck be softer, kinder to myself?" You might envision that some Angel is enwrapping a shawl of soft feathers around your neck… Keep tuning into how the neck itself wants to move… What is the natural wave of your neck at this moment? Is it a quick vibration? Is it a slow big-soft-indulgent ocean wave? Is it a wave that is so subtle that it's barely noticeable? Tune into a neck movement that is absolutely all about softness kindness to yourself…
- Shrug your shoulders a few times and drop-release them down… then be still for a moment and let yourself feel the newfound freedom in your shoulders and neck that this simple movement gave you… breathe deep and tune into the difference between shrugging and releasing… What would it feel like if you didn't have to hold your shoulders up? What does it feel like to completely release the shoulders?
- Do a few indulgent shoulders rotations… At first it might feel like a good stretch. But then soften the movement into a soft wavy trans-like movement. I've found a shoulder movement that involves the arm going back and forth (flipping the palm this way and the other way like a ballet move) doing sort of a figure eight, as if you are trying to droop your shoulder forward, and then kick it backwards. Doing this movement like a soft indulgent wave helps relax all the muscles on the lower angle of the scapula (shoulder blade). If your shoulder is problematic, you may even try bending your body forward to ninety degrees, and shaking your upper body to relax the shoulders. Whatever move you find yourself

comfortable in, and ask yourself, "How can I make these shoulder movement softer, kinder to myself?" Gradually make the wave more subtle... kinder... softer... until the movement is a wave that is unique to you, directed by your subconscious, in accordance with the natural wave of your body.

☯ Bend your torso left without turning or twisting to the left, so that the right side of your torso, the rib cage, lower hip and back are stretched. Now do the same bending right. After a few left and right bends, reduce the move to half the size of the first move, and then make it gentler and more rhythmic like a dance... until the movement starts being just a soft natural wave that frees up your body... You may introduce into this wave a twisting of your body side to side, and a forward and backward snake-like wave of the spine... whichever feels the most releasing for your back. Experiment with this gently, and respect any limitations. Here especially, you need to remember that this movement should not hurt but feel good, soft and indulgent. As you continue the move, tune into more softness from within... until you really feel like the move is being directed subtly by the inner wisdom of your body. Your telltale is that it feels good and brings softness and comfort to your body.

☯ Raise your left arm lazily, and then drop it suddenly... feel the freedom-wave in your shoulder that your left arm drop affected... do the same with your right arm...

☯ Now, let your arms be free to the sides of your body. Start swinging your body from left to right from the waist, all the while letting your arms and shoulders fully release and swing... Now use much less force, and soften the move into a softer and kinder movement... Fully tune into the indulgent subtle wave of your body... Keep reminding yourself to find the way of freedom, lightness, and kindness in every movement... until your movement becomes a trans-like wave of relaxation in the Divine flow of who you Truly are...

☯ Indulge in a few soft rotations of the hips... feel the softness inside you come from your very Soul and into your physical body... Don't force your body into anything. Just allow the subtle movement that's naturally there to come out and guide you... You'd be surprised at how the subtlest of movement can release things and bring you freedom in your lower back. For the lower back especially, the subtler the better. Make your hip rotations a natural soft wave of the body...

☯ Turn this indulgent soft hip rotation into a figure eight with your hip... Keep reminding yourself to make the move subtler and subtler, more and more relaxed... Keep listening to your body's natural wave and letting it guide your movement... keep finding the softness and little freedoms within...

☯ Now start slowly and indulgently kicking your legs forward and slightly to the side in kind of a nonchalant way, as if you're saying "I don't care, I'm high on life..." Make every kick forward more subtle, fun and free... Feel your thighs and butt shake freely with this wave... Feel this freedom wave go all the way trough your buttocks to your lower back muscles... Keep tuning into your body's natural wave and letting it direct the move... your conscious mind should be almost completely turned off at this point.

- Stand on your left leg and allow your right side to dangle a bit so that your right toe lightly touches the ground, and your ankle is doing soft rotations...then flap your calf side-to-side... You can lift each foot and wiggle your toes freely stretching them in all kinds of directions... Keep the movement coming out of the most indulgent place within... Find a softer kinder way to do these movements... Then do the same for the left leg and foot.

- One leg kick that I've found particularly relaxing is lifting the right knee up towards the left side, and then kicking my whole right leg to the right, and then repeating for the other side. You can even have the knee and leg do a soft figure eight. I often get a release and a mini little chiropractic adjustment of the hip joint with this move. But of course, this movement has to be softened into a wave of inner kindness to find its full effectiveness

- Use your hands to lean on something, stand on your left leg, and softly kick your whole right leg backwards... This should send a releasing wave through your Psoas muscle—the walking muscle. Again, after you establish the movement, reduce it to half the force, and then half of that... until you find the particular wave that suits your body at that point—the unique level of softness that completely frees up all of your muscles of the deep abdomen and pelvic area... Repeat for the other side...

- Now be still for a moment and feel the vibration of the subtle wave of energy moving throughout your body... Even though your body has stopped moving, there is still a vibrational movement within your body after all that movement. Just be still and indulge in it for a moment.

Take a deep breath, and envision roots of Light connecting the soles of your feet to the center of the earth. Allow yourself a moment to ground after this deeply meditational movement. Then open your eyes.

By now it should become obvious that all of these moves should feel very good and very indulgent. If something doesn't feel good, don't do it! Listen to your body. Your body-temple is your friend. Remember that all these movements are only suggestions to get you started moving your body in freedom, softness and kindness. Once you get the hang of it, your internal wisdom will most likely start guiding you on many more movements that are most beneficial to your particular body type and issues. Eventually, you'll be such an expert on finding freedom in your body that you'll find that the subtlest of moves—one that barely even feels like you're moving—will induce the mode of freedom and kindness. And finally you'll get to the point that just the thought of Kindness Movements will get you to the point where your spirit rejoices and moves freely within your healthy body and perfect posture.

Happy Back Walk

Happy Back Walk is a wonderful practice on its own. But it also lays the foundation for Nature Walk, as it will help you re-educate your body on better posture, and on how to move with ease and freedom. More than that, Happy Back Walk is a way to integrate the softness, lightness, and freedom of your spirit, which you've established in your body during Kindness Movement, into everyday tasks. And in that, it is the first physical practice we've discussed so far, which facilitates a more powerful integration of your Soul's Creative energy into your physical existence.

Many people take on walking only because their doctor has told them they should do so. They then thrust themselves onto a vigorous treadmill routine, cursing out and being miserable all the way to the finish line. But that type of walk can stress you out and tense up your body, instead of achieving any of the relaxation benefits that we've talked about. Walking doesn't have to be vigorous in order to give you all the benefits that your doctor told you about. Walking should actually be fun! Happy Back Walk can be a pleasurable way to free up your whole body and mind, a time for yourself, a time to let go of troubling thoughts and put some distance between yourself and the mundane, a time to breathe in some fresh air, smell the flowers, get more prana energy from your breath and the sun (or moonlight), and a time to remind yourself of freedom and bliss not only within your physical body, but within your mind and spirit too.

A Few Minutes of Prep Before Happy Back Walk:

First, before each Happy Back Walk, spend a few minutes doing Kindness Movement, only this time, have your walking shoes on, and have the music that you like to use for Kindness Movement playing in your portable music player (such as an iPod or MP3 player), so that once you establish the freedom and softness within your body and mind, you will be able to go straight out for your Happy Back Walk.

When you reach the stillness of a subtle vibration at the end of the Kindness Movement, start walking a few steps around the room, while still remaining in the freedom wave of your body… Let your steps be like the free forward kicking movement of the legs that you just did a minute ago—the one when you felt the kindness wave go all the way up through your buttocks and lower back. Never mind how ridiculous you might feel at first, or how exaggerated your forward kick it… just do what feels good and keeps your lower back, hips and waist in a mode of freedom. Now add to that walk the free-form arm-swinging wave that you did a few moments ago, which freed up your torso. Get your arms swinging freely to the side of your body as you walk, so that your shoulders remain totally free. If you get a few giggles from these over-exaggerated few steps, that's ok. It'll help you get into a happy mode and get your Happy Back Walk started on the right foot.

And don't get all stressed out about time here, either. This whole relaxation symposium should take no more than a few minutes. So that if on a particular day you only have thirty minutes in which to do your walk, it should take you no more than five of those minutes to do this pre-walk Kindness Movement, and you'll still have twenty-five minutes to do a walk that frees up your body as you walk. Also, you may only *need to* do extensive Kindness Movement in the beginning, while you are learning to find freedom in your body, and at times when your life and body are particularly stressed. Most other times, once you've gotten comfortable with Kindness Movement, you'll just be able to recall the feeling of freedom within your body automatically as you start walking, by mentally reminding yourself to get into the mode.

However, you may *choose to* do Kindness Movement daily, just because it feels good, and affects extra freedom in your body. When I first learnt Kindness Movement, I used to do it everywhere… shifting my weight from side to side and doing little hip-figure-eights ever so subtly as I waited to check out in the supermarket, for example; doing subtle shoulder shakes and rotations whenever I stand or sit still; doing soft neck rotation every so often when I sit in front of the computer... I think I still do it, but I am no longer aware of when I'm doing Kindness Movements as it has become such a natural part of me. The interesting thing is that within a few months of introducing this Kindness Movement into my life, my lower back problems completely disappeared, my shoulders and neck issues are monumentally better, and I enjoy walking. No more tensing up, and no more back pain after the walk.

Now Let's Go for a Happy Back Walk:

OK. So after all these introductions, it's now time to get outside and start walking... You may want to switch your music into something a little more happy and upbeat—music that makes you feel joyful and light.

If there is one rule to Happy Back Walk, it's that you should not allow yourself to think any troubling, stressful, or mundane thoughts. Your mind may still wonder to the things that have been on your mind that day. That is perfectly normal. Just remind yourself to postpone worrying about them, put them all out of your mind, and envision placing them in a God Bubble (see *Seven Stages to co-Creating Prosperity From Your Soul*)—an ethereal kind of "I'll think about it tomorrow" bubble of Light in which you place all of your worries, and give them to the Divine to handle and resolve for *you* in the most auspicious way. Remind yourself that the effectiveness of your dealing with any issue, and the solutions you're able to find, are always better, and flow more harmoniously with your Ideal Lifeplan, when your body and mind are rejuvenated by a joyful walk, a restful sleep, nutritious food, and meditation. However, don't stifle the bad thoughts either. Just let them surface, and then let them go, not holding on to any thought, just like we did during our meditations of *Seven Stages to co-Creating Prosperity From Your Soul*. Remind yourself that clearing your mind and *enjoying your walk is your job at this moment*, as part of getting yourself into vibrational resonance with Universal prosperity.

If your lower back usually bothers you, than be very conscious of the subtle Kindness Movement of your hips. Visualizing that your pubic hair is braided into a long braid, and that someone is gently pulling you forward by pulling that braid, does the trick every time. Just the giggles that this image evokes will help you let go. But it'll also help your torso get better aligned over your pelvis and legs, which is the best alignment for the lower back.

As you put each leg in front of the other, softly kick the leg forward in a celebrative nonchalant way, as if you're high on life, and laughing like a big Buddha. As much as this forward kick of the leg is probably going to be subtler than it was during your Kindness Movement, carry the same softness-freedom intent in your mind. You need to feel the quivering wave go up to your thigh and buttocks muscles at the very least, and preferably also to your sacrum, paraspinal, and quadratus lumborum (lower back) muscles. Let the feeling of freedom in your lower back guide your move. You can allow your hips to form a little figure eight as you walk, to help keep it moving in the natural wave of your body. The softer your movement of your hips, the freer your lower back will feel. If you are walking uphill, don't let your back muscles tense up, but tuck in your tummy muscles, as if trying to close a tight zipper; and this will help elongate and free up your lower back muscles. Then once you walking downhill or on level surface, you can go back to the figure eight of the hip and the nonchalant forward kicking of the legs.

Allow your arms to swing freely right and left. They will probably swing so that the right arm swings forward as the left hip and leg go forward, and the left arm will swing forward as the right hip and leg go forward—the leg that goes forward is just naturally coupled with the opposite arm. That is the most natural way to walk that helps keep you balanced, and also helps free up your rib cage (intercostal) and stomach muscles as you walk. But don't take my word for it. Let that movement be directed by what is natural and free for you. Keep reminding yourself not to hold your shoulders up, but to let them be free as they were during your Kindness Movement. And as you take short breaks during your walk, take a few seconds to do little shoulder-circles, a few small soft neck circles, or softly rotate your head right and left... Duplicate some of the moves that freed up your shoulders, neck and back during your pre-walk Kindness Movement for a few seconds, and then continue your walk. Paying attention to flowers, a nice sunset (or sunrise), the beach, or whatever beauty you find on your way will help you tune into the natural rhythms of things, and thus help introduce more softness and freedom into all of your body movement, as well as shift you into higher vibrational resonance with your prosperous Soul Self.

If you are gutsy enough, you may find singing along with the music that you are listening to pretty therapeutic. I have found that even if before the walk I had been in a foul-mood, than if I sing along it takes away the need to cry or yell, and by the end of the walk I usually am pretty happy. My favorite music to sing along is Mozart's opera *The Magic Flute*, so you can imagine how ridiculous I used to feel singing along it at first. I used to walk along the beach far away from the trail and from where people might be looking at me and thinking I was weird. But on a few occasions, people who were walking alongside me didn't seem to think I was weird. They just gave me understanding smiles, as if they too had been there. So I just stopped worrying about what others along the trail thought, and started enjoying the expression of my joy through singing, never mind how unprofessional my voice sounds. My grandmother, for example, loved singing. Through all the joys and sorrows of her life, she uplifted herself by singing. And I had never once heard her sing on tune. She was always off, and sounded terrible. But it didn't matter. She was in a vibration of love and joy as she was singing. I too always feel so elated after singing along with the music, surrounded by nature, freed by this beautiful walk.

So I invite you to experiment with this walk. Experience the relaxation, freedom and happiness that it brings, and feel free to make it your own. Your Happy Back Walk and the Kindness Movement will inevitably take the form that your inner kindness guides them to take. They will be molded to what you need them to do in your life, according to the highest guidance of your Soul. And that is as it should be. Use the time of this walk to appreciate the sites around you, affirm gratitude to your Creator for all the good that is already manifested in your life at this moment, and know that by connecting to that vibration of kindness, freedom and happiness, you are actively pulling more blessings to into your life.

Nature Walk:

Nature Walk is an excellent way to combine walking with meditation. Nature Walk is more than just exercise, and gives you more than just a way to blow off steam. It is very relaxing to be surrounded by Nature. The Nature Walk described here is a very healing practice that uses your meditative power to balance all of your energy centers, dissolve lower vibrational energies, and bring fresh new vital energy into your life. It is essentially the Chakra Clearing Meditation detailed in *Seven Stages to co-Creating Prosperity From Your Soul*, combined with a walk, and further empowered by an active resonance and feed of each chakra by the elements of Nature.

It is true that the Divine energy that feeds you is alive within, through, and all around you all the time, and is unseen. You would not be alive if you weren't constantly fed by Divine life-force energy (Ki). As we have discussed in *Prosperity From Your Soul*, Divine energy feeds you through your energetic bodies, chakras, and nadi and meridian energy channels. When you are in need of extra life-force energy, one way to get it is to breathe more fully, move your body, and employ your free will through visualizations to bring more Ki into you, straight from the Divine. The successful inflowing of additional Divine life-force into your physical being, though, depends on the clarity of your energetic bodies and centers (which may be clear or somewhat clogged at that moment). Another way to get an extra oomph of Ki is to surround yourself with nature, and absorb the extra energy from plants. Plants are also enlivened by the Divine energy of life, but have such tremendous amounts of Ki, that they are happy to give some of it away. The difference between Ki that comes straight from the Divine through your energetic bodies and chakras, and the Ki that you absorb from nature, is that nature's Ki is already stepped down into a vibration that is closer to physical, which is at exactly the right frequency for you to absorb directly into your chakras and nadis (which lead to feeding your physical body and emotions), even if at that moment, your energetic bodies are somewhat clogged. The visualizations of this meditative Nature Walk use your free will to accept the access Divine Ki given away by plants, and absorb it to feed you with fresh living Ki (life-force) energy that is already at the right frequency for you to absorb; the breath pattern helps distribute the accepted Ki into prana in your body; and your conscious intents help direct that energy to dissolve any negativity, completely balance, and heal you. That is why Nature Walk is such a powerful healing process.

In case you're wondering where to find some untouched nature in your area, let's clarify that nature doesn't necessarily have to be a jungle, or a far out wilderness area. Of course it's nice to have access to a beach, a lake, a pretty mountain trail, or a park. But it could just as well be an area that has a few trees or flowers in your neighborhood, or a small garden outside your office on your lunch hour. If you put your mind to it, you can find plenty of beautiful garden spots even in the middle of concrete, alongside a busy street.

I recommend taking a Nature Walk every day, especially at times when you are very stressed, or are going through any kind of transition in your life. If your environment allows it, do a few minutes of Kindness Movement before you go on your Nature Walk. This will help get you into your relaxed kindness-to-self state. Listening to soothing or uplifting music as you walk may help you shift your perspective into a peaceful-joyful mode. Sometimes, it is exactly that inspirational piece of music that makes you feel very light and blissful. I remember the first time I realized how profound the influence of music was on Nature Walk: It was a day that actually started out feeling tired and heavy. But as I started my beach Nature Walk and put on Bach's "Great" toccata in C minor, I felt like I was floating—like my feet were barely touching the ground.

Let's Go on a Nature Walk:

As you start your walk, get your body and mind into a Happy Back Walk mode of freedom and softness. Deepen breath and absorb the fragrance of the air and the vegetation in your area… bend over and smell every rose, jasmine and lavender flower along your route. You may even want to pick a leaf from a bush that is particularly fragrant, such as cedar or mint, lull it in your hands and smell it as you walk. As you intake the air's fragrance, envision that you are absorbing Divine energy from the earth… the trees… the flowers… shrubbery along your way… the birds and the squirrels…

Now start paying attention to different colors of flowers and the vegetation along your path… Envision that Mother Nature is radiating all of her colors as healing energy to you and your life, so that the energy of each color along your route is helping you absorb a particular aspect of Divine Light… until you feel a mutual resonance between you and Nature.

So if you see red flowers along your way, envision that the red flowers are radiating red Light-ray (a differentiated and grounded aspect of Divine Light) energy to heal your root chakra… As you inhale, envision your first chakra absorbing the energy of the red Light-ray from the flower, and as you exhale, envision that you are giving the plant all blocks and negativity, so they can neutralize it and converted it to positive energy of beauty. If there is only a limited amount of red flowers/plants in your area, than you may stand for a few moments in front of it, and do a few deep breaths exchanging energy with it, until you completely unburden your first chakra, and feel energized with the red Light energy of the flower. If there are no red flowers, you can do the same energy exchange with the roots of any plant.

If you see orange flowers along your way, than as you inhale, envision the orange Light radiated by the flowers nurturing and healing your second chakra, and as you exhale, give the plant all that might have been weighing on your second chakra to be neutralized and dissolved… until you can create a harmonious mutual resonance between you and the orange flowers, enhancing your second chakra. In the same way, yellow flowers heal the third chakra; green vegetation and pink flowers heal the heart chakra; cobalt blue vegetation or the color of blue skies radiate the cobalt blue aspect of Divine Light to heal your throat chakra; indigo flowers or indigo late evening skies heal your sixth chakra; and purple flower to heal and open your crown chakra. White flowers can heal all chakras, since white includes all colors of the rainbow. When I see white flowers, I always envision a pure Divine Light completely enveloping me in Its radiance, which creates a magnificent resonance with the flowers as well as with the Divine Her-Himself.

This portion of the Nature Walk in itself can be a very profound healing of all of your energy centers. And you may choose to devote to it your entire Nature Walk. I sometimes do. However, the meditation can continue as follows, and then it becomes a more profound uplifting tool:

Envision that you are one with whichever element of nature that is fulfilling a need in you. For example, if your life has been feeling very heavy lately, you may look upon the skies and the wind whistling in the trees, close your eyes for a moment, and feel oneness with the wind and air element. You may look at the birds with the eyes of your consciousness, and feel oneness of consciousness with them… until you feel that your spirit is soaring with them. If you see prey-birds, you may envision them picking up all of your stresses and all negativities in your life, and eliminating them just like they eat worms or mice that they hunt, and then eliminate it. Do this until you feel your negativity dissolved. If you are depressed, meditate on the sparkle of light reflected on the leaves or on the ocean, and feel oneness with that spark… until you *become* the light of that spark. If you are feeling emotional, confused, or out-of-it, become one with the trees and envision that you too have deep roots extending from the soles of your feet to the center of the Earth… Allow Nature to heal you; absorb from her whatever energy you need; and let her plentitude nourish you with her abundance. Use your inner guidance to merge your consciousness and your vibration with whichever element of nature would vibrationally complete you and bring you into perfect balance at that moment.

When you get back home (or office), stretch well after the walk, preferably on a personal small rug or yoga mat, close to the earth. This meditative walk can get you very blissed out. So it is important to ground yourself afterwards. Remember that grounding does more than just bring you back into wakeful reality. It also helps bring all the healing energies of your meditative walk into your physical reality.

In this chapter, we have begun to cross the second and third bridges between the ethereal co-Creation of your Ideal Life and your here-now reality. Bringing lightness, freedom, and physical health to your body-temple, prepares your body to function more ideally in the face of any new tasks you might undertake as part of your Plan to merge with your Ideal Life (the second bridge); and raising the vibration of your body-temple allows the Infinite Abundance of your Soul pours into your physical reality.

As you start engaging in Joyful Physical Activity, Kindness Movement, and Nature Walk regularly, you'll start seeing a subtle yet noticeable difference in the ease with which you handle certain challenges, your lighthearted attitude towards reality, your feelings of the hope and promise of your new path as a conscious co-Creator, and with those feelings will come a higher degree of harmony with the auspicious synchronistic flow of the Universe.

Chapter 4

Nutritional Harmony

Nutrition also plays a big part of bringing about prosperity from your Soul. The first, obvious significance of nutrition in manifesting prosperity is that nutrition has a huge influence on your wellbeing—bigger than you may realize. And your overall health is certainly a part of the all-inclusive prosperity that you were always meant for.

The second significance of nutrition has to do with your spiritual-energetic resonance with Divine joy. In *Prosperity From your Soul*, we've talked about the importance of joy in co-Creating prosperity. And food is one of life's pleasures. But in order to enjoy good food, without letting that enjoyment limit your feelings of health and freedom within your body-temple, you need to make enlightened decisions about what you allow into your body. You see, metaphysically speaking, food is part of the energy that you integrate from the Universe into yourself, both physically and energetically. And just as you need to weed out naysayers and pessimists from your close circle of friends in order to walk your highest path to success, so too you need to be selective about what you nutritionally become one with, in order to reclaim the health, happiness, and the lightheartedness that would keep you in a prosperity-magnetizing vibration.

In this chapter, we will discuss low-vibrational foods, which make us feel unsatisfied, heavy, lethargic, and sometimes even depressed, versus high-vibrational foods, which make us feel lighter, in better moods, more capable of clear thought, and more energetic and free within our body-temples—all the hallmarks of being able to manifest prosperity from your Soul. There is a very interesting documentary called *Supersize Me*, in which a guy went on a thirty-day diet consisting of McDonalds foods only. The film documents the man's health, as documented by his doctors, before, during, and after the experiment. Before the experiment, the man was eating holistically healthy foods, and was very healthy, as confirmed by his doctors and documented in the video. On the first week of the experiment, the first thing that he noticed was that he was never satisfied with the food: no matter what quantity he ate, about a half-hour to an hour later, he was hungry again. After about three days, he noticed that he started to feel a lack of energy; and by the end of the first week, he felt completely lethargic. By the second week, the man literally started to feel depressed, and could barely get out of bed. By the third week, his cholesterol was sky-high, his liver was completely toxic, he gained much weight, and many of his health parameters were hitting dangerous limits. His doctors were begging him to stop the experiment. He finished the month barely alive, and immediately went on some type of a holistic vegan detox program, which gradually restored his health. I believe that it was only after this documentary came out that McDonalds started to introduce salads and healthy choices. Before that, their only foods were fried and low in nutritional value. And if you think about it, how can anyone co-Create an Ideal Life, when they feel lethargic, fog-headed and depressed? However, rather than dwell on low-vibrational foods, in this chapter, we will focus mostly on the high-vibrational foods that can restore your health, give you the oomph to walk the steps of your Ideal Lifeplan, and bring you into the high vibrational resonance with your Ideal Life of prosperity.

The third layer of interconnectedness between nutrition and prosperity has to do with being in control of your life, as the conscious co-Creator that you now are. There are some stressors in your day-to-day life that you cannot control, at least not at the level of your here-now self. For instance, you do not control the weather, or other people's decisions and behaviors. And there are some medical conditions that are challenging to control. But fortunately, being mindful of how you feed your body-temple is one thing you have absolute control of, and it has a tremendous influence on your physiological wellbeing, as well as your energetic balance and the flow of your spirit.

In your meditations of *Seven Stages to co-Creating Prosperity From Your Soul*, you have experimented with some breathing techniques, and have experienced the subtle but profound affect they have in regulating your moods and states of alertness. In Chapter 3, you have experienced how the simple Kindness Movement can relax your whole body and being, and how Nature Walk can uplift your spirit. Food also has a profound affect on your moods and states of alertness. For example, most people have had a chance to observe how hyperactive children get after eating sugar, and I'm sure you know how much a good cup of coffee gets you going in the morning, and how much a glass of warm milk or herbal tea in the evening soothes you to sleep. For example, I have just eaten a bowl of oatmeal with cinnamon and nutmeg for breakfast, which is making me energetic and giving me a good bowl movement (excuse my candor); but when I wake up stressed, I eat cream of wheat breakfast cooked with milk to calm my stress. Many people have to have their glass of wine with dinner to help them relax at the end of a day. And how many times have you eaten hearty meal of steak, potatoes and chocolate milkshake, and felt afterwards that all was absolutely right with your world? We all know that certain foods have certain effects on us. There is actually a whole science of nutritional medicine to back up these knowings. As it relates to prosperity, you already know that continuously reclaiming the Balance of Grace helps keep your energetic vibration in resonance with the prosperity you want to magnetize into your life. So if something as simple as food could help you control your moods and states of alertness, and by that achieve that precious balance, why not use it?

The fourth layer of connectedness between prosperity and nutrition is that you become what you eat – quite literally. The human body has an amazing capacity of self-healing and regeneration. We see that especially in the amazing rate at which children heal. Even in adults, doctors tell us[1] that every seven to ten years, most of our body cells are renewed, so that every seven to ten years we each have an almost completely new body! This means that what we eat and drink becomes our bodies, and thus becomes part of who we are in a very real way. In the spirit of this knowing, most aboriginal people throughout history have traditionally thanked the spirit of the animal for its sacrifice before eating its flesh. This ceremony was about healing the animal (releasing its spirit and releasing ourselves from the karmic effects of killing it), and clearing the cellular memory of its suffering, so that we do not ingest the negative energy of the animal suffering. So given that you physically and energetically become with what you eat, do you want to become one with pesticides and other harmful chemicals produced in a laboratory? Do you want to clog your Infinite Funnel of Abundance with junk? Or do you want to become one with the highest vibrational ingredients that nature avails you, and open up your Funnel to all the Abundance that the Universe wants to give you? Note that although physiologically what you eat today will make up your body cells in seven years, on a spiritual level the effect is much quicker! Energetically-vibrationally, when you eat junk for lunch, you feel shitty the same day, and when you eat high-vibrational living foods for lunch you feel energetic and wonderful for the rest of the day—ready to reclaim your Ideal Lifepath! This establishes a direct connection between nutrition and co-Creating prosperity from your Soul.

However, nutrition is a huge subject that can fill whole libraries with the many books that had been written about it. This chapter does not attempt to compete with the wealth of knowledge that had been written by nutritional experts. Rather, what this chapter will give you is a *multidimensional basis of knowledge* about nutrition, which can then help you make more enlightened nutritional decisions that incorporate kindness-to-self on all levels. With all due respect to science, once you have some basic facts, your nutritional decisions should be driven by your inner wisdom, based on what is right *for you*. I have summarized here some basic facts about nutrition, just to give you some facts on which to base your nutritional decisions. But the real purpose of this chapter is to help you establish nutrition as a way to nurture not just your stomach, but your whole self—to help you choose only foods that resonate well with your highest wellbeing. This will help you find balance, restore the natural health of your body-temple, and prepare it to be a vessel for bringing forth the enhanced Creative energy of prosperity that's now coming from your Soul and the Divine realms in which It dwells.

The boxed section below contains summarized information about the major food groups[2], the role they each play in our nutrition and health, and a little something about our digestive system[3]. The section that follows—also boxed—contains a summary of some of the diet approaches that are out there on the market today, and the pros and cons of each of them, as I've researched them. The purpose of the boxed sections is not to teach you nutrition or biochemistry, but simply to give you a basis of knowledge on which to base your nutritional decisions, to facilitate a multidimensional kindness-to-self. If you already have a good understanding of these subjects, I invite you to skip the boxed sections and move onto the sections about Kindness Food Principles, Healing Foods, and Spiritual Food Practices – which are the real subjects that this chapter aims to talk about.

If you decide to read the summarized boxed information, please note that it is not important for you to study or memorize it. What is important it is for you to make mental note of any issues that resonate with your inner kindness meter, and become aware of any information mentioned that could contribute to your achieving better health and balance within your body-temple. So as you read, pay special attention to how you *feel*, as these feelings may generate some 'Aha' moments.

Nutritional Basics

The food that we eat is basically divided into two categories: Macronutrients are foods that we consume in larger amounts, while micronutrients are substances that we only need in trace amounts. Macronutrients include carbohydrates, fats, and proteins, while micronutrients include vitamins, minerals, phytonutrients, plant enzymes and antioxidants. And then there is water, which I have moved into the Kindness Food Principle section, because proper hydration, beyond being proper nutrition, is also an important part of kindness-to-self.

Carbohydrates:

Carbohydrates are the basic food that our bodies use for energy. They are produced by plants in a process called photosynthesis—absorbing sun energy, combining it with water and carbon dioxide to produce the oxygen that we breathe and the carbohydrates that we eat.

Chemically, carbohydrates belong to one of three groups, according to the complexity of their molecules: mono-saccharides (glucose) are composed of a simple ring of six carbons, with their respective oxygen-hydrogen (H & OH) groups. Glucose, also known as blood sugar or grape sugar, is the simplest unit of carbohydrates that does not need to be further broken down in the body. *The brain*, for example, *works strictly on glucose.* It therefore absolutely needs glucose and cannot accept any other types of carbohydrates in order to function.

Duo-saccharides are the second group of carbohydrates, and are composed of two rings of six or five carbon atoms tied together, with their respective H and OH groups. These are the different common sugars most of us crave. They differ in the types of bonds between the carbon atoms in their rings, the arrangement of the oxygen and the hydrogen along the rings, and sometimes have a five-carbon, instead of six-carbon ring, as is the case with maltitole. The most common sugars of this group are sucrose (table sugar) and fructose (fruit sugar).

Polysaccharides (starches) are the last members of this exhausting chemistry lesson. They are composed of long chains carbon rings, along with their H and OH groups. Polysaccharides are what we know as starches. They are also used by the body for energy, but are slower to metabolize. That means that the body takes longer and invests more energy to break these large chains, convert them to glucose, and use them for energy. *Thus when eating starches such as natural whole grains, the body is satisfied for a longer period of time from the same quantity of food. It also means that the body burns these carbohydrates on a more even keel.*

Dr. Andrew Weil, the founder of a new branch of medicine called Integrative Medicine (integrating eastern and holistic medicine with allopathic medicine) is an MD that many people regard as a nutritional guru. According to Dr. Weil, *carbohydrates (of a low glycemic index) should make up 50%-60% of our diet.*

Fiber –

Biologically, the structure of plant cells is different from the structure of animal cells in that plant cells have not only the membrane that surrounds each cell, but also a cell-wall.

Nutritionally, when eating plant foods, the cell-wall is what we know as fiber—what used to be called the "roughage".

Fibers can be divided into two groups:
- ☯ The first group contains compounds known as cellulose, lignin (found in whole grains & bran), and hemicellulose (found in whole grains, vegetables, fruits, nuts & seeds). These fibers are insoluble in water, except hemicellulose, which is partially soluble. They retain water, thus making the stool softer and bulkier, which prevents hemorrhoids and constipation. This process also speeds up the passage of food through the digestive tract, which minimizes the absorption of potentially harmful carcinogenic substances by the intestines' wall.
- ☯ The second group of fibers includes gums and pectin, which are soluble in water. They bind bile acids (cholesterol producing substances) and cholesterols, and eliminate them from the body.

Most doctors recommend eating about forty grams of fiber daily, which is about twice what most people consume. The interesting thing about fiber, as it relates to diet, is that since fiber increases the volume of the food, it also helps us feel more full. And this increased fullness does not add calories to our food, since it is not really digestible by our bodies in the normal sense.

Glycemic Index:

Most diets that are out there on the market today, whether they advertise it or not, are based on the glycemic index, including Jenny Craig, NutriSystem, Weight Watchers, and countless other diets. And the principle of the glycemic index is very simple:

Carbohydrates are not the enemy as once thought, and are in fact necessary for a balanced diet. The simpler (more sugary tasting) the carbohydrates, the faster the body digests them, uses them up, and then becomes hungry for more carbs. The more complex (starchy) the carbohydrates, the slower the body uses them up, and the longer the feeling of satiety lasts. Sugars have a high glycemic index because the body metabolizes them immediately, which gives the body immediate high energy, only to crash shortly thereafter, and then crave more sugars. This rollercoaster can go on for years in some people. In contrast, low glycemic index foods fuel the body for a longer period of time on a more even keel. But the story with the glycemic index goes beyond an energetic even keel (which is important to the balance that magnetizes prosperity) and the duration of satiety.

The other part of the story about glycemic index relates to insulin, which is a hormone that has dozens of functions in the body, two of which relate to a healthy diet. High glycemic index foods cause an immediate release of insulin into the blood. One function of insulin is to help the cells and organs of the body absorb glucose, so that they can use it for energy. So far so good. But the second function, which relates to dieting, is that insulin also converts access amounts of glucose to fat for storage, and inhibits the conversion of fat back into glucose for energy use. So the story about the glycemic index is that if you want to lose body fat, you need to eat foods that allow the conversion of body fat back into glucose, so it can be burned as energy that you spend. To do that, we need to eat foods that would not cause large spikes of insulin release.

It is true that all foods contain a combination of carbs, proteins, fats and micronutrients, and no food can be completely carb free or protein free. But the trick is to eat foods with low glycemic index carbs (fruit, vegetable, legumes, nuts, seed, and whole grains) in order to keep insulin release to the minimum necessary, and allow for access stored body fat to be broken down and utilized for energy.

The interesting thing about fruit is that they are sweetened by is the fructose (different chemical composition than glucose or sucrose), which does not cause a release of insulin. Therefore fruits are a fantastic food to eat even if you're trying to lose weight, particularly if you are a sugar junky.

Proteins:

Proteins are the building blocks of life. They make up many of the body tissues such as muscles, bone, the internal structure of a cell, and even DNA which holds our genetic code. They are composed of long chains of molecules called amino acids. There are twenty different amino acids. Eight of those amino acids— considered essential amino acids—need to be ingested from a food source. The other twelve amino acids can be reconstructed by our bodies, using the essential eight.

Proteins are found in animal flesh (beef, bison, lamb, poultry), eggs, and dairy products, but also in legumes, grains, nuts, and seeds.

There are two questions regarding proteins. One is how much should you eat; and the other is what is the best source of protein. If you eat more proteins than your body needs, it can break them down into ketones and use them as energy. But the energy of ketones is not as efficient as the energy provided by glucose, and the brain cannot run on ketones. There are two problems with excessive consumption of protein. One is that the body has to invest a lot of energy to break them apart to use their energy. The other problem is that the byproducts of metabolizing proteins are toxic nitrogen wastes, which must be broken down by the liver and flushed by the kidneys. On the other hand, not consuming enough protein can make us crave too many carbohydrates (and gain weight), and lead to hair loss, feeling weak and brain-fogged, and reduced immune function.

Exactly how much protein is good for us is a much-debated subject. The general consensus is that proteins-rich foods should make up about 20%-30% of our caloric intake. How many grams of protein are essential for us depends on body type, gender, age, and level of activity. The Institute of Medicine and the American Diabetic Association (ADA) advertise that in general, we should eat 0.8 gram of protein per each kilogram (which is about 0.37 gram per pound) of body weight for a sedentary person, and up to 1.8 grams of protein per each kilogram of body weight of the person is physically very active. Naturally, if you exercise a lot, your protein needs would be more towards the 1.8 grams per kilo, versus a sedentary person who needs less protein. Developing children, people recovering from a serious illness, and women who are pregnant or nursing a baby need more protein than most people.

The second (much debated) question is regarding the best source of protein. Vegetarian proteins are the purest in terms of the vibrational energy of the food, but they have one drawback: In most cases, one needs to combine different sources of protein in order to obtain what's called a "complete proteins"—containing all eight essential amino acids—which require time and knowledge. On the other hand, animals provide a rich source of readily available complete proteins, but comes at the price of high calories, high LDL cholesterol, and cruelty to animals, not to mention ingesting all the toxins of an animal that's high up in the food-chain and the energy of the its suffering. This is a debate that your inner-kindness-meter should guide you on—what is the best source of protein *for you*.

Fats:

Fats are used to store energy in the body for future rainy days, as well as for padding and in the structure of various body membranes and tissue. Fats help the digestion of food be a little slower, which gives us a feeling of satiety. They also contribute considerably to taste and enjoyment of the food, as I'm sure you know.

Fats are made of large complex molecules of carbon, hydrogen and oxygen. They are very calorie-dense foods that require lots of energy to assemble, and release much energy when burnt. According to Dr. Weil, fats release nine calories per each gram when burnt, which is more than twice that of carbohydrates (both carbohydrates and proteins release four calories per gram).

As it relates to diet, it is interesting to note that researchers are convinced that the number of fat cells in an individual is set, although they do not know what controls that set number. Gaining weight usually does not increase the number of fat cells in your body, but makes each fat cell hold more fat. Conversely, losing weight just shrinks the size of the same fat cell. There are some claims that the compound CLA, and the amino acid L-Carnitine help reduce belly and waist fat, and some claim that CLA actually reduces the number of fat cells in the body. But according to Dr. Weil, no scientific evidence[4, 5] exists to support that claim. The Zohar Kindness Diet (next chapter) is not predicated on taking any particular food supplements other than any supplements that your inner wisdom may guide you to take.

Fats are divided into saturated and unsaturated. Unsaturated fats are then divided into monounsaturated, and polyunsaturated. There are three types of unsaturated fats considered "essential fatty acids," because of their important health benefits. They are listed in the diagram below. As you review this diagram, note that since the benefits of Omega-6 fatty acids depend on eating it in the right proportion to Omega-3 fatty acids, and since scientists are undecided on what that right proportion is (they also don't know your body as well as you do), than the decision how much of each fatty acid to eat, and from which source, is yet another decision on which your inner wisdom should guide you. Just keep in mind that most of us eat more than enough saturated fat and Omega-6. What we usually don't get enough of is Omega-3 and Omega-9 fatty acids.

Fat Overview Chart:

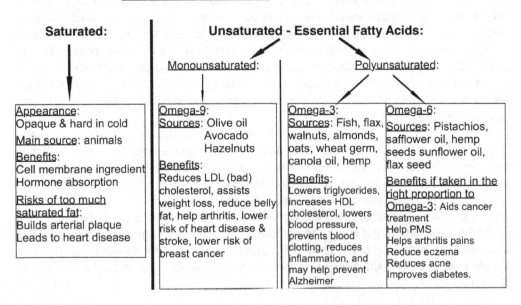

While I've only listed in this diagram the health risks of only saturated fat, any kind of fat is still fat! And since our bodies body can make their own cholesterol given enough fat intake, too much of even the best unsaturated fat can be converted by our bodies to stored fat, which is inevitably saturated, since all animal fat (and humans are still animals) is saturated. So too much of any kind of fat can lead to overweight and heart disease.

However, fats are not the enemy either, provided they are ingested in moderation. Doctors recommend fats to make up 10%-20% of our diet. I say: once you are aware of the facts, use your inner wisdom to judge how much, and what kinds of fat enhance your health, and your emotional-spiritual wellbeing.

Micronutrients:

Micronutrients are called that because we only need trace amounts of them compared to the amounts of macronutrients we need. However, as little of them as we need, they still are monumentally important to our health.

Vitamins –

Vitamins help regulate metabolism by assisting biochemical processes that release energy from digested foods. Vitamins are also co-enzymes in that they combine with enzymes to speed up and facilitate the many chemical reactions that make the body function ideally.

Contrary to what you may think, the best source of vitamins does not come in pill form. The best source actually comes from the fresh fruit and vegetables in their most raw and natural form. Specific cravings of fruit or vegetables may indicate specific vitamins, minerals, or phytonutrients that are deficient in your body, and should therefore help you discern how to be kind to your body-temple and supply the missing nutrients.

While most vitamins are abundant in fruit and vegetables, there are some vitamins that are found primarily in animal flesh. So if you wish to be vegetarian or vegan, you'll need to learn how to get enough of those vitamins from vegetarian sources. For example, vitamin B12 comes mainly from beef, but can also be found in smaller amounts in eggs and milk, or in even smaller amounts in soy, tempeh, miso and seaweed. Vitamin D can be obtained by eating some fish, egg yokes, and dairy products, but can also be gotten from exposure to sunlight for about 15-30 minute a day. Vitamin B2, which is primarily found in beef and dairy products, can also be found in almonds, soy, spinach, Grimini, and Shitake mushrooms.

Minerals –

Minerals are needed for composition and structure of every living cell, as well as for the maintenance of proper body fluid composition, formation of blood and bone, healthy nerve function, and regulation of muscle tone. Minerals are also co-enzymes, enabling the body to perform its functions. In fact, the body's entire chemical balance depends on the balance of minerals.

As minerals are also micronutrients, our bodies only need a minute amount of them to function, compared to other major food groups. Too much minerals can cause mineral toxicity, but that is a rare condition that happens only if you accumulate massive amounts of minerals over a long period of time.

Minerals occur naturally in the rocks of the earth, and are stored in our bodies in bone and muscle tissue. And since plants suck those minerals from the earth through their roots and incorporate them into their cell structures, most of the minerals our bodies require can be abundantly supplied by vegetarian sources. However, some important minerals are obtained mostly by eating animal flesh (beef!), such as iron and zinc. If you wish to become vegetarian/vegan, iron can also be found in soy, nuts, seeds, lentils, kidney beans, chickpeas, black-eyed peas, Swiss chard, tempeh, black beans, prunes, beets greens, tahini, peas, bulgur, raisins, watermelon, millet, bok-soy, and kale. Zinc can also be found in dried beans, sea vegetables, soy, nuts, peas, and seeds. You'll have to research how much of these vegetarian food sources you'd need to eat to supply your body's need for those minerals.

Phytonutrients –

Phytochemicals are substances found in plants that are responsible for giving them their color and flavor. They have a monumental role in preventing disease and cancer. More than two hundred studies show that a diet rich in whole grains, legumes, fruits and vegetables lowers the risk of cancer and other disease. Dr. Weil also notes that micronutrient supplementation in pill form, most likely, fails to provide the phytonutrients of the original plant. Therefore it is far better to eat fruit and vegetables in their natural form than it is to pop a multivitamin for example.

Plant Enzymes –

Plant foods also contain many enzymes that not only help our digestion (such as papaya), but also help prevent cancer and other disease. Like phytonutrients, plant enzymes are also not easily replaced by supplementation. You have to actually eat the fruit/veggie in order to get the benefit.

Antioxidants –

The mystery of antioxidants is not really a complicated one. Unhealthy foods, stress, excessive sun radiation and other factors can interject into our bodies molecules known as free radicals. Free radicals can cause cancer. And antioxidants neutralize these free radicals, and therefore help prevent cancer and other diseases.

To understand the biochemistry in simplistic terms, free radicals are molecules that are missing some electrons, and are therefore unstable in their structure. And since the positive electrical charge of the nucleus of each atom is supposed to be balanced by the negative electrical charge of its cloud of electrons, molecules that are missing electrons are positively charged, and therefore have a strong affinity to complete themselves by "stealing" the missing electrons from another molecule, making it, in turn, unstable. This "stealing" of electrons can cause long chain reactions in the body, which disfigures the attacked molecules, altering their structure and function. Free radicals can interfere with many processes in the body, and ruin cell protein and DNA, which can cause cancer. Antioxidants are simply molecules that readily donate electrons without losing the integrity of their structures, thereby neutralizing the free radicals.

Plants are naturally abundant with antioxidants. The most famous of antioxidants is vitamin C, found in most fruit and vegetables.

Have you heard enough to make you want to eat your fruits and vegetables yet?!

Our Digestive Tract:

When we eat, before the food can be absorbed and utilized by the body, it needs to be dissolved and broken down into smaller molecules. This dissolving and breaking-down process is called **digestion.** The function of the digestive system (also called the GI tract) is then to process ingested foods, and break it down into molecular forms that are then transferred, along with salts and water into the body's internal environment, where they can be distributed to the body-cells by the circulatory system.

The GI tract is a tube running through the body from mouth to anus like a hole in a doughnut, which means that even though the tracts runs through the body, its contents are considered external to the body. The GI tract itself includes the mouth, pharynx, esophagus, stomach, small intestine, and large intestine. Alongside the GI tube, there are accessory organs in the form of salivary glands, liver, gallbladder, and pancreas that are not part of the tract itself, but secrete substances into it via connecting ducts, to help chemically break down the food into smaller molecules.

The opening of the gastrointestinal tract is, of course, the mouth, where chewing starts breaking the food into smaller chunks, and where the saliva's digestive enzymes start the digestive process. At this point however, the food still comprises of relatively large particles containing very large molecules. Most of the digestive process happens in the stomach, where the food stays for four hours, although some digestion happens in the small intestines. Absorption of the smaller molecules produced by digestion takes place through the walls of the small intestines (where the food stays for an additional three hours), into the blood or lymph. In the intestines and colon, there are also some helpful bacteria (probiotics) that help digest indigestible foods.

While digestion, secretion, and absorption are taking place, contractions of smooth muscles along the gastrointestinal tract wall serve to mix the luminal contents with the various secretions, and move the contents through the tract from the mouth to anus.

The digestive system is designed to maximize absorption, and does not regulate the amount of nutrients absorbed or their concentrations in the internal environment. Elimination of the waste products of the body's metabolism is actually not achieved by the digestive tract, but by the lungs and kidneys. In simplistic terms, we exhale (CO_2) or we pee it out. So actually, the materials leaving the digestive system at the anus consists almost entirely of ingestible material that was neither digested nor absorbed—material that never actually became part of the body's internal environment.

Now there is something to be said about the speed at which the food is digested. Doctors tell us that the fastest food moves through the digestive system, the more efficiently the body can absorb its nutrients and discard any possible toxins. From a yogic point of view, slow digestion is a sign of an impending illness. And from an energetic point of view, efficient and optimal digestion goes hand in hand with light energetic bodies and the free flow of spirit.

Diet Approaches Out There

The following is a summary of the diet approaches that are out there today, and some comments about them. In the next chapter, I'll detail the Zohar Kindness Diet, which is a unique diet of adding things to your diet and lifestyle that are kind and nurturing to your whole being. The Zohar Kindness Diet is a well balanced diet, based on sound medical, as well as holistic principles, which will help you along your higher path to success. This overview of other diet approaches is only included here in order to disperse some false assumptions about nutrition that have no medical basis. If you are already familiar with approaches that are out there, or if you just don't feel like it, you can totally skip this section, and go onto Kindness Food Principle.

Atkins, Mayo-Clinic, South Bay Diet & The Likes:

Despite the fact that these diets are yesterday's news, many people are still hooked on them, despite their falsehood. There are only small variations between these diets.

The main principle of these diets is reducing carbs or cutting them off completely. The theory is that the body can break down fats and proteins into smaller molecules that could be utilized to supply energy. The body utilizes carbs first, before it would break fats, or use proteins for energy. The premise of these diets is then to eliminate carbs, in order to force the body to break down fats to use for energy, thus affecting weight loss.

While these diets may work extremely well for short periods of time, they ignore some key points: Although the body can run on the byproducts of proteins (ketones) and fats (fatty acids) for a few weeks, the burning of those for energy is not ideal since the body runs most efficiently on carbs. Additionally, as I've already mentioned, *the brain can only run on glucose*. The brain cannot run on ketones, or on broken down fatty acids. *It must have adequate amounts of glucose in order to function!*

The main drawback of these diets are: they are usually too high in saturated (animal) fats, too protein rich, and dangerously low in the vitamins, minerals, and phytonutrients that fruits and vegetables offer. Another drawback is that these diets do not necessarily encourage exercise.

Low Fat Diets:

Low fat diets are the old style diets, which concentrate on reduction or elimination of fats from the diet. To begin with, these diets completely ignore the whole issue of carb and the body's need for low glycemic index carbs. But with regards to fats, while there is nothing wrong with reducing our overall fat intake (especially saturated fat), attention should be given to eating enough essential fatty acids, which as their name suggests, are absolutely essential to our health.

Food Combining Diet:

This diet was developed by Dr. William Howard Hay in the 1920's. Dr. Hay theorized that eating fruit and vegetables produced alkaline end product after digestion, and eating processed and refined food left high acidic end product after digestion. He also theorized that each type of food requires different enzymes to digest it: carbohydrates requiring alkaline-based enzyme to digest, and protein require acid based enzyme to digest. Therefore carbs must not be combined with proteins or sour fruit, so that the alkaline and acid would not cause a problem in digestion. This diet advocated eating specific "alkaline foods" combinations, such as fruit and nuts in the morning, protein and salad for lunch, and a starchy food with vegetable for dinner.

Later interpretations of the Hay diet explained that eating carbs makes the pancreas secrete insulin, which not only helps the cells absorb glucose, but also drives fats to the body, convert the fats into storage, and prevents the body from utilizing stored fats. However, if you are only eating carbs with no fat, there is no fat to be stored; and if then on another meal you only eat proteins and fat with no carbs, than there is no insulin released, and therefore nothing to drive the storage of fat. These later developments of this diet also advocate abstaining from drinking liquids during the meal so as not to dilute the digestive enzymes.

The problem with these food-combining diets is that the theory behind them is not based on science. First, in 1935 Dr. Stewart Baxter showed that the pancreas secretes digestive enzymes regardless of whether proteins or carbs are eaten. Second, the notion of abstaining from ingesting liquids during the meal because they may "dilute the digestive enzymes" is commented on by all physicians as bullshit, since digestive enzymes are abundant in the GI tract. Drinking enough water is crucial to health and there is no way that drinking water would harm digestion. Moreover, each area of the digestive tract has its own specific pH, so as to maximize the efficiency of the digestive enzymes secreted into it. In fact, pH is very tightly regulated throughout the body. So no food combination is going to mess that up. Even when we eat a mouthful of all macronutrients together in one bite, each of them is going to be digested ideally in its respective area of the digestive tract, perfectly supported by an ideal pH and an abundance of digestive enzymes.

Alkaline Diets:

The Alkaline diet, which has been re-popularized in recent years by Edgar Cayce, D.C. Jarvis, Herman Aihara, and Robert Young professes that eating only certain foods, and drinking "alkaline water" (produced by a machine that you'd spend thousands of dollars for), is better for your health, prevent disease, and produces easy weight loss. This diet has been under the heavy scrutiny of the National Council Against Health Fraud. As stated above, the pH environment in each zone within the digestive system is very tightly regulated by the body, as perfectly suited for the various enzymes secreted into each zone. The stomach for example is highly acidic. So no matter how many "alkaline" foods you eat, it is still going to be bathing in acid for four hours while digestion takes place in the stomach. Beyond that, the blood's pH is also very tightly regulated between 7.35-7.45 by the homeostatic mechanisms of the body. Doctors tell us that a blood pH above 7.45 (too alkaline) causes a serious medical condition called alkalosis, which can result in hypokalemia and hypocalcaemia.

The only shred of truth in the so-called "alkalizing of your body" is that if you eat too much protein, its byproducts are acidic. The same is true about overeating sugar, or eating processed foods in any amount – they all have acidic byproducts after digestion. Dr. Weil notes that the normal way that the body gets rid of acidity is by breathing out carbon dioxide, but that Western diet, which contain too much processed foods, sugar and protein, "can lead to a very low level of 'metabolic acidosis.' The key words here are 'very low level' (true metabolic acidosis is usually the result of kidney failure or other serious disease, not of dietary imbalances)." This low-grade metabolic acidosis leads the body to take out some calcium from the bones in order to offset the acidity. Integrative Medicine physician Tieraona Low Dog recommends eating *nine servings of fruit and vegetables* a day to balance the acidity of meat, sugar, and processed foods, thus preventing the body's taking out calcium from the bones (osteoporosis).[6] (A serving is half a cup of fruit or vegetables, or one cup of leafy vegetables.)

As noted by many physicians, the benefits of the alkaline diet are merely a result of eating more fruit, vegetables and whole grains. So it's not about the acidity or alkalinity of the food. It's about eating fruit, vegetable, nuts, legumes, seeds, and whole grain. But isn't that what we've been talking about all along?

Counting Calories or Points:

The premise of these diets is actually pretty sound: to lose weight, one must spend more calories than they intake. Many people have lost considerable weight and regained their health with diets like Weight Watchers, which simplifies caloric counting into points counting. The points take into account the fat content versus fiber content of the foods.

The downside is: losing weight and keeping it off requires one to be on those diets for at least ten years, even if they lost the weight in only six months. Most people who go on these diets lose considerable weight, but then gain it all back plus some, when they go off the system.

The other drawback relates to quality of life: Do you really want to spend your life counting calories/points, feeling like you need to be punished for eating? Or do you want to enjoy the pleasure of food, celebrate your life, be kind to yourself, and magnetize all-inclusive prosperity into your life?

The Zone:

The zone is a reasonably balanced diet. It does distinguish between good and bad fats, and between good and bad carbohydrates. And it does encourage people to exercise and drink lots of water. The only drawback of The Zone diet is that it looks at food as a drug to be used to manipulate the body's hormones and metabolism, which is a horrible way to look at food. Food is a source of pleasure that should be rejoiced with. It is a blessing and an opportunity to celebrate the abundance in your life and the bounty of blessings that God is giving you every day, even in your 'now' reality.

Ayurveda:

The purpose of Ayurveda is not to lose weight, but rather to heal and maintain quality of life and longevity, by recognizing the body's natural ability to heal itself, as well as nature and natural's food ability to assist that healing.

There are several components to Ayurveda:
- Balance of the five elements in the body – ether being related to the cavities of the body; air being related to motion of the heart, lungs, nervous system and sensory impulses; fire relating to light and the life-energy of our metabolism, digestion, vision, and intelligence; water relating to fluids in the body via secretion, digestive juices, mucous membrane, and blood; and earth relating to all structures in the body.
- Equilibrium of the three doshas or physical constitutions – Vata, Pitta & Kapha, each having a long list of characteristics that are attributed to them. The theory is that each of us exhibits aspects of all three doshas, but has one dosha that is more closely associated with us.
- Vitality and balance of digestive fire—agni, which is achieved by the proper balance of doshas.

☯ Balance, production, and elimination of the three malas (waste products)—urine, feces, and sweat

☯ Balance of the six tastes in every meal – sour, salty, sweet, pungent (spicy), bitter, and astringent.

I have nothing bad to say about the Ayurveda diet, except that it requires great care and discipline in the planning and preparation of food. The Ayurveda diet is normally practiced as a part of a whole Ayurveda-Hindu based lifestyle. For that reason, if you are seeking to live by this diet and philosophy, you should study this complex system in depth, and consult a professional Ayurvedic healer.

Macrobiotics:

Macrobiotics was developed in the late nineteenth century by Dr. Sagen Ishisuka, who aimed to combine the principles of Western medicine with Traditional Oriental Medicine to develop a system promoting health, harmony with nature, happiness and long life. The premise is that food is the basis for health, and the best food is natural, whole, unrefined, locally grown food eaten in season. So far so good. Actually, so far so excellent!

The macrobiotics diet is a vegan diet, which promotes chewing each bite at least a hundred times, and heavy reliance on whole grains, nuts, seeds and legumes. It teaches to balance yin and yang in the body by balancing food intake between the five tastes: sour, salty, sweet, pungent (spicy), and bitter.

The Macrobiotics diet is a very good diet. I have nothing bad to say about it, as it seems to be based on solid health principles of both Eastern philosophy and Western medicine. I know some people who have gone on this macrobiotics diet who have lost weight and regained excellent health thanks to this diet. However, all people I've talked to, who have gone on that diet and were able to stay on it for a while admit that they spent several hours a day in the kitchen preparing the food. I myself have tried to go on a macrobiotics diet and have failed. There is a macrobiotic restaurant in Santa Monica (California), in which I've eaten many times. And I have to say that despite the fact that the food is vegan, every time I eat at that restaurant, I feel comfortably satisfied (not overly stuffed), light, and fairly balanced in my state of mind. It's possible that they just balance the five tastes of the foods better, or that their dishes contain just the right combination of foods to supply enough complete protein. At any rate, I have talked to many people who, like me, have tried the macrobiotic diet and couldn't do it. They were hungry all the time, and were craving animal protein.

So if you like the macrobiotic idea, than you should study it more carefully, and learn how to balance the five tastes, how to combine the yin and yang on your plate, and how to replace animal flesh with the proper combination of vegan foods that will provide you with complete proteins, as well as vitamins and minerals. One online review of this diet claims that perhaps this wonderful macrobiotics diet is best suited for petite Asian people, who are culturally and physiologically already conditioned to survive on rice and soy.

Kindness Food Principles

Now that we understand some of the basics of nutrition, let's talk about how to integrate kindness-to-self into our nutritional habits, as a way of allowing Divine Abundance energy to flow into our lives through our Infinite Funnel of Abundance.

Of course, nurturing has many components, some of which come from food. Being nutritionally kind to yourself starts with the physical attributes of the food that you are putting into your body-temple. Are you putting into your body-temple junk? Or are you truly nurturing it with healthy foods that are in alignment with whom you Truly are? Being nutritionally kind to yourself goes beyond just the physical aspect. As human beings, we all have a need for mental, emotional, and spiritual nurturing, as a condition of restoring our True Selves and allowing them to flow freely into our body-temples on a daily basis. The amount of mental-emotional nurturing that you get greatly affects what you are then inspired (or driven) to eat, and how much of the food's energy your body either holds onto or releases. High-vibrational foods can also feed you on a spiritual-energetic level, which makes the food much more enjoyable and satisfying. Moreover, high-vibrational foods actually have a healing, mind sharpening, energizing affect that helps ready you for the actions required to merge with your Ideal Lifeplan. They make you feel peaceful, light and happy, and thus help bring you into an energetic vibration that resonates with, and therefore magnetizes prosperity. So you see, food is not just an indulgence. It is an integral part of living a Truly abundant life of all-inclusive prosperity.

The information above has established the physical basis for feeding your body well on a physical level. Kindness Food Principles will help you incorporate mental, emotional, and spiritual nurturing into the nutritional kindness that you are now going to start showing yourself.

Water:

Few if any chemical reactions happen without water. Water is a natural catalyzer for all life-supporting processes. That is why NASA, in its search for extraterrestrial life, concentrates on finding liquid or even frozen water as a first telltale that a planet could support life. Our human body is composed of nearly 70% water. Beyond facilitating literally every process in the body, water also helps maintain body temperature, and carry waste material out of the body, all of which are essential to homeostasis (the internal life-supporting stability of our body's temperature, pH, and all other body-environment parameters).

Our bodies lose water in many ways: Most of the water (about 1.5 liters a day) is lost through urination as we eliminate the byproducts of metabolism. Additional water is lost in sweat, which helps cool the body to maintain its steady temperature. More water is lost in our bowl movement, and even more moisture is lost through our lungs' breathing. Sweat, breath and bowl movement account for loss of another liter a day of water from our bodies.

Drinking enough water helps the body's immune system. The liquids are first metabolized and pass through our intestines, then seep into the blood stream and lymphatic fluid through the intestinal wall. The briefly increased volume of the lymphatic fluid passes through the lymph nodes, which are our hotspots for fighting disease. And of course, on its way out to the kidneys and urethra the liquid collects toxins from the blood to be extracted.

The point is that we all have to be mindful of drinking enough water. Research shows that dehydration is a major contributor to fatigue. Dehydration is often initially mistaken by the body for hunger. Thus when you are suddenly tired, or suddenly feel hungry even though you've just eaten, drink water first, before you figure out your need for rest or food.

How much water is enough? Healthcare professionals say that drinking an average of 8-9 cups of water per day is a minimum. However, bear in mind that if you live in a hot climate you lose a lot more liquids through your sweat pours. And if it's a dry climate, you won't even notice that you're losing so much, since the sweat evaporates. Also, if you are very active physically, you also lose additional water through sweat. If you drink coffee or other caffeinated drinks you lose additional water, since caffeine is a diuretic. Alcohol is also a diuretic. So for each caffeinated or alcoholic drink you have, you need to drink an additional cup of water beyond your normal intake. And keep in mind that eight or nine cups a day is an approximation. It does not account for different body weights and physiques.

The yogic approach makes it easy: A good rule of thumb is to drink half of your body weight in ounces. So if you weight 160 lbs., you need to drink eighty ounces of water (or other non-caffeinated, non alcoholic drink) per day, which is about ten cups. It is good practice to hydrate yourself in the morning and early afternoon hours, so that you wouldn't have to drink a whole bunch of water at night and wake up to pee at every hour of the night.

As a kindness-to-self practice, taking little breaks from your busy day to sip your cold bottle of mineral water could provide you with just the right kind of mental break, in which to breathe more deeply, remind yourself how fabulous you are, and bring in more of the energy of your Soul.

Whole Foods:

What are whole foods? Whole foods are foods that are consumed in a state that is as close as possible to their natural form—the state in which they appear in nature.[7] They include fresh (hopefully organic) fruits, vegetables, whole grains, legumes, seeds, nuts, seaweeds, herbs, spices, naturally occurring oils, and natural seasoning. Whole foods have had little to no processing, have not been denatured or adulterated by artificial ingredients, additives, coloring, or preservatives, and are therefore rich with natural nutrients, fiber, and flavor.

Whether you believe that nature is the product of evolution or that God is the driving force behind this evolution (which in my view are not mutually exclusive concepts), Mother Nature has had millions of years to perfect the products that she offers us. Most substances that our bodies need are abundant in Nature in just the right amounts for our bodies, if we just follow our inner wisdom and eat natural foods.

Historically speaking, the industrial revolution gave us the option for mass production and distribution of food, in order to help prevent world hunger. Thus we began to manufacture foods using many chemical and industrial processes, not knowing their harmful effects. But consider that prehistorically, and for the majority of our existence on Earth, people lived in tribal societies that subsisted on what they hunted and gathered from nature, yet nothing was missing. In fact, that lifestyle ensured that the perfect balance was maintained not only between people of different tribes, but also between man and nature, which produced a healthy balance within each person. The closer we get to eating food in its completely natural form, the better chance we give our bodies to naturally purge out toxins, and restore its natural perfect health.

Whole grains are of particular interest since they have also been properly researched and found to contain much fiber, important nutrients, and antioxidants. Studies show that eating whole grains helps reduce cholesterols, overweight, blood pressure, and the risk of chronic diseases, such as diabetes and heart disease.

But if you think scientific research is all that, take a look at the history of diet. Every ten years comes a completely new diet fad that negates and the validity of the diet that scientists previously believed in. The point is that the right balance of the nutrients necessary to support our health already occur in the right amount and balance in nature, perfected by millions of years of evolution. Some people who are used to only organic wholesome foods actually start feeling sick if they suddenly eat overly processed food full of unpronounceable ingredients. For example, I love gefilte fish, which is "meatball" made from fish that my grandmother used to make each Friday evening. But since preparing gefilte fish is such a complicated production, I used to occasionally buy it in a jar from the kosher section of the supermarket. And for many years, I was perfectly fine eating the gefilte fish from the jar. But in recent years—since I've been eating a diet of mostly wholesome, organic, healthy foods, I find that my stomach reacts violently to the preservatives present in the jarred gefilte fish. I guess I have become one of those people who cannot tolerate preservatives and unpronounceable ingredients. As you start adding more wholesome foods to your diet, you'll find that your body can tell the difference. You'll feel more energetic and light when you eat wholesome foods. And you'll find that it sustains you for longer. For me for example, when I am a guest in someone's house, and they only have white bread, French fries, and processed foods, I feel hungry all the time, and find that I need to eat more of it to feel full. At home, where I've been eating wholesome foods for many years, I feel full from less food. And that is something to think about, particularly if you are trying to lose weight.

Beyond the physiology of whole foods' nutritional value, there lies the energetic reality: wholesome foods give you a chance to become one with the Nature that God has Created, in a pure way. And it is this pure unadulterated Nature that contains a pure form of Divine energy, as it was originally Created for our healing and nurturing. This makes wholesome foods the highest vibrational food in existence.

Organics Versus Conventional:

Organic food are grown without chemical pesticides, pesticides, insecticides, fungicides, and the like, and are also free from GMO (genetically modified organisms).

Personal benefits of eating organic foods are: avoidance of harmful chemicals, GMO, hormones, and antibiotics, as well as enjoying the better nutrients and better taste of organically grown foods. The enhanced nutrient and taste are partially the result of the soil being nourished with sustainable practices, giving the fruit/veggies more nutrients and a better flavor. I personally can tell the difference (in most cases) in texture and taste between organic and non-organic produce. Some people also have a higher sense of social responsibility, and are moved to eat organic foods by reasons such as preserving our echo-systems, reducing pollution, protecting our water and soil, preserving agricultural diversity, supporting farming, and keeping our children's future safe—all valid reasons.

However, organic foods are more expensive these days (although I personally find that in most cases, organic costs just a few cents extra, and tastes much better). Therefore, if money is an issue in your selection of food—if being able to feed your family is on the balance here, than perhaps buying non-organic foods may be the kinder choice for yourself and your family.

What is GMO?

Genetically engineering and modifying our foods started for the benevolent purposes of improving food, increasing yield, and resistance to pests. This was traditionally done by genetically splinting the genetic code (DNA) of the plant we want to eat and produce, with the DNA of another organism that possesses the beneficial qualities we want to introduce. Genetically splint the DNA of each cell with pesticide-like organisms makes it so that its harmful effects cannot be washed off like sprayed pesticides could be washed off of a fruit or a vegetable. What scares me and a lot of scientists about, for example, forcing antibiotic genes into the DNA of the plant with a "gene gun," is overriding nature's defenses—unlike Mother Nature, who has had millions of years to experiment with the results of each change she introduces, we lack the years of research to back up our actions, so their long term affects on our health are still unknown.

When it comes to the flow of spirit within the food, needless to say that genetically modifying God's handiwork, and replacing it with harmful chemicals greatly inhibits the Divine flow of spirit within the foods.

But again, I am presenting here two sides of the coin: organic food is slightly more expensive, but it adds tremendous benefits to your health and overall wellbeing. You have to be the one to make the decision on what is kindest for you and your family, based on the circumstances of your life and your inner wisdom.

Local & in Season Produce:

In today's food environment, we are blessed with such an abundant of foods from all over the world year round that you may ask, "Why is it important at all to eat fruit and vegetables that are locally grown?"

People who advocate eating locally grown, in-season food site the cost of fuel for hauling the food from a remote region of origin, which add to atmospheric pollution, and the altering of global agricultural economy. But again, this is a choice that you're going to have to make. Eating only fruit and vegetables that are in season at the area where you live can considerably limit your choices of produce. I mean, what if you live in Alaska and it's winter? On the other hand, kindness-to-self may dictate avoiding the preservatives, additives, and processing necessary to store the produce during its long commute to your table. Even if the veggies are not canned, but are just sitting in a container being flown to you, they are still oxidizing, which causes degradation of nutrients, freshness, and taste. You might also consider that some of the juiciest, mouth-watering, best quality fruit and vegetables, including many heirloom varieties, are only available at your local farmers' market.

Energetically, locally grown foods bring you into better harmony with your natural environment. For example, it is well known even in the scientific community that honey and bee pollen should be eaten from local farmers in order to adapt your immune system to the local allergens and reduce allergies.

However, limiting your choices may not always be the kindest thing to do. I too occasionally indulge in a mouth-watering-juicy sweet fresh pineapple, which is grown nowhere near Southern California where I live. But you don't have to make a once-and-for-all decision about any of these choices. Just keep this information in the back of your mind, and keep making decisions, on an everyday basis, that are kind to yourself, your family, and your environment,

Living Versus Dead Foods:

A few years ago, I went to a Chinese medicine doctor, who told me that I had "liver-chi stagnation" (whatever that means), and that to cure it, I needed to cook my vegetables rather than eat them raw, since this would increases the flow of chi in the body. Later I learnt that this is a common recommendation that all Chinese medicine doctors make for any kind of chi stagnation in people; and there is always some kind of chi that is stagnating.

On the other hand, the new hip vegan trend is to eat only raw foods with nothing cooked over 118°F. They profess that raw foods provide the full spectrum of nutrients for clean burning energy, and the complete spectrum of vitamins and minerals, as well as the enzymes needed to metabolize the food (never mind the fact that digestive enzymes are abundant in our bodies). The limitation of not heating anything over 118°F is due to the fact that the plant's enzymes are destroyed above this temperature. Now, it is true that some nutrients, especially vitamins, get destroyed with heat, light, air, and contact with metal (cutting knife). It is also true that cooking carbs, for example, in many cases raises their glycemic index, which does not support a weight loss diet. And of course I acknowledge that raw foods retain their original chi. But there is more to the story.

Dr. Weil gives the pros and cons of raw food diet on his web site: He sees the benefits of eating raw foods as providing much fruit, vegetables, nuts, and seeds, all of which are essential to a healthy diet. The raw food diet also avoids animal products, which then avoids the animal toxins and the risk of overloading on proteins. But he points out the many advantages of cooking foods: "Many of the vitamins and minerals found in vegetables (tomatoes, carrots) are less bioavailable when you eat these foods raw than when they're cooked…" Another point he makes, which seems monumentally important to me, is that many toxins that occur naturally in edible roots, stems, leaves, and seeds are destroyed in the cooking, such as in celery, mushrooms, and alfalfa sprouts to name a few. Dr. Weil notes some new studies that suggest that although body mass index was lower in raw food eaters, their bone mass was unhealthily low.

I am not suggesting that you go all raw tomorrow morning, or that you cook all your foods. I am also not suggesting that you thoroughly investigate each and every vegetable you are about to eat, to see whether to cook it or not; that would be tedious. But everything is good in moderation. And finding the most harmonious balance between raw living foods and a juicily grilled steak depends on what works for you personally. Some of your cravings can provide an excellent source of information on what your body needs at any given point. If you regularly crave a certain food, or food cooked in a particular way, you might do a little research on the benefits of that food, or the benefits of cooking versus eating it raw, as the case may be. I'm willing to bet that you'll find that something in the food you're craving that is beneficial for your health, and that (aside from overindulgence in the wrong kinds of sources for any missing nutrients) your instincts were trying to lead you in the right direction. For example, I've hated eating raw tomatoes ever since I was a child, but have always loved tomato soup, but throughout my young adult life I have tried to force myself to eat raw tomatoes. It wasn't until I read Dr. Weil's book *Eating Well For Optimum Health* that I realized that tomatoes are actually more beneficial for my health cooked and not raw. My instincts and internal wisdom have never stirred me wrong. And I am not unique in that. I believe that we were all given healthy instincts. We just need to re-learn to listen to them.

Vegetarian Versus Animal Foods:

There are quite a few vegetarian styles out there. Most vegetarians do eat some animal products such as eggs and dairy products. Yogic diet avoids eggs but include dairy. And vegans and macrobiotic diets don't include any animal (no eggs, no milk) products at all. I've heard the terms "nothing with eyes" and "nothing that had a mother" mentioned amongst some vegans.

People choose vegetarian diet for a variety of reasons. Some people choose it from purely humanitarian reasons: avoiding cruelty to animals. Others avoid eating animals because of their high place in the food chain, and the resultant high levels of toxins that their flesh accumulates. Yogis reason that beyond the humanitarian reasons, the process of the animal being slaughtered leaves an extremely negative energetic imprint of fear and pain in their flesh, which as spiritual beings we should not become one with. Many vegetarians simply take the energetic approach of becoming one with the plant kingdom. Although most of them would not express it quite in those term, the idea is that since plants have a Ruach (spirit) but not a Nefesh (animal instinct, see Chapter 1 of *Prosperity From Your Soul)*, they are not tainted by the low vibrational fear that often influences the Nefesh, so their essence is purely that of the high vibrational living spirits (Ruach). As much as I enjoy a good juicy steak every now and then, I acknowledge that I am less aggressive, calmer, and dwell in a higher vibration when I eat vegan. And of course, I would never dream of eating animal flesh before I teach/initiate someone into Reiki.

However, eating animal flesh is not all bad. In fact, there are many benefits to eating animal flesh. Eating animal flesh helps maintain a healthy bone density. Animal flesh also provides a ready, rich source of complete proteins, as well as some vitamins and minerals that are hard to find from vegetarian sources. For example, lean beef provides a great source not only of complete proteins, but also of selenium, vitamin B12, B6, iron, zinc and phosphorus. While it is possible to come by all of those nutrients from vegetarian sources, it takes much knowledge, attention, and preparation to do so. You would have to eat a gallon or two or kale or winter greens to come by the amount of iron that you get from just four ounces of beef. Plus, you would not only have to research which nutrients are needed, how much of it you need, and where to get it from, but also you would have to spend time to obtain and prepare those two gallons of kale. And that's just one mineral! We haven't even begun to talk about the other minerals and vitamins, and correctly combining foods to come up with complete proteins in every meal.

So where is the happy medium? One interesting approach to counter humanitarian attacks against eating animal products is presented by Ester Hicks, who claims to channel a higher entity she calls Abraham. While asked about vegetarian versus eating animal flesh, Abraham answers through Mrs. Hicks (I'm paraphrasing) that the animals that end up on our plates come into this incarnation clearly knowing that they are going to sacrifice their lives and become our food, and they don't mind doing it. On a high level, they do so lovingly and by choice. That is an interesting approach. An approach I resonate with a lot more is the Native American tradition, which teaches us to only take from nature what you need (not being greedy), and also to take the time after each kill, to thank the spirit of the animal for its sacrifice. In our case, thanking the animal for its sacrifice could take place after you buy the meat, while cooking it, or just before you eat it. I usually do the blessing and thanking twice: once as I start cooking the meat, and then again when it is on my plate, just before I eat it.

If you love to eat animal products as much as I do, one solution to the issue of the toxins that may be contained in animal products is to try and eat mostly organic or otherwise all-natural, grass-fed or vegetarian-fed animals, which reduces the amount of toxins. A solution to the issue of the energetic imprint of the animal's suffering on its flesh is to do a little ceremonial prayer before you eat animal flesh. I personally reiki my food and thank God for all my blessings before I eat each meal. As I do so, I also intend for the reiki energy to cleanse the food from the energetic imprint of the animal suffering, and briefly send reiki distant healing to the animal to thank if for its sacrifice. Your inner wisdom will guide you on a ceremony that is appropriate for you.

The key is to find a balance that is best for you: You can eat some vegetarian/vegan meals, while indulging in animal products in others. Use your inner guidance to tell you how much animal flesh, and how much fruit, vegetables, nuts, grains, seeds and legumes to eat, and what is the balance that is most harmonious for you.

If you are already one of those light-vibrational vegetarians, and generally feel healthy, vibrant, and bursting with energy, then I salute you. In my history as a Kundalini yoga teacher, I have gone on and off the yogic diet for many years. I find that when I eat vegetarian I do feel lighter and more bursting with energy, but after a while I have trouble focusing, and crave beef. I personally cannot fathom how women in their menstruation age can exist on a vegan diet without craving beef. This may be due to my own inability to properly research and prepare a vegetarian diet that contains all the nutrients my body needs. But it may just be that human beings—as our teeth structure, the relatively short length of our intestines, and our lack of ability to digest fiber suggest—are meant to be omnivores, which means that we are not meant to exist solely on a vegetarian diet; we are meant to also eat meat. On the other hand, I know how high-vibrational the vegan diet makes me feel when I go on it.

Where is the balance? The art of life in this reality is to find the happy medium between dwelling in your Soul Self, and being grounded into this existence – joy being the one vibration that both your Soul Self and your here-now self agree on. And that applies to food also. I think that if there is anything you can get from this long introduction to a very simple concept, it should be to find the balance that works *for you*. Because only your inner wisdom can guide you to harness all this information to find the perfect balance between the high vibrational spirit of the food, and the here-now quality of the food. So tune into your inner kindness meter, and be the kindest you can be to yourself, your family, and your environment.

Healing foods

The right foods, prepared with the good intents, and eaten with an air of "I'm fabulous" can have an incredibly healing affect. And there are three categories of healing foods:

Wholesome:

In the first category of healing foods are foods that are high vibrational because they are organic, wholesome, fresh, and in-season. They include fruit, vegetables, nuts, seeds, legumes and whole grains. In short, foods that are close to nature, and as such, contain the highest vibration of spiritual energy, because they are as close as you can get to the bountiful harvest that our Earth Mother (and Heavenly Father) has given us.

Containing Special Nutrients:

The second kind of healing foods are foods that have been scientifically found to contain specific nutrients that are healthy and may remedy certain health issues. There is actually a whole science of nutritional medicine, and the effect that each food has on our health. Many books have been written about that. Here are just a few examples:

- Lower Cholesterol – If you have high cholesterol it is especially important for you to eat plenty of Omega-3 rich foods, such as fish, oats, walnuts, flaxseed, chia seeds, and almonds, since Omega 3 is known to decrease the bad cholesterol and increase the good one, effectively lowering your cholesterol.
- Immune – Since vitamin-C is known to boost the immune system, vitamin-C rich foods, such as orange, grapefruit, lemon, and rose hip tea are healing foods for immune issues.
- Himalayan salt – contains many healthy minerals. Eaten in moderate amounts instead of regular salt can help reduce salt cravings, as well as treat migraines due to its magnesium content.
- Coconut Water – is a drink that replaces the electrolytes the natural way—a much healthier way than sports drinks. It will help you feel refreshed. And is also one of the only things I can hold down during a migraine attack.
- Herbal tea infusions containing specific herbs with known healing qualities
- Healing herbs in pill or tincture form
- Foods found to contain particular nutrients that can heal particular health ailments

Emotional & Spiritual Food Value:

The third kind of healing foods are foods that have been prepared with love, while feeling happy, after a good meditation, or foods that you have otherwise imbued with high-vibrational intent for yourself and your guests. This is food that have absorbed the love energy that you radiate, and the vibration of uplifting music.

The movie *Like Water For Chocolate* took this notion to the extreme to make a point. One scene in the movie shows a woman crying the deep heartfelt tears over her separation from her Soulmate while cooking for her sister's wedding. And in the next scene, they show all the people eating the food that she has cooked suddenly starting to cry and yearn for their long-lost loves. As humoristic as these movie scenes are, there is actual spiritual truth behind that idea: food does absorb the energy that you radiate as you prepare it. For example, we all know that mom's chicken noodle soup heals a head cold. But medically speaking, there is very little scientific basis for this miraculous healing that we all experience, beyond maybe the ingestion of liquids, and the warm salt water which temporarily reduces throat infection. Yet we all know it works wonders to heal our head colds and other ailments. So what is it about mom's chicken soup that heals?

Another example is: growing up, my family used to gather at my grandma's every Saturday for lunch—the special Tshulnt (a special Jewish stew cooked overnight) and Klops (Yiddish for meatloaf) that she used to make for us. Today I would give every last penny I own just to sit with her one more time and eat her Tshulnt and Klops. As a child, I have watched my Safta (=grandmother) prepare this meal many times. And I can tell you, knowing what I know now about cooking, that there are no tangible ingredients that make her recipe so unique. The first time I tried making my Safta's tshulnt and Klops from the recipes and exact instructions that my mother passed on to me, it actually came out tasting pretty bland. And that's when I realized what the secret ingredient in my Safta's cooking was—an ingredient that made her cooking rich with flavor, mouth-watering juicy, and cravable beyond any food I will ever craved – Love! All through Friday afternoon and Saturday morning, my Safta was excited that we were coming, that she would get to see us and give us all of her love and her goodness. Although she worked hard to prepare the Shabbat (=Saturday) meal, as she prepared the food, she used to hum happy tunes, and sometimes devotional songs that she learnt in her childhood. Despite the hard work, Safta was radiant with Love, as she was preparing the food for us. And I cannot count how many times her food healed me… everything from soar throat to a broken heart.

Another example from my grandma's cooking is chopped liver. From a physical health perspective, it is well known that despite the fact that liver is rich with iron, it is one of the worse foods you can eat, because the liver is where an animal stores all its body-toxins. So when you eat it, you intake not only the iron, but also the toxins that were accumulated in that animal's liver. However, for me personally, chopped liver is one of my top healing foods. Because when I eat chopped liver, in my heart, I feel like I'm sitting in my Safta's little kitchen all over again, like she is still standing in that kitchen humming her happy tunes, giving me occasional hugs, lovingly listening to all of my concerns, worries, hopes and dreams… and making chopped liver especially for me. And in those moments—as I bask in the memories of my grandmother, I somehow still feel her immense love for me. So who cares if this one tablespoon of chopped liver has some minute amount of toxins? It nurtures me to the core, and makes me feel beloved! And when something nurtures you to the very core of your being, and makes you feel so deeply beloved, than unless it's cyanide, it is your ultimate healing food.

So the scope of healing foods stretches way beyond the physical. Healing foods include foods that have specific meaning for you. Just like me, I'm sure that when you think about it, you too would find some foods that are healing for you in a special way.

Then the next question becomes: in the absence of someone who loves us so dearly, how do we reproduce the healing affect of our grandmothers' (or mamas') cooking? To begin to answer that, let us remember that God's Love is what composes this whole multiverse. It is the essence and living spirit within you. All you need do is be aware of it, open up your heart, and allow God to pour into your being. So in the next section are some suggested practices that can help you imbue your food with healing love energy. And I can tell you from experience that ever since I have started blessing the foods that I cook with love and Reiki energy, everybody who comes to my house not only enjoys them, but also starts seriously craving them. I have a flight attendant friend who, while living in Maine, bids difficult schedules necessitating long commutes, just so she could come to my house and eat the blessed wholesome food that I cook with love. I have included a few meditational practices I use in preparation and enjoyment of the food, which I thought might give you a start.

Spiritual Food Practices

To start imbuing your food with nurturing love energy, the first step is to change your way of thinking about food. Start thinking of food not merely as a survival necessity, but as a form of nourishing your whole self, and as an anchor to ground your Soul's spiritual energy into this physical reality. When you prepare your foods in a way that imbues it with Soul's love for you, and with an "I'm fabulous" feeling, even the strictest diet can feel much more nourishing.

The second obvious step is taking the time to really enjoy your meals. This goes beyond chewing well to get your digestive juices going. As you stand in the kitchen preparing the food, you can play some inspiring and uplifting music; take a few deeper breaths; do some Kindness Movement to free up your body; and remind yourself of joy. You might even decorate the plate as you serve the food, even if you are serving it only to yourself and eating alone. I do all that every day, even when I dine alone. You can go as far as putting a nice tablecloth, large dinner napkins; and lighting candles for your dinner, as a way to remind yourself that you are a beloved child of God. She-He wants you to enjoy, treat yourself well, and know that you are worthy.

You already know (see *Prosperity From Your Soul*) that expressing gratitude for what's already in your life, as well as for the blessings that you trust are on their way, are huge components of your ability to co-Create prosperity in your life. Meals are a great opportunity to take the time to remind yourself to be grateful, since you are already taking time away from your hectic schedule to have them. Christian and Catholic people are used to this idea of blessing the food. Religious Jews usually say particular prayers for specific foods. Sikhs chant three long "Sat Nam" with palms in prayer pose before their meal. But blessing your food does not necessarily have to be a religious practice (if there is anything that I myself am devout about, it's never to conform to any one particular organized religion; to honor them all; but to cultivate my own pure and untainted connection to the Divine). Blessing the food, and expressing your gratitude for the blessings that are already in your life, is a way to energetically open yourself up for more blessings from the Universe. When I reiki my food before I eat, I thank God for the blessings that are already in my life, but also for those blessings that I wish to amplify in my life—the health, love, happiness and prosperity that are still coming— intending that as I ingest the food, I would become one with all of those Divine blessings that I wish to bring into my life at that moment. Even if you are not a reiki practitioner, you too can find your own unique way to bless your food in a way that makes you feel blessed as you eat it. And feeling blessed is a huge part of what drives your energetic vibration into a resonance that attracts to you the prosperity you seek. So make each meal an opportunity to breathe deeply, nurture your health, and to uplift your spirit, your day, and your mood. Make it an auspicious opportunity to tune into how fabulous you are in that moment, and raise your energetic vibration to co-Create an attractive resonance with prosperity from your Soul.

On a somewhat mundane level, a big part of nutritional kindness-to-self is to start planning your next meal as soon as you recognize that you are starting to become hungry. Don't wait until you are hungry enough to devour an elephant. Start planning your next meal when you are starting to feel that you are going to be hungry soon. This way, you'll have enough time to prepare the food with joy (or choose a restaurant that offers kindness foods), eat your meal joyfully and leisurely, and bless your food to imbue it with your co-Creation intents.

Safta's Pre-Cooking Meditation

To be quite honest, my grandmother never actually meditated. In fact, she didn't even know what meditation was. I call this meditation Safta's Pre-Cooking Meditation, to honor her memory, and because my Safta was the epitome of love. She didn't *need* to meditate to tune into, and dwell in a vibration of love. She had enough love to give everyone, even strangers. And especially when she was cooking for us, she dwelled in such a state of joy and motherly love that her very essence brought forth for us Divine Love.

My question for years was: In the absence of someone who loves you and prepares the foods for you with such deep love, how can you-yourself embody such high-vibratory-Love that would overspill and imbue the food with spiritual nurturing love? This meditation was given to me as the answer to this question. The meditation can help you shed off lower vibrational energies, and get into an energetic vibration of love and nurturing that comes from your Soul. This can help you dwell in a nurturing vibration of Love when you prepare the foods, so that you can imbue it with this nurturing Love energy.

Music Selection –

To set up for this meditation, put on music that inspires you to feel the deepest feeling of love. For example, my Safta had a special connection with music, as her father was a Cantor rabbi.

She sometimes used to listen to classical music on the radio while preparing the food for us on a Saturday morning. But more often than not, she would hum songs from her childhood that connected her with the loving memory of her parents, and affirmed her love of life during the preparation of the meal.

As you can understand from this example, the music that you choose during the preparation of the food is a very personal choice, one that also depends on the kind of blessing that you are trying to imbue your life with. As an example from my musical selection, when I am preparing and eating a relatively quick lunch, I usually choose uppity-up music like Vivaldi, or cheerful devotional- yogic songs. But while preparing and enjoying dinner after a day that takes my all, I put on music that reminds me of the deepest love of my Soul. This music sometime brings a few tears into my eyes, but it help me connect energetically and emotionally with a deep place of love within. The idea is for the music to help you tune into love, re-experience it within yourself, imbue your food with that love, and then ingest the food with the intent of blessing yourself with more of that love.

The Meditation ~

Sit quietly with yourself for a few moments in a comfortable position. Start deepening your breath as you say a little prayer of your choosing to call upon Divine Love… With each inhalation, envision pink Light coming straight from the heart of the Divine, and entering your chest area, and spreading through your entire being… And with each exhalation, envision that the Light that you have called onto yourself instantly turns to incandescent Divine white light, and spreads from your heart center to engulf your entire being…

Your thoughts may initially wonder as thoughts always do. Just let those thoughts surface and then let them go. Keep bringing your mind back to inhaling the pink Light of Divine Love into your chest, letting it fill every part of your body, letting the Light turn into incandescent white Light within you, and than letting it spread throughout your aura as you exhale… Gently put your soft left palm on your chest, and your right palm over it, to give yourself a very nurtured feeling…

As you continue this process, envision your aura becoming bigger, brighter, and more saturated in the incandescent pinkish-white Light, representing Divine Love. After a while, you'll feel that your heart and God's heart are one continuous beam of Light pulsating as One with each breath, and you will feel bright, happy, completely immersed in Love.

Now bring your attention to the people you are about to cook for (even if you are cooking just for yourself, and certainly if you are cooking for a loved one)… Concentrate for a few moments on the beautiful essence of each of these beautiful Souls… Think about what you love about them, how much you love them, and what a joy it is to have them in your life… However, as you think about the people that you are cooking for, do not dwell on their human shortcomings, or on what irritates you about them, but on their Divine potential—their True Selves. And don't allow yourself to veer from dwelling in the Divine Love of the incandescent pinkish-white Light that you are now basking in… This may help you develop a higher love for the people in your life, which is unaffected by their human shortcomings, as it helps you see them from the perspective of dwelling in Divine Love.

To end the meditation, take a few deep breaths envisioning roots of Light extending from your root chakra and the soles of your feet to the center of the earth, grounding into you and your life all the Love energy that you have just invoked. But do not ground yourself completely. Stay in a somewhat meditative state; keep the inspirational music on; keep your breath naturally deep; and keep envisioning yourself in the bubble of incandescent pinkish-white Light… Gently get up, and start cooking. As you cook, envision the food that you are preparing imbued with this Divine Light-Love that you are now channeling through you. Set the intent that as your guests eat the food, they will be internalizing the high vibration of Love-Light that you are bathing in right now. Continue breathing in Love-Light until you feel yourself so immersed in Divine Love, that you know that sharing it would only serve to magnify it.

In this chapter, we have touched on some of the principles of nutritional kindness, healing foods, and spiritual food practices. Notice that I laid out the information in as neutral a way as I could, as the discussions of this chapter were only meant to help you weigh in the facts, and contemplate some of the options of spiritual kindness-to-self as they comes into play nutritionally, so that you can then engage your considerable inner wisdom to decide what's right *for you*.

Being kind to yourself when it comes to food rids you and your body of toxins and lower vibrational energy, and helps you dwell in a peaceful yet upbeat prosperity-magnetizing vibration. Physically speaking, it prepares your body-vessel for the activities that you are now planning to integrate into your life in order to merge its current reality with that of your Ideal Lifeplan. Energetically, kindness and spiritual food practices make energetic room in your body-temple, as the anchor of Soul energy, for receiving the enhanced flow of Creative energy into your life, through your Infinite Funnel of Abundance (your energetic bodies being the funnel that allows the pouring of Heavenly energy into your physical reality). So practicing nutritional kindness can help you establishes a lifestyle that is vibrant, upbeat, ready to host all the blessings precipitated upon you by the Universe.

In the next chapter, I introduce the Zohar Kindness Diet – a revolutionary diet that is based on *adding* things to your diet and lifestyle, not taking them away. While not everyone needs to lose weight, the Zohar Kindness Diet is all about helping your body find its own perfect balance. The next chapter will give you some food for thought on ways to achieve the nurturing of your whole being, as well as some more specific directives on how you may introduce kindness-to-self into your nutritional habits and lifestyle. The next chapter also ties together everything we've talked about in into a system that's easy to follow, and can help you ready your body-temple and lifestyle for receiving True prosperity from your Soul.

Chapter 5

The Zohar Kindness ~~Diet~~ Lifestyle

When I first wrote this chapter, it was simply called "The Zohar Kindness Diet." Later, I changed the name to "The Zohar Kindness Lifestyle," because I realized that while it contains some diet mindfulness and *can* help you lose weight if you need to lose some, this chapter is really more about a lifestyle of kindness-to-self, and integrating the practices that we have discussed into clear guidelines that could help you shift into a balanced, healthy, and happy state of being, which is more in line with the loving radiance of your Soul. For as we've discussed, it is this balanced, happy state—the Balance of Grace—that will help you ground the Infinite prosperity of your Soul into your here-now reality. The reason I added the name Zohar to the name of the diet is not so much because Zohar is my True spiritual name, but because the word "zohar," in biblical Hebrew, means Divine radiance. And it is my prayer and wish that this kindness lifestyle will help you bring your own Divine radiance into your here-now existence.

Still, why am I keeping the word "Diet" as part of the name of the chapter? Statistics tell us[1] that one of three Americans is overweight or obese. Obesity extends to children: one quarter of two to five-year-olds and one third of school age children are also overweight or obese. And we all know the health risks of obesity. But let's hold our horses here! This is not a medical book about your health. How does overweight relate to co-Creating prosperity? And how do we achieve an ideal body shape and weight, the kind way? This is the subject of this chapter.

First let's answer the first question: There are several relations between shaping your body-temple to a weight that is ideal *for you* and co-Creating prosperity in your life. That is not to say that obese people cannot be wealthy. But if we are talking about all-inclusive prosperity from your Soul, there is something to be said for being comfortable in your body-temple—just being comfortable in your own skin. And there are several aspects to why being comfortable in your body-vessel is important to prosperity from your Soul, the first of which is that perfect balance and radiant health are integral parts of the all-inclusive prosperity from your Soul. From a practical here-now perspective, as I have found out from my own experience, access weight can also limit your ease of movement, stamina, and consequently the extent to which you are capable of acting on your co-Creative insights. From a purely metaphysical standpoint, the energy blockages imposed by the access weight can limit the free flow of Creative energy into your body-vessel and through your Infinite Funnel of Abundance, and consequently they can also limit the extent to which you can ground all that new prosperity into manifestation in your life.

However, contrary to what most diets would tell you, the best way to bring your body-temple into its ideal weight is to actually eat more, not less, and to add more things into your daily nurturing habits. So in this diet, the more the merrier—the more you eat and bring into your life, the more weight you'll lose, and the more your body-temple, mind, and emotions will stabilize into the perfect balance for you. But there is a time and a reason for every thing under Heaven, yes? And in the case of this diet, there is the matter of what, specifically, you need to eat more of; when/how often to eat it; and what other food you are to bring into yourself in order to vibrationally resonate with radiant health, blissful happiness, and Infinite prosperity – from your Soul.

Your Diet Motivation

Before we start talking about weight control, I want to emphasize one point: you are a beloved child of your Creator. Your beauty does not depend on your weight or your external appearance, but on the radiance of your True essence. If you want to lose weight, the best motivation is to do it for yourself – to be healthier, to feel lighter and freer in your body, to be able to do the things you want to do with ease, and to be more in touch with your physical here-now self, so you can more fully ground joy and abundance into your here-now reality. I know that some overweight situations are unhealthy. But no one needs to look like a model, to be healthy and comfortable in his or her own body. Some curves might actually look nice on you. And your approval and love of yourself should *not* depend on your financial achievements, your fame and fortune, other people's approval, and certainly not on your weight.

However, I know from personal experience that feeling this way is much easier said than done. Most people spend about three hours each night watching television, and most of us go to movies occasionally. And in ninety-nine percent of movies and television shows, the actors and actresses are always stick-figure-lean and in perfect shape. And of course, if it's a good show or movie, we identify with its characters, and see ourselves in them. Then we close the TV and look at ourselves in the mirror and lo and behold – we don't look at all like them! And so we start this somewhat conscious process of continually beating ourselves up for not looking like the movie stars we just identified with. Most of us do this without even knowing it. And so it has become the norm to think of thin people as successful and worthy, and of overweight people as losers. But consider where all these stigmas are coming from: Movies? Magazine adds featuring twelve-year-old stick-figure models? Actors whose sole job in life in between movie productions is popping supplements and spending five hours each day at the gym, in order to look the way they do? (And I've seen them at the gym doing it.) We need to learn to separate the reality of movies and magazine adds from the reality of our lives.

Consider that about a hundred years ago, in most Western cultures, it was considered beautiful to be full-figured. Botticelli did not paint stick-figured women or men. Neither did Michelangelo, Monet, or Degas. They all painted men and women who they considered beautiful—full figured and curvy. And if you go back ten-thousand years to hunters and gatherers societies, a person who was overweight was considered rich and successful, since one had to be a good hunter (or huntress), or be married to a great hunter-warrior, in order to have the opportunity for so much surplus that would allow him or her to become overweight. And that way of life sustained human kind for the majority of its existence. So which stigma is correct and where do we find the balance?

The reality of it is that every person has a body weight and figure that are ideal for him/her, which does not necessarily conform to the rigid body mass indexes. Some people have heavier bone structure. Others have narrow bone structure or a petite physique. A weight that works for one person may not work for another, and what works at age twenty, may not work in one's thirties, forties, or fifties. We are all different. Our DNA is different. Our build is different. And the essence of who we are is different. And that is as it should be.

For example, I am tall (5'9") and have strong large bone structure. From high school until I hit age 33, I maintained a weight of about 145 pounds pretty steadily. But throughout my twenties, despite the fact that I was slender, I wished that I had been one of those petite women who weigh 125 lbs. I also wished that I were a few inches shorter. I now lovingly accept that I am just not meant to be 5'5" tall, or weigh 125 pounds. Even at 145 pounds, I was extremely slender. When I was 33, I accepted a job as an airline pilot, which necessitated working at hours that were changing all the time, sitting in the cockpit all day, and eating terminal junk food, while on the road bouncing between airports and hotels (the only food I had access to). So I started gaining about ten pounds per every year of working at the airline. When my weight hit 97 pounds over my now appealing weight of 145 pounds, my doctor told me that my weight presents a health risk. At that point, I cognitively knew it was time to do something about my weight. But for some reason, I continued eating pasta with cream sauce, steaks, tiramisu cakes, chocolate mousses, and many other unkind foods. In other words, the cognitive knowledge that my health was at risk still didn't drive me to start a diet. My motivation to start a diet came when I visited my friends in Arkansas, and wanted to do fun things with them. I noticed that it was difficult for me to hike with them, as I felt heavy like my feet were made of lead, and I was huffing and puffing with every step. It was difficult for me to fit into their lovely little sports car; I couldn't bend as my belly was in the way. My body felt chunky, and it was difficult for me to stand in the kitchen and cook the gourmet dinners I wanted to cook for the three of us. That was when I knew *I wanted to* start a diet: not because of how I looked to other people; not even because my doctor said about my health was at risk. *What motivated me was how I felt*, compared to how I remembered I could feel. As I meditated deeply, my inner wisdom showed me that the extra weight was limiting my freedom and ease of movement within my own body, and restricting the flow of Ki within my body-temple. I tuned into the vitality and zest of life I used to feel when I was lighter and more connected to my body, and I deeply yearned to feel that zest of life and lightness within me again. That was the deep motivation that convinced me to lose weight. Because of the spiritual path I have been walking through life, I knew that my own radiance and self-love are Divinely sourced, and didn't depend on my weight. So when I decided on a weight goal, I knew I didn't necessarily need to go back to my twenties' weight of 145 pounds. I knew that I could still love my body and feel free and beautiful if I went down to 155, or even 170 pounds.

Our beauty originates from within—from our Divine radiance and the essence of who we Truly are. And I truly believe that our energetic essence and what we energetically project is what people see when they look at us. How many times have you seen a skinny woman who radiates a nervous "I hate myself" energy, and even though she has the potential to be beautiful, because she hasn't tuned into her own radiance and inner beauty, no one notices her. On the other hand, how many times have you seen a curvy or even obese woman, who is happy, confident, accomplished, radiant, graceful, and dressed the part, and the head of every man in the room turns to look at her in admiration. And by the way, the same works for men. There have been plenty of times that I was attracted to a heavy-set guy because of what he radiated, and completely ignored a hunky guy standing in the same room because he projected a negative attitude about himself. On one occasion, I turned down a gorgeous Italian man, who owned several restaurants and a beautiful sailboat in the Caribbean's, and went home with an obese, broke diving instructor, simply because of what they each projected. I believe that when we start losing weight, it's not the weight loss itself that makes people look at us. It's the fact that we've turned our attention to approving of, and loving ourselves, and so we feel healthier, lighter and more beautiful, and we radiate that air of "I'm fabulous."

The biggest factor that determines the success of your diet is your motivation. And there are several levels of motivation. If other people around you have told you (or showed you) that you need to lose weight, it may give you a weak motivation to start a diet. But since deep down inside you already know your self worth does not depend on your weight, it may not give you a strong motivation. Not fitting into the clothes that you like can also provide a weak motivation for diet. But again, this is not a strong motivation, since you may actually like going out and buying new clothes. If your doctor has told you that you need to lose weight for health reasons, than that provide a much stronger motivation for losing weight. But the knowledge that your weight situation poses health risks is still just a cognitive knowledge, which may or may not filter into the level of feeling it.

The only motivation that can sustain you through weeks, months or even years of dieting are feelings and emotions. It is the deep conviction of your internal wisdom telling you that you *want* to be and feel healthier. And *wanting* to lose weight is very different than knowing that you ought to. Desiring something deeply to the core of your being is the only motivation that is deeply anchored in your Soul Self. And since you already know how powerful the Will of your Soul is, only when your goal is supported by your Soul, will it become easier for you to have the determination to make permanent changes in your life that will support your higher goals for manifestation. Remember that diet is a small but important step for manifestation of your overall Plan. Having your diet steps anchored in Soul-wisdom will help you put yourself first in a graceful way, even in social eating situations. It will keep you motivated, and help you carry a positive visualization for positive results.

What's Your Ideal Weight?

There are many formulas for calculating one's ideal body weight. I won't bore you with them. Despite my strong affinity with math and science, the Body Mass Index has always been too complex for me to bother with, and its results are a number that doesn't quite mean anything in our daily lives. I have always disliked the fact that I must depend on a written chart to measure myself up. What makes formulas kind of obsolete is that each one of us knows when he or she is overweight and when they are not. We each know when we feel free within our bodies—when we fit into our skinny jeans, and when we do not. Am I right?

And there are two more reasons why knowing how much weight to lose and how long your projected diet road is are not important: First, you will find the Zohar Kindness Diet so nurturing and easy to do, that you will not want to stop it once you start. Second, the Zohar Kindness Diet is not really a "diet" per se, but a shift into a kinder, happier lifestyle that resonates with prosperity from your Soul. As you will see, it is a diet of adding things (not taking things away) that allows your body to find its own weight/caloric balance. So when you reach your ideal weight, your body's internal wisdom will naturally guide you, and your weight loss will naturally stop. And you will still be eating and nurturing yourself according to the Zohar Kindness Diet principles. So there is no need to put an end point or a target weight in mind. You will feel fabulous and radiant doing this diet.

All that being said, if you still want a formula for figuring the weight that you should shoot for, a much simpler formula for calculating your ideal body weight is the one published in 1871 by the French surgeon Dr. P.P. Broca. It is a formula that was very popular in Israel when I grew up, and has always been very easy for me to use. I'm hoping it would be easy for you too. The original formula was published in the metric system, but I have worked out the formula's conversion into the Imperial system of measurements that is more popular here in the States. As you glance at this formula, keep in mind that I'm not advocating use of any formula to find out what your ideal weight is. I'm merely providing you with a means to get a ballpark figure what weight to shoot for, if that is what you wish:

<u>Formula #1 – Your Ideal Weight</u>:

<u>Metric</u>: [Height (in centimeters) – 110 = Ideal Weight (in Kilograms)] ±10% for men, ±15% for women

<u>Imperial</u>: [Height (inches) x 5.6 – 242 = Ideal Weight (lbs.)] ±10% for men, ±15% for women

So for example, plugging my own measurements into this formula:
69" x 5.6 – 242 = 144 lbs.   144.4 + 15% = 166   144.4 – 15% = 123
Notice that even according to this formula, things are not as cut and dry or as precise as the body mass index table would have you believe. There is a wide range of weights that would still be acceptable for each individual, even from a medical perspective. In my case, my good weight ranges from 123 to 166. That's a 43 pounds range, which in my view allows for the variation in build and in how we each choose to carry ourselves. Some people actually like themselves a bit curvier. Some people don't mind carrying around just a few extra pounds, so that they may allow themselves to more fully enjoy food as one of the joys of life. And yet others take more joy in

having an athletic physique. Even scientific formulas allow for a range that leaves room for your inner wisdom to guide you as to the most ideal weight for you.

Putting the formula aside, know that the ideal weight for you is the one that makes you *feel* good. Do you feel sensual and in touch with your body? Is it easy for you to move around and physically do the things you want to do? Do you feel vital and youthful? Remember that *weight is just one tool of measuring the health of your body-temple*. Since the purpose of this whole physical existence is to enrich your Soul, it is absolutely imperative that you be kind to yourself at every step of the way. Give yourself time to reach your weight loss goals; be accepting and non-judgmental of yourself if you have an occasional craving; listen to what your body is telling you at every step of the way; and accept that some days are not meant for you to exercise if your body is legitimately tired, while on other days, kindness-to-self dictates that you do push yourself to do more for your health. Weigh everything on the balance of kindness.

What Affects Weight Gain or Loss?

Scientifically speaking, weight control is governed by an extremely simple formula. Now don't get alarmed! We are not going to dwell on any formulas here. I am just presenting this simple formula in order to establish a basis for the wisdom and kindness-to-self that you are going to be practicing. Think of this formula as a sink full of water, in which the faucet is constantly on pouring in water, and the drain is also partially open for water to flow out. Well, if the sink is filled to a certain level, than if you want to decrease the water level in the sink, then you either have to decrease the flow of incoming water from the faucet, or increase the drainage. In this analogy, the level of water in the sink is analogous to your current weight; the water incoming from the faucet is analogous to food that you eat; and the drainage of the sink is analogous to your expenditure of energy throughout your day. Weight, like all other things in the universe is energy. The food that you eat gets converted to energy in the body, which is either spent (drained like water out of the sink) through your daily activity, or converted to fat for storage in your body (which is analogous to raising the level of water in the sink to have more reserve). Scientists measure the energy of the foods you eat, as well as the energy you spend in units called calories. So plain and simple, if you eat more energy (food) than you spend, the access energy is then stored in your body as fat, increasing your weight. To lose weight, you must either reduce what you eat, exercise more, or a combination of both. So far, it sounds simple enough, right? I've expressed this principle as a very simple formula (since the conversion factor of 3500 is an approximation, you can regard this formula as a rule of thumb, really):

<u>Formula #2 – Weight Gain or Loss:</u>
(Caloric Intake – Caloric Expenditure) ÷ 3500 = Weight Loss/Gain (in lbs.)

Now don't get all bent out of shape about calories or formulas. Zohar Kindness Diet will not have you counting calorie, points or anything of the kind. And we are not going to get stuck on formulas either. The formula is given here just to simplify all that you might have heard about diet, and what makes it work. Calories is just a measurement of energy that allows us to compare the energy derived from the food we eat to the energy we spend during the same timeframe, say a day or a week. As a side note here, what I've referred to it as calories in the above formula, is scientifically referred to as kilocalories (kCal). I have referred to it as calorie for simplicity's sake, since most diet books and online resources use the same simplification. And 3,500 are the *approximate* number those calories that make up one pound. Most calorie-counting diets count the caloric intake per day. Also most nutritional information that provides daily intake recommendations refers to caloric intake in a twenty-four-hour period. However, since daily weight fluctuations are small and reflect liquid variations in the body, most diets shoot for a weekly measurement of weight loss.

All that being said, I'm not a big supporter of counting calories or points, and I do not have a very high opinion of eating pre-measured canned food (such as in Nutrisystem, for example) either. Eating pre-boxed canned foods is not my idea of being kind to yourself. Neither is putting yourself in the mental cage of counting calories or points.

Now, just to put things in perspective: all this formula really means is that in order to lose weight, you have to spend more energy than you intake. But it doesn't say anything about reducing the volume of the food you eat, your satiety from the food, or your enjoyment of it. In fact, as I've already said, the Zohar Kindness Diet is a diet of *increasing* what you put into yourself.

To start seeing how you could lose weight by increasing what you put into yourself, let's look at the bigger picture here: while scientifically, the simplicity of this formula holds true for any weight control program, even scientists agree that **there are many factors influencing both variables in the equation:** There are many factors affecting how many calories you eat; there are many factors affecting how many calories you spend; and there are factors affecting how fast your body is willing to let go of its access weight. There are also other factors at play here, which most scientific based diets have thus far missed. Some of these factors are emotional-mental, and others are purely a matter of the flow of energy within your energetic bodies. To understand what we are going to increase in this diet, and why, let us now look at the many factors affecting both the intake and expenditure variables of the formula.

As you read through the many factors affecting caloric intake and expenditure, pay attention to your feelings. You may get some 'Aha' moments when you read through the particular factors that affect you. And as you do, you may want to write them down, and then meditate on what you can do to remedy these factors.

Multidimensional Factors that Control Caloric Intake:

If you feel like you are eating more than you should, or are constantly hungry, than there must be a reason for it: you are probably deprived in some way, either physically, emotionally, mentally, or spiritually. And what I am suggesting here is the opposite of what other diet books suggest. Although scientists would accept the physical layer of deprivation, and perhaps even the emotional layer—factors affecting your drive to eat, most scientists would not acknowledge the spiritual influence on caloric intake. And that's okay; science will catch up one day to the technologies afforded by spiritual advancement.

Each of us already has within them the highest wisdom to guide our lives. So instead of continuing to deprive ourselves, the Divine wisdom within can help guide us each to nurture ourselves and replace what is missing. I believe that just by nurturing yourself properly on all levels, and by letting self-kindness be your guide, you can make a huge stride towards keeping your weight under the control of your Higher Self.

<u>Physical Factors Influencing Increased Caloric Intake –</u>

Water & Dehydration – there has been a number of studies[2] that suggest that when we don't drink enough water, the body's first reaction to thirst is fatigue, and the second is hunger. So in many cases, people feel hungry despite having eaten enough, not because they really need to eat, but because they are dehydrated. The solution to that is simple. If you are hungry before you think you should be, it never hurts to hydrate yourself properly first. Then, if you just drank plenty of water, and are still hungry, by all means, eat! But water intake is one of the things we are going to increase in Zohar Kindness Diet. As we've discussed in the previous chapter, you should be drinking half of your body weight in ounces (160 lbs. → 80 oz. of water → 10 glasses).

Fatigue – lack of good quality sleep and rest are monumental factors driving people to excessive eating. When the body is sleep deprived, it turns to the most immediate source of energy it can find—food, especially overly rich foods like low grade (sugary) carbohydrates, saturated fats, and fatty animal proteins—comfort foods. As we have discussed in Chapter 2, getting adequate sleep is an integral part of your overall health, but especially so if you have cravings for comfort food and binges of unhealthy eating. You'd be in awe of how easily your cravings will disappear or subside once you give yourself to a good night sleep of eight hours.

Number of Meals – According to most dieticians, if you go more than three or four hours without eating, your hunger level, and thus how much you eat at your next meal increases way beyond what you need to eat in order to sustain or lose weight. According to naturopathic doctor Natasha Turner[3], eating at least every three to four hours "will improve your fat loss by preventing excess insulin, allowing leptin to work its magic on appetite control and metabolism, and by balancing the stress hormone cortisol." And as we'll see a bit later in this chapter, the hormone leptin is closely related to producing a feeling of satiety. Many dieticians[4] recommend eating three meals and three snacks throughout the day, as a way to curve down the appetite during the meals and thus keep the caloric intake lower.

Meal Content – Each meal should be balanced and filling, with the heaviest meal of the day at breakfast. This prevents starting the day on a hungry note, which prevents overeating throughout the day. We will spend the rest of this chapter talking about what to eat to actually feel full, yet not stuffed and lethargic. But based on the considerations discussed in the last chapter, you already know that eating a bunch of processed foods with unpronounceable ingredients will most likely not satisfy you. On the other hand, eating wholesome, preferably organic foods, rich with fresh and in-season vegetables and fruit will fill you up more, and help you stay full for longer, not to mention keep your energy level up so you can burn more calories and feel happier.

Lack of Nutritional Value in the Food Eaten – you might be eating lots of calories and even heavy meals, but if you are not getting the important nutrients you need, your body feels starved, and is thus going to keep prompting you to eat more and more, until you give it the nutrients it needs. Your body is designed to heal and sustain itself in a most natural way. So craving and prompting you to eat more is just one way that the body heals itself by letting you know when certain nutrients are missing from your diets. This can take the form of eating higher caloric intake, or specific cravings. For example, a friend of mine used to always drown her food in salt, until I suggested that perhaps this big salt craving was simply her body's way to get some missing minerals, not necessarily sodium chloride. I suggested that she either takes minerals either in pill form, or replace the regular white salt with pink Himalayan salt, which contains many of the important minerals that our bodies need. It took her a long while to listen to my recommendation, but when she did, within a week, she noticed that she was using only a fraction of the amount of salt she used to use. This is a classic case of – when you give the body what it needs, it won't drive you to crave unhealthy things.

The best way to cure cravings is to simply try to add more wholesome foods into your diet—more vegetables, fruit, legumes, whole grains, nuts, and seeds. You can also do what I did with beef: At a certain period of time when I was suffering form severe frequent migraines, I was heavily craving beef, which made me go off the yogic-vegetarian diet. I needed to eat beef almost daily, as beef helped me "finish off" a migraine. Despite the fact that I love the taste of beef, I understood that eating beef every day increased my cholesterol and could be unhealthy. I also felt heavy in my body, and desired to restore my ability to feel light and free within my body-temple. So I researched, and found out that it wasn't the complete proteins that I was craving, since chicken had even more protein than beef per gram and per caloric intake. It was, most likely, craving iron or vitamin B12, since those are mineral/vitamin that occur mostly in beef. I found an herbal supplement that has those nutrients in pill form. And ever since I've been taking this natural supplement, I am no longer a slave of the missing nutrients. I eat beef only when I choose to rejoice in the pleasure of the experience. And all it took was a simple online search to find out the solution to the riddle of the missing nutrients.

So I encourage you to do the same for any particular food craving you may have. Start by asking yourself (and asking Google) whether there are any particular nutritional benefits provided by the particular food you are craving. If there are, can you get those nutritional benefits from eating a more healthful natural food?

Prehistoric Craving Factor – Our struggle with dieting is, for the most part, a struggle to reconcile our prehistoric craving factor—our genetic code predisposing us to crave lots of carbs and fats—with the abundance of modern life, an abundance that's apparent on every supermarket shelf and probably also in your fridge.

From anthropological and medical standpoints[5], our bodies crave sugar because it provides an immediate boost of energy. We are genetically predisposed to enjoy starchy foods because they can be easily converted to glucose and used for energy, or converted and stored as fat in our bodies, for rainy days when food is less available. Although this notion may seem ludicrous to most people in today's day and age when food is so plentiful to most, our ancestors were hunters and gatherers who survived on the flesh of animals they hunted, and grains and roots they found.

The hunter-gatherer lifestyle was feast or famine—sometimes there was a lot of gain to be hunted and roots/grains to be gathered; while other times the people had to survive off of the surplus of fat stored in their bodies, until things got better. Carbohydrates in general, let alone sugar, were not readily available. So naturally, it was mostly those people who had a genetic predisposition to crave sugar and starch, and to store its access energy as fat in their bodies, that were able to survive. And through the evolutionary process of natural selection, those who survived were the ones who were able to pass their gene pool to us. Thus to some degree, our brains and bodies are genetically programmed to like sugary and starchy foods.

However, there is a way to overcome these cravings: If you provide your body adequate amounts of carbohydrates from vegetables, whole grains, and legumes, all of which have a low glycemic indexes, than your body will have adequate supply of carbohydrates that lend themselves to more efficient use over a longer period of time after eating, and consequently will crave less sugars. I have put this method to the test, and it works a hundred percent of the time.

The story with fats is similar. Fats are rich foods that provide a tremendous amount of concentrated energy, which can be used or stored as fat for rainy days. Protein is the ace in the hole—the molecules that can be converted to both fats and to carbs. And again, those of our ancestors who craved and loved fatty food were more predisposed to survive, and thus were able to pass their gene pool down to us. But again, if you provide your body with adequate amounts of lean proteins and essential fatty acids from seeds, nuts, whole grains, and legumes, your cravings and dependency on animal protein and fatty foods like beef, butter, fried foods, bacon, and the likes will naturally subside.

Mental-Emotional Factors Influencing Increased Caloric Intake –

In many cases, cravings and overeating have an emotional origin. This doesn't negate the fact that when you are driven to eat more, you genuinely feel hungry. But in the spirit of kindness-to-self, if there is one thing you can do while reading this list of emotional craving factors, besides note which factors apply to you, it is letting go of any self-judgment about it.

Stress – unfortunately, stress eating is something most of us are familiar with. Physiologically, stress activates the 'fight-or-flight' response of our sympathetic nervous system, just like our ancestors when they were about to go on a hunt or battle. Most marathon runners are seen gulping down mountains of pasta weeks before a run. This is because they know that the body's most immediate source of energy is the glycogen that's stored in the muscles and liver. During strenuous activity such as running a marathon, once the glycogen storage runs out, one "hits a wall" as the body now has to break down fat and convert it to energy[6]. Despite the fact that you could be stressed and sedentary at the same time, and despite the fact that most stresses in our modern lives are mental-emotional (not physical), stress is still regarded by the body as preparation for a strenuous or even extreme (depending on the level of stress) physical activity, such as a battle, a hunt, or a marathon. Doctors also tell us that high levels of cortisol—the stress hormone—reduce the body's sensitivity to leptin, which is the hormone that produces the feeling of satiety. The bottom line is, when stressed, your body drives you to overeat.

But stress itself can be subtle. And if it extends over long period, you may not even recognize that you are stressed. Most of us have come to accept the demands of our hectic lives as normal, stretching ourselves thin while trying to satisfy everyone else in our lives. And during this whole rat-race, we forget our own need for nurturing and relaxation, and instead, we munch on something to calm down our nerves.

If you are eating out of edginess and restlessness, go and work it out: Go for a run, do your joyful physical activity, or go blow off some steam, and then meditate to get to the core of what's making you nervous. Better yet, go on a Nature Walk. To remedy stress eating, you should add joyful physical activity, and some meditational Me Time into your day.

Eating out of Boredom – many of us eat when we are bored. We sit in front of TV and it is only natural for us to go for the potato chips, nachos, and the likes. Discarding the cases in which you eat nachos because your body is not getting enough minerals and is craving the salt (or you could be craving complex whole grain carbs), if you really are eating just out of boredom, than *please* stop!

However, when I say stop, I don't mean that you should cut yourself off the nachos, cold turkey. That is not the way of the Zohar Kindness Diet. The way to make yourself stop with the nachos, or whatever your craving may be, is to first give yourself something more worthwhile. If you are just plain bored, realize that there is so much more that you could do with your time. Go outside and do something really enjoyable, something that resonates with all of who you are and makes you joyous all the way to the tips of your toes. Or utilize that time to take some of the steps implementing your Ideal Lifeplan.

Even while you are relaxing in front of TV, you could be reclining and giving yourself back the love you deserve, by just setting the intent to nurture yourself and being in an 'I'm fabulous' mind frame. I do reiki healing on myself throughout my sofa-TV time. That is the way I choose to give myself back the love and nurturing, and restore my "I'm worthy and fabulous" feeling. Adding meditations and fun activities can make your life feel more full, which can go a long way to getting your boredom-eating to wane down on its own.

Habit – If you are eating out of habit, try to replace the nachos with organic baby carrots, or cut celery stalks; you can even make a fun dip from my recipes in Appendix A. Experiment with some healthy snacks, and see how you feel with them. If you are still craving nachos (or whatever it is that you are craving), than you are either hungry, in which case it would be more beneficial for you to prepare a good nutritious meal for yourself, or you are missing a particular nutrient present in the food you crave munching on, maybe the salt and minerals if it's a salty food, maybe complex carbohydrates, probably sleep if you're craving sweets. And as we have discussed, there are always more nutritious ways to satisfy a cravings for particular nutrients.

Refuge – Feeling weighed down by the difficulty of life's challenges many times drives many people to find refuge in food. Know that you are a beloved child of God who is supported on every level, at every step of your way. You have many Angels, Spirit Guides, and helpers to help you along your path of life. You already know that all challenges you face are presented to you by your own Soul Self, in order to give you opportunity for growth. You also already know that you always have the power to surmount all challenges, either by facing them with the right attitude and at the right time, or by choosing a different path that is more in line with your Soul's highest plan for you in this lifetime. So challenges are good opportunities in your life. The meditational processes of *Seven Stages to co-Creating Prosperity From Your Soul*, especially some of the processes discussed in Chapters 3 and 4 of that book, can help you take advantage of these opportunities in your life, so that you don't need to drown your sorrows in food.

Feeling Deprived – lack of nurturing and love makes us eat more for several reasons. Many of us were told as kids, "be a good boy/girl, finish off your plate," which has stamped into our subconscious the notion that if we eat more, we would be more worthy of love and approval. As children, we were also gratified by our parents with food (candy), which makes us subconsciously equate food with love and reward. But once you realize this, you can give yourself the love and approval you need. Wake up every morning, look yourself in the mirror, and tell the image of your here-now self how much you love and approve of him/her. And from that place of self-love and acceptance, you will be able to derive a level of self-validation that does not depend on finishing off your plate, or approval by others. Of course, if you are a reiki practitioner, giving yourself daily reiki healing sessions will go a long way towards getting yourself to *feel* nurtured and beloved, rather than deprived.

Beyond daily rewarding yourself with adequate sleep, fun physical activity, some Me Time, and the added nutrients contained in vegetables, fruit, whole grains, legumes, seeds, and nuts, you might also consider rewarding yourself with little things that do not depend on food, say a conversation with a dear friend you have not seen in a long time, wearing a festive shirt you haven't allowed yourself to wear because it was too dressy, or even occasionally buying yourself little gifts – just because. I usually buy myself little crystals, or all-natural aromatherapy soaps to rewards myself. Although your selection of self-gifts may be different than mine, those little gifts, which usually only cost less than five dollars, go a long way towards alleviating any deprivation you might be feeling, and to getting you in a mode of feeling worthy, validated, and fabulous.

Low Self Esteem – Sometimes, low self-esteem drives people to a resignation attitude. They say to themselves, "well, I'm already fat, so it won't matter if I eat more of those cream puffs." But the reality of it is that your beauty does not depend on your outside looks. It is God's radiance within you that makes you beautiful. And it could shine brighter and be freer to express itself within your body-temple, if you truly treat your body as the temple for your Soul. All you need do to cure this resignation attitude is believe and tune into the radiance of your Soul. I'm not saying never to indulge in deserts. I'm saying indulge only when your inner wisdom guide instructs you to indulge, not because you are addicted to sugar. You should practice self-validation and kindness-to-self every day.

<u>Spiritual-Energetic Factors Influencing Increased Caloric Intake</u> –

There are spiritual-energetic reasons for cravings and overeating. What we truly crave, whether we know it or not, is Love (the all-encompassing kind), and nurturing of our Spirit.

Weak Aura – In yogic terms, our auras are the electromagnetic fields that protect us and contain our life-force energy. When the aura is weak or shrunk, we unconsciously but automatically seek to enlarge it by employing different techniques: we either engage in what I call "retail therapy"— bringing into our energy field a bunch of new things we don't really need, in an effort to enlarge our auras; or we overeat in an unconscious effort to enlarge our physical body in order to give us the layer of protection that's missing because of our shrunk/weak aura. A way to remedy this problem is simply to do some deep breathing, envisioning a large bubble of white Light around you – putting your free will into action, using the pureness of your intent to gather around you some extra Divine Light to strengthen and enlarge your aura.

Feeling Detached – feeling alone in the world, detached from Divine and the rest of Creation, leads many people to eat anything and everything in an unconscious effort to become One with it, and perhaps then become One with the rest of Creation. Once you are aware that that's what you are doing, you can engage more deeply in some of the meditational practices (especially Zohar Breath Meditation, detailed in *Seven Stages to co-Creating Prosperity From Your Soul*) that reconnect with your Soul Self, and by extension, with the Divine, and all of Creation.

Replenishing Energetic Leaks – some of us are natural givers. This means that whenever we are asked for something, or are confronted by people who take our energy, we are naturally inclined to oblige out of the goodness of our hearts. And if this situation lasts for an extended period of time, or if those energy takers are permanently in your life, this situation can create an imbalance or an energy leak through energetic entanglement cords, through which you are unconsciously giving your personal energy away. Other factors may be little tears in your aura as a result of past injuries. And since food is a giver of energy, many of us unconsciously turn to food in order to replenish the drained energy. However, doing some visualizations of colored light around you (see Chapter 2 of *Seven Stages to co-Creating Prosperity From Your Soul*), and especially Cord Cutting Meditation (see Chapter 4 of *Seven Stages to co-Creating Prosperity From Your Soul*) will do wonders to cure any tears or holes in your aura, and to dissolve unhealthy energetic cords, respectively. As these meditational processes will help you surround yourself with healing energy, they will eliminate the need for overeating, since the energy will no longer be missing, not to mention the wonderful benefits of these meditations/visualizations in keeping your energy apparatus clear of debris, and ready to funnel in True abundance from the Divine.

Of course, all that being said about all the reasons for overeating, the objective in life is to experience love, happiness, and joy. So abstinence of anything does not necessarily bring joy or happiness. But neither does overindulgence which can lead feeling heavy and uncomfortable with your body-temple. As in anything, moderation is the key. And the moderation I'm talking about is the one that your inner wisdom and kindness meters guide you to, because the only one who really knows which side of kindness balance you should practice at each point—when to indulge, and when to push yourself to eat healthier—is your Soul Self.

Multidimensional Factors Affecting Caloric Spending:

Most trainers and diet experts proclaim that simple laziness is our cause for overweight. But if you've learnt anything in this book series, you probably already know that things are never that cut and dry, and that there are always several layers to reality. And so it is with caloric spending too. Sure, there are physical and physiological reasons causing one's caloric spending to be low, but there are also emotional, mental and spiritual reasons, all of which we will discuss. Again, as you read these factors, pay attention to thoughts that pass through your mind, and feelings that these lines evoke in you, so that you may ascertain for yourself which factors are true for you.

Physical Factors Affecting Caloric Spending –

Heredity – To a certain degree, on the purely physiological level of reality, the predisposition to high or low metabolic rate (the rate at which your body burns calories) is genetic. But this doesn't mean that if you're overweight right now, you'll always be overweight, because your genetics is only your starting point, not the end result. So first of all, cut yourself some slack. Be kind to yourself. And know that *your destiny is very much in your hand. You can be anything you want to be* that is in line with your True Self, and this includes your physique.

Metabolism Slowdown Induced by Self-Starvation – It is vastly agreed upon by athletic trainers and scientists alike that cutting down caloric intake causes the body to lower its metabolism, therefore keeping the #1 Formula above at a standstill. For example, if you lower your caloric intake from 2400 a day to 1700 a day, your body will soon find a way to slow its metabolism and burn only 1700 calories per day (unless you are boosting your metabolism up by physical exercise), and you will have achieved nothing. Although there are many supplements that claim to boost metabolism, they are usually full of caffeine (MaHuang and Guarana are just two example), which makes you jittery, nervous, and agitated. Doctors tell us that although coffee and caffeine boost your level of alertness and thus help burn a few extra calories, caffeine also decreases our sensitivity to insulin, which may cause insulin resistance, resulting in high blood sugar and weight gain. The bottom line is – eat! Do not starve yourself. In fact most new diets advocate eating smaller meals as often as five times a day. This scientifically supports my philosophy of how profoundly kindness-to-self supports a healthy weight loss diet.

Number of Meals – According to most dieticians and doctors[3, 4], going more than three or four hours between meals not only builds up an elephant appetite for the next meal, but also slows down metabolism, which means that you burn less calories throughout your day.

Meal Schedule – Have you ever heard the old adage: "eat breakfast like a king, lunch like a queen and dinner like a pauper?" Well, according to dieticians, there is some truth to it. Dieticians profess that the heaviest meals of your day should be both breakfast and lunch, since eating them early enough in the day gives your body plenty of time to digest the food. Also as far as caloric burn rate, your metabolism is faster early in the day. So if your largest meal is breakfast, this gives your body the most amount of time to not only digest, but also to burn the calories of the food you intake. It is recommended that you do not eat a breakfast that is loaded with carbs, as carbs will make you sluggish and slow down your metabolism (caloric burn). On the other hand, I don't believe in bombarding your body with densely caloric foods right as you open your eyes. The old all-American breakfast, with bacon, a triple egg omelet, hash brown, toast, and butter, is not what I would consider kindness-to-self, and it is certainly not kind to your arteries. That breakfast will make you pretty lethargic and heavy. Each of your meals should be sensible, yet nutritious and balanced meal. I recommend that, keeping all of these recommendations in mind, you employ your own inner wisdom to construct your meal schedule according to what you feel is kindest to you.

Glycemic Index & Insulin – As explained in the section about glycemic index in the previous chapter, eating a lot of high glycemic index carbs gives the body lots of surplus to be converted and stored as fat. It also causes the liver to secrete more insulin, causing high spikes of insulin in the blood, which helps convert those carbs to fat, and prevents breakdown of the stored fat for energy. In recent years, there seems to be a consensus that eating carbohydrates of low glycemic index in balance with lean proteins, healthy essential fatty acids (3 & 9), and lots of fruit and vegetables is key to keeping production of insulin to a minimum, therefore allowing the body to release stored fats and use it for metabolism. To that affect, Zohar Kindness Diet aims to add lots of vegetables, fruits, whole grains, legumes, nuts, and seeds, which are all low glycemic index carbs. This will make you crave less and less white bread, white sugar and the likes. And I've put this to the test: every time I cook organic brown and wild rice, along with plenty of vegetables and some lean proteins, I don't feel the need to eat chips, crackers, white bread, deserts, and the like. When I am too lazy to cook my grains and prepare my vegetables, I start raiding my munchies cabinet about an hour after the meal.

Sedentary Habits – Let us not overlook the obvious: some people, for one reason or another, just lead a sedentary life. There are various reasons why people are sedentary. It could be due to a physical illness, spending too much time at an office job, being overwhelmed by life chores to the point of exhaustion, emotional-mental exhaustion combined with a habit of alleviating it by watching TV. But no, don't think of yourself as lazy. If you become adamant about giving yourself the love, kindness and nurturing that you need, you will stop feeling the need to spend long hours sedentary, TV watching. As discussed in Chapter 1, a good place to start is just stake out an hour each day for your Me Time. Adopt a fun activity that is somewhat physical, and is so enjoyable for you that it nurtures your spirit and connects you to your Soul Self. Nature Walk is a good one. Don't think of it as exercising or punishment. Think of it as rewarding yourself with an activity that pleasures you, which just happens to be physical and meditational in nature.

The Yogic Perspective – In yogic terms, efficiency of digestion and elimination, as well as properly functioning nervous, circulatory, lymphatic, and glandular systems are essential to the regulation of the body's metabolism, and therefore weight control. From the yogic point of view, anything we eat should either be used or eliminated within 24 to 48 hours.

Ancient yogis have constructed specific yoga sets, or kriyas (a kriya is a series or actions—poses and exercises—that has a specific concentrated effect), that they believe have the power to cleanse your body and restore its systems to perfect operation. Although I personally have practiced these yoga sets and have taught them to others, with the perspective of what I know now, I'm not sure whether it was the specific yoga poses that made us all feel great, the fact that we all believed they were going to restore our bodies and spirits, or just the fact that we were deep-breathing, engaging in a physical activity that was enjoyable to us at the time, which moved our Ki around. I believe that the activity you engage in does not have to be that strenuous to have positive results for your body, mind, and spirit. Nor do you have to pretzel your body into ridiculously demanding yoga poses in order to find balance and peace, unless of course yoga is your preferred physical activity, which brings you joy.

To restore your body, mind, and spirit into perfect balance, simply employ the wisdom and healing powers of your Soul, to help you find your own balance of kindness among all the elements of your life: joyful physical activity, sleep, meditation, social activities that nurture you, your Ideal-Lifework, and living a lifestyle of kindness and joy.

Mental-Emotional Factors Affecting Caloric Spending –

Stress – Besides driving you to stress-eat, stress also affects how quickly (if at all) the body is ready to release access weight. It activates the 'fight-or-flight' response, which drives the body to hold on tightly to all of its stored fats and not release it. This is because genetically, we are built just like our ancestors, whose biggest stress was when they had to go hunting or into battle. Just as before battle, stress automatically induces in our bodies to store fat, in an effort to ensure that we'd have enough energy stores to last us throughout the hunt/battle. Biologically speaking, when we are stressed, our bodies still think that we are about to go on a hunt or a battle, even if nowadays our battles are mostly with our bosses, our coworkers, traffic, or just the battlefield of life.

So if your life is stressful, staking out your Me Time, in which to meditationally relax or do your joyful physical activity, is not just an indulgence. It is a necessity for your cardiac and overall health, as well as your diet. Finding peace is as important to diet as exercising.

Energetic Factors Affecting Caloric Spending –

Energy Blocks & Negativity – If energetic debris and blocks (see Chapters 3 & 4 of *Seven Stages to co-Creating Prosperity From Your Soul* for how to get rid of those) are allowed to accumulate over time, they can cause illness in the body-temple, or can manifest as various physiological processes that prevent the body from releasing stored fat. But again, this is not a judgment. Even after the profound meditations you did in Chapter 4 of *Seven Stages to co-Creating Prosperity From Your Soul*, we all accumulate energetic debris as we go through our day-to-day lives. That's just part of the human experience. The important thing is what you do about it, and how you rise up to the challenges that life presents you. Keep engaging in some of the processes and meditations detailed in *Seven Stages to co-Creating Prosperity From Your Soul*, to help you let go of stress on a daily basis, and to keep letting go of themes that do not serve your Ideal Lifepath of prosperity. You now know better than to allow yourself to get sucked into stress, anger and the like. And you have an important path to walk as a conscious co-Creator of your life. Helping the body let go of access weight is just one byproduct of keeping your energetic apparatus clear, and your energetic bodies light. Prosperity coming through your Infinite Funnel of Abundance is another welcome byproduct.

Prana – How we breathe affects not only our moods and readiness states, but also our weight. Taking deep breath of fresh air is not just relaxing, but also nourishes the body fundamentally, by enhancing your life-force energy that enters your body-vessel. Air is a medium that helps distribute Ki energy throughout your body systems in a most balanced way, which enlivens their operation. Breathing also helps your body-temple release all the energies that do not serve its highest good. So start being aware of your breath. Make it a point to take some deep breaths in the course of your day, even when you are not meditating. In time, you will find that it relaxes you and makes you feel lighter and freer in your body.

Loss of Vitality – As we've discussed, childhood traumas, stress, negativity and anger create energetic blocks in the perfect flow of life-force energy through our charkas and light bodies. These energetic blocks can greatly affect not only our body's ability to release energy (calories), but also our level of our vitality, and thus how active we are able to stay (our metabolic rate) throughout the day. As a result, energetic blockages have a direct slow-down affect on how many calories we spend. They can also play a major role slowing down elimination, and hindering the proper function of all other body systems. In extreme cases, they can sometimes cause a person to be ill enough to become bed ridden, which would make it hard to keep an active life and spend as many calories as you intake.

If you have already manifested an illness that steals away your vitality or your ability to be active, take small steps. Start with five minutes of long deep breathing a day to restore your vitality. Start adding fruit, vegetables, nuts, grains, seeds, and legumes to your diet. It is extra important that they be fresh, organic and in season (from a farmer's market) to the extent possible. These simple practices will start introducing more vital energy from nature into your body-temple. As you prepare your fresh foods, hold your hands over the plate and envision Divine white Light energy coming through the crown of your head, flooding over your heart center, and radiating out of your palms to bless your food. Since we all channel Divine Ki, this practice is similar to imbuing your food with reiki energy. It will help bring more living fresh Ki into your body via your food. You can also put the palms of your hands on your body (on various chakras and organs), and use the same visualization to channel extra amounts of Divine Ki to heal yourself. Then when you feel a bit better, add to your day a few minutes of kindness movement, little Nature Walks (start with five minutes and then build on that), or whatever fun physical activity you are able to do. If you are suffering from an illness for which you are under strict medical supervision, ask your doctor if gentle physical activity is ok. In most cases it will be, but you should ask. If you are suffering from extreme obesity, swimming or water walking are excellent for you (as I'm sure your doctor will agree), since your body weight is supported by the water. In all cases, and especially when you are already suffering form an illness or a loss of vitality, it is very important that any physical activities you add are *enjoyable* for you.

The bottom line of this section is: If you're not hungry, don't eat! When you have an urge to put something in your mouth just for the sake of crunching, ask yourself: "Am I really hungry? Maybe this is just thirst in disguise? Or is this stress/boredom/emotional eating? Is this just an old non-serving habit to munch on something during another activity (say– cookies with coffee; chips while watching a ball game)?" You now have the tools to analyze the root cause of your munching urges, and obtain wisdom from your Soul on the healthiest, kindest substitute for each urge.

However by the same token, if you find yourself snacking on everything under the sun, you might actually be hungry. And if so, it is better that you lovingly prepare a nutritious meal for yourself, and eat it leisurely and with joy, than it is to keep snacking and snacking and snacking on processed, nutritiously-devoid foods.

What Produces Satiety?

As you understood from the previous sections, if all you wanted to do is simply sustain your weight, then your daily caloric intake should be equal to your caloric expenditure. And in that case, the number of calories you'd have to eat per day to function (sustain weight) is called your Basal Metabolic Rate, which is also easily to calculate:

Formula #3 – Basal Metabolic Rate (How many calories you need to consume to sustain weight)[8]:
BMR (women) = [655 + (4.3 x Weight in lbs.) + (4.7 x Height in inches) - (4.7 x Age in years)] x 1.2*
BMR (men) = [66 + (6.3 x Weight in lbs.) + (12.9 x Height in inches) - (6.8 x Age in years)] x 1.2*

*Multiply, instead, by 1.3 if you are lightly active, by 1.4 if you are moderately active, by 1.5 if you are highly active, or by 1.6 if you are do hard physical labor or intensive training.

In order to lose weight, you must either reduce the number of calories that you eat per day, or increase your caloric expenditure (activity), or a little of both. But this is where we're going to dump all formulas. Because the real issue is: how does one reduce caloric intake, without an automatic reduction in metabolism? I mean, obviously kindness-to-self can really help here. So how should one reduce their caloric intake and/or increase caloric spending while still being kind to oneself? That is, how do we reduce the calories of what we eat without feeling hungry or deprived? To answer that, we have to know what causes hunger and satiety in the body. While it seems that the exact mechanisms that controls hunger and satiety still eludes scientists, here are some of their theories:

Part of the mechanism is actually in the brain, in the two parts of the hypothalamus that process hunger or satiety signals from the body. It is the brain that, once it processes the body's signals, sends a signal that the body is full or hungry. Now the main debate is about the many signals that influence these two centers[9].

Most researchers agree, however, that satiety is the result of high levels of blood glucose, and food being present in the stomach and intestines. However, an article by the Department of Health[10] sites a research which proves that *fullness of the stomach and intestines does not depend on caloric intake, but on the volume of food*[11, 12]. One study[13] actually introduced air to increase the volume of the food (by making the food into a milkshake), which produced a bigger feeling of satiety than without the air. Another study[14] introduced water into the same exact food content, by making a casserole into a soup containing the same calories and nutrients, but a bigger volume. The study proved that people who ate the bigger volume were fuller and consumed less calories.

Another factor that researchers seem to agree on is that it takes about twenty minutes for the stomach and intestines to signal that they are full, for blood glucose to rise, and for certain hormone levels to reach the brain, and give it signals that then get interpreted as a feeling of fullness.

One of the newest and still not fully understood factors in satiety is the hormone leptin. Leptin is produced by the body's fat cells. Increased levels of leptin in the blood signal the brain that there is plenty of fat stored in the body, which causes the brain to suppress appetite and increase metabolic rate[15]. It would seem, then, that an increased level of leptin would be beneficial for diet. It is believed, though, that most obese people become resistant or desensitized to the signals that the leptin in their system gives the brain[16]. However, doctors who advocate "The Leptin Diet", explain that getting adequate quality sleep, as well as eating plenty of foods rich in fiber and water, such as vegetables, fruits, whole grains, legumes, nuts, and seeds, raise the leptin levels, which in turn makes your brain signal fullness, suppress your appetite, and increase your metabolic rate. But even if researchers are unsure of the exact method to raise leptin levels, doesn't this advocacy of getting enough sleep, and eating plenty vegetables, fruits, whole grains, legumes, nuts, and seeds sound familiar? Isn't that what we've been talking about all along?

Aside from all kinds of fads, simple high school biology teaches us that the stomach is actually elastic[17]: The more you eat, the more you want to eat because your elastic stomach has stretched; and the less you eat, the less you want to eat, because your elastic stomach has shrunk. That is why in most diets, it is recommended to eat more meals of a smaller portion, so that you train your stomach to shrink, produce satiety from less food consumed, and as a result, you are not walking around hungry while you diet.

The latest fad on the diet arena, which actually has lots of scientific truth to it, is the glycemic index and glycemic load diets. Glycemic index is not just a fancy idea. Besides the story with the insulin (see previous chapter), the lower the glycemic index of the food, the longer it takes your body to digest it. And if you think about satiety as resulting from having some volume of food in the stomach and intestines, than the longer it takes the body to digest the food, the longer the food will remain in the stomach and intestines, giving them some volume, the longer it will take before you feel hungry again. After eating a slice of white wheat bread, you may get hungry an hour later. When you eat a slice of whole-wheat seeded bread (lower glycemic index) of the same caloric intake, you'll stay full for a bit longer. But if instead you eat a small bowl of whole grains of the same caloric value, you'll be full for much longer. I find that when I load up on potato chips I am hungry again very shortly afterwards. But when I eat the same amount of brown &

wild rice with some broccoli, for example, I stay full for at least a few good hours. So that's why eating low glycemic index carbs plays a real role in your diet.

However, you know what they say about too much of a good thing. Even low GI carbs are still carbs. So eating excessive amounts of them is still not conducive to weight loss. To express that idea, scientists have recently come up with something they call a glycemic load, which is a mathematical expression combining the glycemic index of a food with the number of carbohydrates grams that are available in a portion. So for example, watermelon is pretty sweet, and has a relatively high glycemic index of 72, but is composed of mostly water. So three-quarters of a cup of watermelon only has only six grams of available carbs, bringing its glycemic load to 4. In terms of glycemic load values, scientists say that 1-10 is considered low, 11-19 is medium, and 20+ is high. I have included the glycemic load formula, as well as a list of foods and their glycemic indexes and loads in Appendix B, in case you want to look at those.

However, just as counting calories and points is also not my idea of kindness-to-self, neither is calculating glycemic loads. Once you've integrated kindness into your nutritional habits, and even during the integration, you should be enjoying your food, not counting calories, points, grams, glycemic loads, or anything of the sort. For that reason, the Zohar Kindness Diet will give you specific plate composition rules of thumb, which are very easy to follow, and will produce the fabulous dietetic results, as well as help you integrate kindness and joy into a lifestyle that will lead you towards your Ideal Lifepath of prosperity.

Body Organs that Support Weight Loss

If you ask a medical doctors which organs of the body are involved in weight management, he or she will tell you: the liver, thyroid gland, adrenal glands, and of course, the omentum. But while most doctors maintain that the only time you have to worry about these organs is when illness has occurred,[7] holistic nutritionists and naturopathic physicians maintain that the thing to do is prevent disease, by holistically taking care of one's health before any illness occurs.

So let's see, from a holistic nutrition standpoint, how each of these organs is involved in weight management, and what you can do to naturally support its operation.

Liver:

The number one organ that is involved in weight management is the liver. The liver is the major fat burning organ of the body, producing bile to help break down and absorb fat. Normal liver function include the filtering of toxins and waist products from the blood, transforming them into substances that can be extracted via the kidneys/urine, or dumping them via the bile duct into the digestive system to be eliminated as feces. The liver also has major functions in regulating blood glucose, insulin, estrogen/testosterone, immunity, and in the production and removal of insulin.[18]

Holistic dieticians and naturopathic physicians tell us that improper nutrition (eating foods that contain high fructose corn syrup, hydrogenated fats, unpronounceable chemical additives, food dyes, preservatives, as well as foods that are processed, too rich with saturated fats, and/or too high in salt), alcohol drinking, as well as emotional-mental stress, can all put undue stress on the liver, and cause it to become slightly inflamed. It may not be an inflammation of the liver strong enough to warrant a diagnosis of illness by your doctor, but this stress and low-grade inflammation of the liver are said to be major causes of fat buildup in the body, especially in the belly area.

Not everyone suffers from stressed, inflamed, or fatty liver. Short of getting a liver function blood test by your doctor, liver issues can be detected by paying closer attention to your body symptoms, such as fatigue, insomnia, brain-fog, digestive issues, low energy, cravings, and excessive thirst and urination. If you have those symptoms, than it would be wise to detox your liver even if you are not trying to lose weight. The good news is that to detox the liver, you do not have to take medications, or even go on a crazy liver-cleanse or juice fast. There are gentler ways to cleanse and detox your liver:

First off, stop smoking, reduce alcoholic beverages to a minimum, take medications only when you have to, and ditch the processed foods. If you start reading labels of foods you buy, it becomes easy to put back on the shelf foods that include ingredients like high fructose corn syrup, hydrogenated fat, food coloring, preservatives, hormones, additives, and other unpronounceable ingredients. In his book *Eating Well For Optimum Health,* doctor Weil has a very comprehensive chapter on buying foods and looking at food labels.

If you like to take herbs, there are some herbs that affect a healthy and natural liver detox, such as milk thistle, dandelion, burdock, turmeric, and mint[19]. There is also a long list of foods that can naturally detox the liver and support its healthy function: garlic, grapefruit, beets, carrots, green tea, leafy green vegetables, avocado, apples, olive oil, whole grains, cruciferous vegetables (cauliflower, broccoli, and the like), lemons, limes, walnuts, and cabbage.[20] As you can see and will continue to see in the Zohar Kindness Diet, we don't have to go far out of our way to cleanse the liver. As part of the nutritional kindness-to-self that you will be integrating into your lifestyle, you'll be eating lots of these healthy vegetables and whole grains anyway, as well as healthy oils and nuts that contain essential fatty acids.

Thyroid:

The thyroid gland, located at the front of the neck, helps our bodies regulate metabolism. It secretes thyroid hormones, which help the body use energy, and stay warm, amongst other functions. In simplistic terms, the thyroid regulates the metabolism, or the activity level of the body, measured as Basal Metabolic Rate (BMR). And if the BMR—the amount of energy needed to sustain the body's activities—is too low (due to an underactive thyroid), it means that the number of calories that the person needs to eat to sustain weight would be low, and thus the number of calories that this person has to eat if he or she wanted to lose weight would be even lower.

But again, while medical doctors will say not to worry about the thyroid unless you have a diagnosed illness in the thyroid, naturopathic doctors will tell you that if you feel like your metabolism is a little sluggish, than your thyroid is not functioning ideally. And rather than wait passively for illness to strike, the thing to do is to load up on the are eleven specific nutrients that support a health of the thyroid the natural way: iodine, selenium, zinc, copper, iron, vitamins A, C, E, B2, B3 and B6.[21]

- ☯ Foods that contain Iodine are sea vegetables, seafood, such as haddock, clams, salmon, shrimp, oysters, and sardines, as well as eggs, spinach, garlic, asparagus, mushrooms, summer squash, lima beans, and sesame seed.
- ☯ Foods that are high in selenium are: tuna, mushroom, beef, sunflower seeds, Brazil nuts, and halibut.
- ☯ Foods that are rich in zinc are: beef, turkey, lamb, fresh oysters, sardines, walnuts, sunflower seed, Brazil nuts, pecans, almonds, split peas, ginger, and whole grains.
- ☯ Foods that are high in copper are: crabmeat, oysters, lobsters, beef, nuts, sunflower seeds, beans, shitake mushrooms, barley, tomatoes, and dark chocolate.
- ☯ Foods that are rich in iron are: meat, oysters, clams, spinach, lentils, white beans, and pumpkin seeds.
- ☯ Foods rich in vitamin A are: beans, asparagus, leafy greens, parsley, peppers, strawberries, guava, papaya, and kiwi.
- ☯ Vitamin E rich foods are: peanuts, almonds, sunflower seeds, beans, asparagus and leafy greens.
- ☯ Foods rich in vitamin B2 are: egg yolks, meat, and also wild rice, wheat germ, mushrooms and almonds.
- ☯ Foods rich in vitamin B3 are: poultry, peanuts, wheat bran, and rice bran.
- ☯ Foods rich in vitamin B6 are: fish, bananas, brown rice, wheat germ, sunflower seeds, walnuts, and beans.

From this diverse list of foods that support the health of the thyroid (and therefore contribute to healthy weight management), you can see that with the right kindness balance, almost every natural whole food, especially vegetables, fruit, beans, whole grains, nuts, and seeds, as well as seafood and lean meat in moderation, can be healthy for you and support not only weight management but also a healthy body-temple.

Adrenal Glands:

It is a well-known fact that stress has an adverse affect on weight loss. And the organs that govern how stress affects our body are the adrenal gland. When we are stressed, the adrenal glands activate the "fight-or-flight" response in the body, by secreting adrenaline and cortisol, which provide the body with an extra oomph of energy. So far so good. However, increased levels of cortisol (the stress hormone) reduce the body's sensitivity to leptin (the hormone that makes us feel full), which causes us to want to eat more. And although we are no longer fighting our neighboring tribes or hunting for our foods, the constant stresses of our modern lives still cause our adrenal glands to secrete too much cortisol and adrenaline.[22]

The solution to adrenal stress is simple: Don't stress! To reduce physiologic stress, doctors tell us that we need to actually increase the number and frequency of healthy, nutritious, but sensible (smaller portions) meals throughout the day, in order to keep blood sugar balanced, and by that, prevent excessive cortisol from being secreted. To avoid and reduce emotional stress, meditate, engage in some of the meditative practices brought forth in *Seven Stages to co-Creating Prosperity From Your Soul*, or practice a relaxation technique of your own, and absolutely stake out your Me Time hour each day. That supports the idea behind this Zohar Kindness Diet in a big way—you need to increase the overall amount of nurturing and kindness that you show to yourself in order to stabilize your body weight to its ideal value.

Omentum:

The omentum is the membranous fatty tissue that covers and supports the intestines and the organs of the lower abdomen. Although the omentum has a vital function in our bodies, excessive fat deposits in it cause central obesity.

Natural remedies to reduce omentum fat are: getting adequate sleep, walking, eating whole grains, and getting enough Omega-3 fatty acid. Some super foods rumored to[23] specifically reduce belly fat are: almonds, watermelon, beans, celery, cucumbers, tomatoes, avocado, apples, tart cherries, and pineapple. Again we see that eating lots of vegetables, fruit, and beans are part of the key to healthy living.

Kindness Diet Meditation

As explained in previous chapters, each person is already connected to the Infinite Divine Funnel of Love, kindness, joy, health, prosperity, and... All-There-Is. So whatever it is that you need or want, you are, or have the capacity to be connected to it via your Soul. You may also recall from our discussions in *Prosperity From Your Soul* that your consciousness is an integral part of Divine Intelligence. Therefore it is through your Soul that you are also connected to the bank of all Universal knowledge that exists. On a here-now level, even from a scientific point of view, your brain manages thousands functions per second, most of which you are completely unaware of: your body knows how to breathe on its own, send the right enzymes and hormones to the right places at the right time, digest food, maintain homeostasis, rebuild itself... and a whole array of other functions, all of which happen automatically. So on both the highly spiritual level and the here-now subconscious level, your body and being are highly guided as to which nutrients are good for you, and what your needs are at any given moment. As you've already found out in *Seven Stages to co-Creating Prosperity From Your Soul*, deeply listening to your Soul's wisdom is of paramount importance to your highest Lifepath of prosperity. Soul wisdom is not only important to nourishing your spirit with kindness and love, but also to nourishing your body with the nutrients it needs to muster the vitality and health that would allow you to reclaim your Ideal Lifepath.

This meditation will help you tune into this wisdom to learn: the causes of your overweight (if you are overweight), the causes for any unhealthy cravings you may have, the best solutions to these causes and cravings, and the best joyful physical activity that you should add to your life.

So on a quiet evening, cleanse, protect, and bless you space (see Chapter 1 of *Seven Stages to co-Creating Prosperity From Your Soul*) in preparation for a meditation. Put relaxing non-verbal music that would help you tune into your core. Light a candle that you've blessed with your intent, and place it on a coffee table, so that when you sit and meditate, the flame of the candle will be at about your eye level. Sit comfortably on your meditation pillows, with your spine erect but not stiff, your chin slightly tucked in, and your shoulders relaxed down. Begin focusing on your breath…

Deepen your breath so that with every inhalation your breath is slightly deeper than the one before. Now open your eyes halfway, and begin hazily (off focus) looking at the hue around the light of the candle. This focus on the candle is a known technique for developing your intuition. Troubling thoughts from your day may surface, and that's okay. Don't stifle them. Just let them come up and then let them go, returning your attention to the light of the candle. After a few moments, you'll start feeling the, hopefully familiar, meditational peace.

Now in the peaceful stillness that you've reached, have a conversation with your subconscious. This is similar to Zohar Breath (see Chapter 2 of *Seven Stages to co-Creating Prosperity From Your Soul)* in that your higher consciousness (the observer within you) is the one leading the meditation. Or if you've read *Seven Stages to co-Creating Prosperity From Your Soul* and have mastered Zohar Breath Meditation, you can certainly have Soul Self lead the meditation, since tuning into the wisdom of your Soul keep the insights that you get high vibrational. But this time, we are attempting to get answers from a deep here-now aspect of yourself—your body's intelligence.

So after a few deep breaths, go deep into your subconscious. Close your eyes just a bit more (although not completely closed), and envision that you are walking down into a cave deep within the womb of the earth, and you are taking this candle with you to light your way into some answers. Set the intent that as you go down into the earth-womb, you will be going deep down into your subconscious, and communicating with the innate intelligence of your body-temple.

You (the conscious observer within you that is leading the meditation) are now going to ask your subconscious mind some questions. So now when you get to a peaceful place that you feel is tuned into your depth, ask your deep subconscious:

- ☯ What purpose did the access weight serve in your life up until now?
- ☯ Did it induce an important change in your life?
- ☯ Was it serving as a layer of energetic protection?
- ☯ Did it "serve" as protection in another way, such as keeping your mate away, out of fear?
- ☯ Was it subconsciously triggered by fear or other non-serving conditioning?
- ☯ In light of what you know now, does this access weight still serve a purpose for you?
- ☯ What is the Ideal way to serve the same purpose for your highest wellbeing, without experiencing this heaviness within your body-temple? I.e., what is the Ideal solution to your overweight situation, from the highest perspective possible?

After posing each question, get back into the natural deep breathing… continue hazily staring at the candle and envisioning yourself within the womb of the earth… and re-achieve meditative stillness. Now, within your re-established meditative stillness, the answers may come to you as visions that you see coming from the light of the candle; you may be "seeing" the answers-visions in the eyes of your mind (clairvoyance), "hearing" them spoken within your mind (clairaudience); you may tune into certain feelings as your answer (clairsentience); or you may just have a deep knowing of what the answers are, without knowing how you suddenly know (claircognizance). Either way is fine.

Once you've received some answers that resonate within you as Truth, you are ready to move to the next stage of this meditation. The next set of questions that you need to ask yourself will ascertain what the reason for any unhealthy cravings you may have. Ask yourself:

- With regards to unhealthy cravings, what is the reason you are craving these things?
- Are there any specific nutrients missing from your diet?
- Lack of sleep? Accumulative fatigue?
- Are you skipping meals?
- Are you missing spiritual-emotional nurturing?
- What is the Ideal way for you to supply your body-temple with the missing nutrients, from a healthy source that would serve your highest wellbeing?

Once the observer in you poses the questions, go back into deep breathing, and envisioning that you are in the womb of the earth—in your depth—letting the light of the candle shine your way. Physically, keep hazily gazing at the candle through two-tenths-open, eight-tenths-closed eyes, and letting go of all but the impressions that are "coming to you" from your subconscious. The next set of questions will help you learn what physical exercise serves your best interest. Ask yourself:

- What physical activity were you good at as a child? Which of them did you thoroughly enjoy?
- What physical activities would you still enjoy today? Remember that this doesn't have to be strenuous or laborious. It doesn't have to be pumping weights at the gym or running for several hours each week. It just has to be something physical that you enjoy.
- Which of those physical activities would you have easy access to in your current life situation?
- Which of these joyful physical activities serve your highest-best interest to engage in? How often?

You may want to do some automatic writing (see Chapter 1 of *Seven Stages to co-Creating Prosperity From Your Soul*) to note the information that comes to you. At the end of the process, envision yourself leisurely climbing back up from the womb of the earth to the surface; take a few active deep breaths to signal the body to come back into wakeful consciousness, open your eyes, and stretch. This should help you come back into a wakeful ordinary state of mind, and feel refreshed yet calm.

After the meditation, you may use your logical here-now self to organize your insights into steps that you can follow. You may have already had some ideas as you read through the multidimensional reasons for increased caloric intake and for decreased caloric spending. And during this meditation, those ideas may have already started to crystalize into insights and decisions of what you need to add into your diet and lifestyle to help your body find its healthy balance and ideal weight.

For example, when I started my own Zohar Kindness Diet, I noticed I was having uncontrollable cravings for sesame pretzels. I was determined to stop these cravings, since pretzels are made of white wheat and have a very high glycemic index, which were counterproductive to my diet. So one evening I started to experiment. At first, I thought it was the carbs that I was craving, so that evening, I ate a healthy serving of barley. But I was still craving the pretzels. So then I assumed it was the salt in the pretzel that I was craving, so I cooked myself a couple of artichokes, and ate them dipped in lots of the mineral-rich Himalayan salt. But I was still craving the pretzels. The next morning, as I was doing my morning meditation and reiki self-healing, I received an insight that what I actually craving were some of the minerals present in the sesame, which were helping relieve my migraines. This insight reverberated within me as truth, and I decided to research it. I went online, searched for the nutrients of sesame seeds, and discovered that sesame seeds were rich in calcium and magnesium, both of which play a major role in relieving migraines. So I started sprinkling sesame seed on just about every food I was having, adding up to about two teaspoons of sesame seeds per day. Soon after I started loading up on sesame seed, I noticed that I no longer craved the sesame pretzels. And that helped my diet a lot. So whatever unhealthy cravings you might have, you too are perfectly capable of meditating and researching the missing nutrients that would stop them. Adding the missing ingredients, whether that's love, emotional nurturing, or a particular physical nutrient, will help stop cravings and overeating, and drive your body to find it's healthy weight and balance again.

The Zohar Kindness ~~Diet~~ Lifestyle

I have already said that the Zohar Kindness Lifestyle is a diet of adding things, not taking things away. Kindness-to-self is not just a loftier-than-thou idea. Multidimensionally exercising kindness-to-self ensures that the body will indeed be ready to let go of access fat.

Now let us fine-tune our understanding of why adding things will cause weight loss: The overall concept is that one becomes overweight as a result of something being out of balance either energetically, emotionally, mentally, or physically. As you restore harmony and balance into your body-temple and life, your spirit will flow more freely within your body-temple, and on a physical level, your body systems will start functioning more ideally, which will enable your body to naturally restore your weight to its ideal value. Our bodies have an amazing healing ability. They are designed to seek balance and health. And with the Zohar Kindness Lifestyle, this balance, health, and restoration of your body's ideal weight happen naturally and effortlessly.

This being said, it is good to loosely keep in mind that in order to lose weight, one must consume less calories than one spends. That is a physical fact. And traditionally, dieticians and doctors have always advocated one of three ways to achieve that: consuming fewer calories, increasing caloric spending, or a combination of the two. However, there is another way, and that is the way of the Zohar Kindness Diet – the diet of adding things. Because the only way to decrease caloric intake without feeling hungry or deprived is to increase real living nutrients and self-nurturing on all levels; and the only way increase caloric spending while still being kind to yourself is to spend those extra calories doing something that is fun and puts you in a state of joy and bliss. That is the only way to restore a healthy body-weight while still being kind to yourself, and staying in an energetic vibration of abundance.

In terms of food, the main foods that we are increasing in this diet are foods that are rich in real living nutrients, high in water and fiber (high in volume), but low in saturated fats and glycemic load, and are thus able to satisfy us with fewer calories. As you might have guessed, these are vegetables, fruit, legumes, whole grains, nuts, and seeds.

But food is not all we're adding. There are also many lifestyle things, the addition of which can help bring your caloric intake-to-expenditure ratio into balance. And there are also many emotional and energetic components that we are doing to increase. Nutritionally speaking, increasing the energetic vibration of the foods you eat has a tremendous affect on the satiety effect of these foods. As we talked about in chapter 4, food that is high-vibrational is simply more satisfying. And increasing the spiritual-energetic vibration of the food and your enjoyment of it can be done in a number of ways, starting from eating more wholesome foods, spending enough time lovingly preparing your veggies in appetizing ways, increasing the time that you give yourself to really enjoy your meal (which also gives the brain plenty of time to get the fullness signals), and blessing the food through your prayerful intent. All of these practices increase the energy of the food, which increases the satiety you derive from fewer calories.

Besides holistic food practices, we are going to be increasing things that are going to help nurture you physiologically, by making sure you're getting enough good quality sleep; mentally, by achieving mental peace through adding meditation; emotionally, by rewarding yourself in various ways; and spiritually, by tuning into your Soul Self.

All of this adding will nurture your body, mind, emotions, and spirit so well, that you will naturally and effortlessly let go of unhealthy, calorie-loaded, nutrient-empty foods. Trust me, after a week or two of eating healthy foods, your body's natural affinity to foods that are healthy, fresh, and wholesome will be restored, and you will start craving those healthy foods. It is my belief that the human body is naturally built to want natural foods. This tendency is very apparent in babies. I remember babysitting my then eight-months-old nephew, and placing in front of him a bowl of chocolate and a bowl of strawberries. And the baby's hands would always naturally go for the strawberries. I have seen this with many of my friends' babies: at a young enough age, before preschool and the media have inserted the idea of sweets and junk-foods into the kids' minds, a baby's hand would almost always go towards very basic foods in their natural state. I have seen many babies grab celery to munch on, and not cheese-sticks, carrots and not steak. Of course I understand that as parents, there is always a misguided fear that the baby would not get enough protein, which make parents ignore their kids' natural instincts push on them overly rich foods. We start teaching our kids to eat the fatty protein-rich foods at a pretty young age, which distorts their natural affinity for wholesome, plant-based foods. And by the time they reach kindergarten, they have already learnt to want potato chips, sugary snacks with food colorings, and the like. But underlying all of the unhealthy things that we have learnt to crave as adults, our body's natural affinity still is to Kindness Foods – wholesome, organic, fresh, and 'living.'

Now, the reason I say to *keep in the back our your mind* that the aim is to *naturally* wane down your dependence on unhealthy, overly rich foods is that here is the way the diet is going to work: **as you add healthy ingredients to your diet and lifestyle, your craving for processed foods that are energy-dense and nutrient-poor—foods that are high in saturated fats and glycemic loads—will wind down on its own, and your body will naturally find its perfect balance.** Therefore, there is no need to really count calories. There is no need to starve yourself. There is no need for self-deprivation of any kind! In fact, as we have seen, self-deprivation is as counterproductive to weight loss as it is to magnetizing prosperity from your Soul into your life.

Because the Zohar Kindness Diet is more than just a diet. Beyond helping you restore your body-vessel into its ideal weight and balance, it is also a way to integrate the energy of kindness, joy, and love into your life through your nutritional, self-nurturing habits. It also helps you be more receptive to the enhanced Creative energy coming through your Infinite Funnel of Abundance, and prepare your body-vessel to act on all of your creative ideas. And when you think about it in this light, adding joy and self-nurturing is not just an indulgent, lofty idea. It not only helps you let go of access weight, but also plays a vital role in manifesting prosperity from your Soul into this physical realm.

Now let us see more specifically what we are adding, and why.

Lifestyle Additions

Before we get to the food section of the diet, it is easier to start your Kindness Diet by adding the necessary things to your lifestyle. Be gradual about the things that you add. You may even choose to add one thing per week, so that the changes don't feel overwhelming. Listen to your inner kindness meter when you introduce these changes, and add only the things that make your heart sing.

Sleep:

Adjust your day so you can get at least eight hours of peaceful, uninterrupted sleep per night. Remember that you need additional time to unwind and relax, and some time to shift gears to be refreshed and ready for your day in the morning. Following the steps detailed in Chapter 2 will help you get a deeper more peaceful sleep.

As we've already discussed, the first thing that happens when you are sleep deprived is that your body tries to find other sources for the missing energy. So you go on devouring anything and everything you can lay your hands on, especially sugar. So getting eight hours of quality sleep each night will stop this overeating, and is thus a key ingredient that facilitates weight loss.

Deep Breathing:

How we breathe greatly affect our diet and energy metabolism. From a yogic perspective, getting a full natural breath (inflating the belly as well as your lungs) increases lung capacity, strengthens the nervous system, reduces stress, and strengthens the immune system. It also helps release emotional-energetic blocks, and increases the amount of life-force (prana) you intake, your vitality, as well as your subtle connection to All-There-Is through internalizing the prana energy. As you can see, all of these are beneficial to weight loss, as well as to the co-Creation of prosperity.

So what should you do? I understand you won't just suddenly start breathing full natural breaths for the rest of your life just because you've read this section. But you may want to remind yourself to take a few deeper breaths now and again throughout your day. Just start by taking what I call "Breath Brakes." It doesn't have to even take two minutes. Just take a few seconds to stop your mental activity, deepen your breath, re-center yourself, remind yourself of the joy of who you Truly are and all that is possible for you... and then carry on. You'll find that just taking a few deeper breaths introduces more peace, joy, and even hope into your day.

Me Time:

As we have discussed in Chapter 1, staking out at least one hour each day for your Me Time is essential for freeing up your mind from the troubles of your day, meditationally nurturing yourself, and reminding yourself of the joys of living. And these feelings go a long way to effectively reduce cravings, as well as for co-Creating your Ideal Lifepath of prosperity. If you have some weight to lose, you may choose to devote some of your Me Time to your chosen Joyful Physical Activity, and in that case, it also contributes to your daily expenditure of calories.

Joyful Physical Activity

In Chapter 2, we have seen the physiological, psychological, and spiritual values of adding a joyful physical activity to your day. From a diet perspective, exercise does more than just burn more calories during the minutes that you exercise. It is a well-known fact that muscle tissue burns calories at a faster rate than other tissue. Toned muscles are calorie-burning machines. And the more exercise you do, the better toned your muscles will be, which in turn would help you burn more calories per day even when you are at rest.

Exercise also boosts up your metabolic rate, which means that it speeds up how fast you burn calories and get rid of stored body-fat. But it does so not only during the actual time that you exercise. As you may have noticed, your heart rate, breathing, body-heat, and energies are accelerated for several hours after you are done exercising, which means that you continue to burn calories at a faster rate for several hours after exercising.

Of course, on an energetic level, Joyful Physical Activity helps move your Ki, which can be significant in removing the energetic blocks that are responsible for holding on to the access weight.

If you do enough Joyful Physical Activity, it can also help you burn calories in a way that could be significant in your caloric expenditure-to-intake balance. Below are some examples of pleasurable activities, and the caloric expenditure that they produce. Again, I am not advocating counting calories, or pushing yourself to do any strenuous exercise. The table below is just to demonstrate that you *can* lose about a half to three-quarters-of a pound per week without even dieting, just by adding a joyful physical exercise.

	Activity:	Caloric Burn:	Need to do:	To Lose...
180 lbs. Person	Walking @ 3mph	156 Cal/30 min	6 x 1-hour	0.53 lb./week
	Hiking with backpack	264 Cal/30 min	5 x 45-min	0.57 lb./week
	Swimming 40 yds/min	375 Cal/30 min	4 x 45-min	0.64 lb./week
	Skiing downhill	399 Cal/30 min	2.5 hours	0.57 lb./week
	Bicycling @ 10 mph	435 Cal/30 min	4 x 31-min	0.51 lb./week
220 lbs. Person	Walking @ 3mph	171 Cal/30 min	6 x 1-hour	0.59 lb./week
	Hiking with backpack	291 Cal/30 min	5 x 45-min	0.62 lb./week
	Swimming 40 yds/min	447 Cal/30 min	4 x 45-min	0.77 lb./week
	Skiing downhill	420 Cal/30 min	2.5 hours	0.6 lb./week
	Bicycling @ 10 mph	636 Cal/30 min	4 x 31-min	0.75 lb./week

Notice I didn't include in this table pumping weight at the gym, or attacking the elliptical trainer. I included only activities that could be perceived as fun. So don't think of exercising as a chore. Think of it as something fun that you are rewarding yourself with. For the real value of exercising is getting yourself into a habit of finding your Me Time in the course of your day, and doing something with it that is pleasurable for you, and energizes you to find again the joy of living.

As it pertains to the Zohar Kindness Lifestyle, it is extra important that the physical activity you add is joyful for you. Frontally attacking the treadmill or elliptical trainer at the gym on a day in which you are feeling weak, sleep deprived, or hungry will get your body into starvation mode, and it will not release any access fat. The same goes for doing any activity that is so stressful for you that it activates the "fight-or-flight" response in your body. So if you want to increase your metabolism, and encourage your body to let go of access fat, you must choose an activity that is enjoyable for you. And from an energetic-spiritual perspective, the more enjoyable the physical activity you choose, the more freely and harmoniously your Soul's energy will move within your body-temple, and the lighter you'll feel energetically, emotionally, and consequently physically. A good joyful physical activity to add is Nature Walk, which as I hope you've already found out, can give you peace of mind, clarity, a feeling of lightness, and a blissful balance.

But there is another, more practical, benefit to shifting your exercise into a Joyful Physical Activity: Many people lead hectic lives, and don't have time to exercise every day. I mean, if you have to carve time out of your busy day for something, you're much more apt to do it for an enjoyable beach walk than you are for twenty boring minutes on the treadmill. Besides the likely factor, when it comes to using physical activity to boost up your metabolic rate, the longer your physical activity, the more calories you'll burn. And if you don't have time to exercise every day, then on the days that you do exercise, in order to lose weight you probably need to do more than twenty minutes; you probably need forty minutes or an hour. And the most torturous way that I can think of, to get in forty minutes of exercise, is on the treadmill or the elliptical trainer at an indoors gym, where someone else has chosen the (unbearably loud) music for me, where I'm stuck in front of a TV screen showing infomercials and ridiculous soap operas, and smelling everyone else's sweat. On the other hand, if I'm listening to the music of my choice or just listening to the waves crashing and the birds singing, smelling the fresh scent of flowers, breathing refreshing ocean air, and looking at the afternoon "diamonds" on the ocean, than I'm likely to walk for two or three hours without even noticing it. I know that walking outdoors is not always possible in all climates. So use your inner guidance to choose the Joyful Physical Activity that is best suited for your situation. The point is: when you find the physical activity that's ideal *for you*, it would be great if you can vacate a few hours, or best leave the rest of your day open, so you can be free to enjoy and let yourself go. Leave your watch in the car, breathe deeply the fragrance of life, and just enjoy yourself. This is the best way to boost your metabolic rate, while experiencing joy, moving your Ki around, and renewing the co-Creative energy that's pouring in through your Infinite Funnel of Abundance.

Over and above the caloric benefits of exercise, I find that even if I woke up tired and upset, doing a Nature Walk (Chapter 2), a meditative swim, or a RezoDance not only improves my moods tremendously and instills peace, but also enables me to be more productive for the rest of the day, on top of which I sleep better at night.

Adequate Time to Do things:

As we've discussed in Chapter 1, today's economy and societal pressure to succeed tend to put everyone in a go-go-go mode of achieving as much as possible in as little time as possible. This makes most people take on way too many responsibilities, and cram way too many things into their daily To Do list, which leads to stress. Now imagine what it would be like if you could have more than enough time to do every task in your life with leisure and joy. No deadlines. No rush. Just do everything leisurely and joyfully. If you start being realistic about your daily To Do list, and not demand from yourself being a superman/superwoman, you'll suddenly notice that there is so much less stress in your life. And one thing you'll notice is that on those days that you took your time to enjoy everything that you do, you have less unhealthy food cravings. So give yourself a break. It's okay if you only accomplished five out of the ten things you intended to do today.

You can always complete the other tasks another day. But did you enjoy yourself today? Did you feel peace and satisfaction from your daily activities today?

Meals:

In nutrition and diet science, it is a well-known fact that having more meals of smaller portions boosts the metabolism, and helps weight loss. So adding small meals and healthy snacks is one of the easiest things you can do to boost up your diet. Do not worry about overeating. As you add healthy snacks and small meals to your day, you will be less hungry when the scheduled meal comes, so it would be easier for you to eat the kind foods first, and avoid the unkind foods.

Meal Time:

Allocating time out of your day for eating is important even if it's only thirty minutes per meal. Beyond the importance of chewing your food adequately to awaken your digestive enzymes, give yourself enough time to really relax and enjoy the meal. Your digestion and elimination will be more efficient that way, and support your diet efforts. Enjoying your meals will also boost up your level of enjoyment of your whole day. You can take this mealtime to reflect on your day and count your blessings. Make every meal an occasion to stop and meditate on all the things in your life at present moment that you are grateful for. This will imbue the foods you eat with the energy of gratitude, which will increase the energy of the food as well as magnetize more blessings into your life. It is a tremendous manifestation tool.

Spiritual & Emotional Nurturing:

As we have seen, lack of spiritual and emotional nurturing are big factors that drive both sides of the diet equation into imbalance—they drive us to eat more than is healthy for us, and they drive the body to hold onto fat and not let it go. So nurturing yourself spiritually and emotionally is of paramount importance on your path to restoring the perfect balance of your body-temple. For starters, I recommend doing a Self Nurturing Meditation (see *Seven Stages to co-Creating Prosperity From Your Soul*) every day. But also, find different ways to reward yourself with (non food) things that remind you how beloved you are. Go get a massage; go sunbathe; go to a beautiful place and just absorb its beauty; hug and caress yourself to remind yourself of softness and nurturing; and look at yourself in the mirror and affirm your beauty! If you are a reiki practitioner, reiking yourself is incredibly effective in restoring balance and nurturing yourself. The point is, there are millions ways to give yourself the emotional and spiritual nurturing that you deserve, which do not depend on food. Just choose one that works well for you!

Mental Relaxation:

Almost any meditation can help you unload worries, and give you some peace of mind, which will help your body let go of fat more easily. One valid process to achieve mental relaxation throughout your day, which you might consider, is writing all of your worries in To Do lists that you will leisurely handle later, when the time is right. Or consider using some of the meditational processes discussed in *Seven Stages to co-Creating Prosperity From Your Soul*, to give you peace of mind. Just choose one or a few meditations or processes that resonate with you, and use them daily to empty your mind from the round-and-round troubling thoughts, and restore peaceful clarity.

Group Support:

It is always easier to do a diet when you have made a pact with a friend or a family member. Even though in this diet we are not subtracting anything but adding, having a support system could help you persist with your new path, rather than falling back on old habits. Because as I've found out, whether you fall back on old non-serving habits or you stick with your new path is a mental-emotional switch—it's a mode change. You either fall back on the mode of indulging in every juicy-steak-French-fries-and-milkshake craving you have and feeling heavy, or you switch into a mode of vitality, lightness, and agility in your body-temple, and craving only salads and light foods—you either cling to the old need-to-feel-overly-full-and-heavy internal self-image, or you cultivate a new healthy-and-light-feeling 'me' image. And one thing that could help you make that switch on a continuous basis is having someone close to you or a support group that you create for yourself, with whom you can compare notes on what fun thing you've added today; healthy and light food recipes you've discovered; how light and energetic yet satisfied you felt; and how inches and pounds have shed off. It's like joining the "let's hike, eat alfalfa sprouts and nuts, and feel light and happy" crowd, instead of the "let's drink beer, eat potato chips, and commiserate" crowd. Within this support, you can increase the emotional nurturing, as well as the encouragement that you give each other to be kind to yourselves, which will help all of you drive your caloric equations towards balance and harmony.

Above all, at this beginning stage of your Zohar Kindness Diet, the biggest thing you can add is self-validation and non-judgment. Remember: you want all these changes to be nurturing and kind enough that you would want to sustain them over a long period of time. So don't force yourself into anything. Just add a little bit of these kindness practices at a time, until you are ready to add some kindness foods into your life.

Kindness Foods to Increase

In general, we are increasing the volume of foods that are high in fiber, water, micronutrients, and have a low glycemic load of carbohydrates, namely – vegetables, fruits, legumes, whole grains, nuts, and seeds. Since you'll be eating the foods in this category first (see Plate Composition & Orientation below), the volume of calorically dense foods on your plate will naturally decrease, but the overall volume of foods, and their nutritional value will increase, which will help you to get more satisfied with less calories. For example, when you are very hungry, you could probably go for a sixteen-ounce steak and some home-fried potatoes, but not if you've first had a big salad, a bowl of yummy vegetable soup, or a veggie casserole (made with low-fat milk instead of cream).

In that case, once you've had your delicious veggies, you would probably only be hungry enough to eat only 6 ounces of, say chicken breast or fish grilled with fresh Italian seasoning, garlic, and a spray olive oil, with perhaps a cup of quinoa or barley. Do you see what I mean? And vegetables don't have to be boring. You don't have to think throughout your meal of how much you are depriving yourself by eating them. Have your steak if you want it. I dare you to eat a sixteen-ounce steak after two cups of deliciously prepared vegetables with savory seasoning and a creative flair. I don't think you could do it even if you wanted to, and I don't think you're going to want to.

Other ingredients that we are adding to your food are the spices, condiments, and loving preparations that increase the foods energy. For example, you don't have to just steam your broccoli, carrots and cauliflower with salt. That's boring. How about, instead, adding to your broccoli some Himalayan salt, fresh ground pepper, a bit of fresh garlic, and a spray of olive oil, wrapping your baby-broccoli in aluminum foil, and grilling them? Doesn't that sound yummier? Even if you do steam your veggies, what about making for them my eggplant dip, tahini, or chipotle-ranch dressing? I promise you that any of these dips/dressings would add such flair to your vegetables that you won't want to stop eating them. Or let's say you wanted to eat zucchini and eggplants. Raw, these vegetables are boring, I agree. But how about rubbing them with sea-salt, fresh ground pepper, and Herbs-of-Provence spice, and then sautéing them with a touch of olive oil, and then sprinkling with just a little fresh parmigiano-reggiano cheese and a few pine nuts? Not boring anymore, right? Even asparagus doesn't have to be boring. You can lay them on a baking pan, add some sea salt, a few drops of water, fresh garlic, and add a 2-3 teaspoons of low-fat ricotta cheese, a few shaves of parmigiano-reggiano, and a little spray of olive oil, cover it with a sheet of aluminum foil and bake it, and you'll be in awe of just how delicious it is. It's true that the ricotta and parmigiano-reggiano add a few calories of saturated fat. But for a pound of asparagus, three teaspoons of cheese won't hurt your diet, and it'll increase your enjoyment of the food tenfold. This is how a little can go a long way, when you add good seasoning to your vegetables. Even vegetables that are starting to sag can be made delicious: Let's say that you have asparagus, mushrooms, onions, garlic, and tomatoes that need to be cooked. Chop all the veggies to fairly small size, spray a skillet with hazelnut oil, and start sautéing… first the onion and garlic, then the mushrooms and tomatoes, then the asparagus pieces, then you add low-fat milk to make all the veggies "swim" in the milk. Add sea-salt, fresh pepper, two drops of Worcestershire sauce, a tablespoon of flour to thicken it, and then a sprinkle (very little) of parmigiano-reggiano cheese… and – presto! You have a low-fat "cream" sauce you can put on your brown-and-wild rice, on other grains, or even on your vegetables. And these are just a few, off-the-top-of-my-head ideas on how to use a little seasoning to spark up your veggies. Once you get creative with cooking your veggies, you'll find a world of flavor and gourmet cooking hidden in them. I have included a few more ideas on how to make your veggies yummy in Appendix A. I invite you to experiment with them, and modify them according to your creative talents.

All of this adding of vegetables, fruit, legumes, whole grains, seeds, and nuts, plus the addition of flavor to your veggies, and the lifestyle spiritual addition detailed above, will greatly enhance your enjoyment and satisfaction of the foods, leading you to naturally need a lower caloric intake. That is the idea behind the Zohar Kindness Diet.

However, in order to be somewhat mindful of decreasing your caloric intake, let's clarify what exactly you are increasing. We will talk about how much to eat of each type of food later in this chapter, in the section about what to eat. For now, let's discuss the three categories of foods that you'll be adding: Main foods to add, foods to increase in moderation, and foods to gradually and kindly wean off of.

Main Foods to Add:

Water –

As explained above, hunger is one of the first signals of dehydration, even if you've just eaten. And don't let anybody fool you and tell you that drinking water before or during a meal dilutes your digestive enzymes. That is physiologically impossible, since the body has an abundance of digestive enzymes. Getting even subtly dehydrated can lead to not only hunger, but also loss of vitality, fatigue, and mental confusion, all of which reduce the productivity and joy of your day, which in turn reduces the amount of calories you are able to spend during your day. So drink plenty of water. The yogic rule of thumb is to drink half your body weight in ounces (so if you weigh 160 lbs., you should drink 80 oz. of water per day, or 10 cups), and if you exercise and perspire, you need to drink even more.

Fruit juices can hydrate you, but they are loaded with calories. On the other hand, alcoholic and caffeinated drinks are diuretics. This means that they cause you to lose more fluid than you intake. Alcohol also reduces your body's natural fluid retention. So if you think that coffee or a cold beer count for your hydration balance, think again. You need to add two extra glasses of water to replace the fluid lost from every glass of caffeinated or alcoholic beverage.

I myself love the taste of good spring water. But since many people don't like the taste of plain water, here are some suggestions on how to enhance the taste of your water, without adding too much sugar or calories to it:

- ❧ Lemon Water – something I mainly do in restaurants, where the lemonade is unbearably sweet and the water tastes terrible, is I order a glass of water with a plate of lemons or limes on the side. Then I squeeze a bunch of lemons and limes into the water. You'd be amazed at how tasty it is once you wean yourself off of any sugar dependency. And the lemons also help rid the water of impurities.

- ❧ Mint Water – Take a handful of organic fresh mint leaves, and place them in a large cup or a small teapot. Add boiling water to it, and let it steep for a while into a dark and minty tea. Then, pour the water onto a large jar, and refrigerate. You can then pour more hot water the teapot with the mint leaves, to make more tea, and once it too steeps for a while, add that to your refrigerated jug. Refrigerate the mint tea for a while, and then drink it cold.

- ❧ Fruit Water – Cut some organic fresh fruit into small cubes. Use whatever you have that's tasty and in season. It could be watermelon, apple, orange, pineapple, peach, or anything you have at hand. There should be about a cup of cut fruit for every liter of water. Place the fruit into a jar, and add water. Let the jar with the fruit sit in the refrigerator for several hours to absorb the flavor of the fruit. The water will then have a very subtle fruity taste, and yet absorb only a miniscule amount of calories from the fruit. It is so refreshing, that you'll want to load up on this water. And by the way, once you drink up all the water in the jug, you can add more water and let it sit again for several hours or overnight to absorb the flavor of the fruit. The same cut fruit is good for several days.

- ☯ <u>Juice spritzer</u> – another idea on how to make water tasty without adding too many calories is to mix a tiny little bit of natural juice with water or seltzer. So for example, one drink that I love is mixing about 1/8 of a cup of grapefruit or orange juice with cold water or club soda. It adds only a smidge of calories, but is very tasty.

- ☯ <u>Flower Essences</u> – Flower essences are tinctures of different flowers, which are expelled in the presence of alcohol. The idea is that as you ingest the vibrational essence of the flower captured in the tincture, you bring into yourself the various spiritual and healing qualities of the flower. You usually put just a few drops of flower essence into a glass of water, but it gives the water a nice taste, and helps harmonize your energies. You can think of it as having a little liquor in your water, kind of like having a little schnapps in the middle of your day.

So now that you know that water is not just a necessity to restores your vitality, but can also be tasty, there is no reason not to indulge in some flavored water.

<u>Greens</u> –

The main tangible on-your-plate foods that we are adding in an unlimited amount are vegetables and fruit.

But when I say vegetables, I do not mean French fries. Potatoes are not the enemy, but they are starchy carbohydrate, which in most forms of cooking have a pretty high glycemic index, and even a higher glycemic load. And French-fries are as their name suggest fried, in most cases with trans-fatty acids that are unhealthy. So when I say increase your vegetable intake, I mean real vegetables, such as leafy greens, cucumbers, tomatoes, carrots, broccoli, artichoke, cauliflower, asparagus… the list can go on and on. When it comes to non-starchy vegetables, don't worry about the calories. And as we've begun to explore above, vegetables do not have to be boring or lacking in flavor. There are so many ways to make your vegetables tasty: from stir-fries, to soufflés (see my low-fat soufflé in Appendix A), to casseroles, to baking, grilling, and sautéing vegetables with different spices. Vegetable based foods can be very gourmet eating. In appendix A, I have given a few easy recipes for tasty vegetable-based foods.

As far as cooking your vegetables versus eating them raw, listen to your inner guidance. It might be easier to start with cooking most of your veggies, and then gradually introducing more and more fresh veggies, until you find your balance. A good balance is eating half of your veggies cooked, and half of them raw (salad). Also, even when cooked, most vegetables are tastier, and retain more of their original nutrients, when they are slightly crunchy. So for example, broccoli should never be cooked for more than four or five minutes. It should not be soft enough to be mashed, but be cooked only until it gets a darker color.

Fruit are also one of the foods you should add plenty of. The sugar that fruit contain is not sucrose, but fructose, which does not induce a release of insulin. Therefore fruit have low glycemic index. And since most fruit have high water content, the amount of available carbs in them is usually low, which makes their glycemic load pretty low (except for bananas, which are very high in fructose, and therefore high in carbs). Plus, I believe that if you finish your meal with a fruit, you'll have less of a need to indulge in ice cream, cake, and the like.

As you indulge in vegetables and fruit, your cravings of fatty, high-carbs, and processed foods will subside naturally, and along with that, your caloric intake. But don't worry; this is not one of those crazy diets that would have you existing only on leaves. You will still eat plenty of substantial foods. But you'll notice an interesting thing happening soon after you start indulging in healthy food – you'll start craving fresh vegetables. How odd is that? It was odd for me when I started craving vegetables and fruit, but a welcome change.

Meals & Healthy Snacks –

Eat Often! Eating smaller meals at shorter interval helps boost metabolism, and will eliminate any feeling of deprivation, which will in turn eliminate mental-emotional factors from offsetting your intake-expenditure energy balance. Listen to what your body is telling you, and know when you are starting to get hungry. Start planning your next meal or healthy snack as soon as you start feeling like you might get hungry soon. This will reduce hunger-stress, which will reduce the amount of cortisol—the stress hormone—that's secreted in your body, which will allow your body to be sensitive to leptin—the hormone that signals satiety. In simple terms, eating smaller meals and healthy snacks in shorter intervals helps portion control, so that you don't let yourself get hungry enough to eat a horse. It also helps imbue your subconscious with the feeling of being nurtured, so that your body would be more willing to let go of access weight more readily. It is good to eat at least three healthy and balanced meals, and at least two healthy snacks, so a total of five small meals a day.

There are many combinations of healthy foods that are yummy and fun to eat, which could make healthy snacks. Here are a few ideas:

- Carrots and celery sticks dipped in low fat cottage cheese
- Fruit and nuts
- Soy-nuts (I actually like them roasted & lightly salted)
- Fruit with oats sprinkled on top
- Low-fat yogurt with berries, and a little sprinkle of organic raw honey on top
- Pumpkin/sunflower seeds
- Smoothies you make yourself with frozen berries, some fresh fruit, low-fat yogurt, banana, a natural juice, and with no sugar added

Foods to Add in Moderation:

Besides water, vegetables, and fruit, you should always make sure you eat enough macronutrients: low glycemic index carbs, lean protein, and essential fatty acids. These are foods that have many health benefits and will help reduce your cravings for unhealthy foods. That is, making sure you get enough lean protein, and complex, low glycemic index carbs will help you avoid going down on that mountain of nachos you would otherwise go for. It also prevents you from craving sweets and overly rich deserts shortly after your meal.

However, the foods I've included in this category are also somewhat high in calories, as well as carb or fat content. They are complex, low glycemic index carbs, with all the essential fatty acids that they contain, but you know what they say about too much of a good thing. Even the lowest glycemic index food, with enough available carb grams (dense in carbs), becomes a food with a high glycemic load food, which does not support a weight loss diet. And when it comes to fat, since our bodies know how to make their own cholesterol, than too much of even the best essential fatty acids can turn into cholesterol and stored fat in the body.

Still, this is still a category of things that we are adding to our diets, because of the good nutrients that are in these foods. Just make sure that you've added more vegetables and fruit to your plate than the foods in this category (see Plate Composition & Orientation section later in this chapter), and that you actually eat your vegetables and fruit before you eat the foods in this category.

Legumes –

Beans are a fabulous diet food, since they contain lots of fiber and lots of protein. They also contain essential fatty acids, and are a good source of omega-3. It is true that beans do not provide you with complete proteins, since they do not contain all eight essential amino acids. But if you combine them properly with other protein-rich foods (see later in this chapter), they can make up a complete protein.

Because beans have such a high fiber and protein contents and such a low fat content, they make you full quicker (reducing your craving for unkind foods), which makes them an excellent diet food.

However, they are not without carbohydrates. True – the carbs that they contain are of a low glycemic index, and in moderate amounts, translate into a nice medium glycemic load. But if you start eating excessive amounts of beans, you will load up on too many carbs than is beneficial for balanced nutrition. So again with beans, moderation is the key, unless you're talking about soy beans, in which case you can have an 'all-you-can-eat' breakfast, lunch and dinner buffet of tofu, soy beans, soy nuts, and edamame, dipped in soy milk…(just kidding). You'll be as skinny as a stick in no time. But soybeans aside, add beans to your diet in moderation.

Whole Grains –

Organic whole grains are among the healthiest form of carbohydrates there are, especially if you eat them as close to their natural form as possible: brown and wild rice instead of white rice, bulgur, quinoa, barley, millet, and the likes. I actually like to buy an organic rice mix that contains long-grain brown rice, wild rice, whole grain Wahani rice, and whole grain black Japonica rice, all of which are whole grains. It's the only kind of rice I cook. Most whole grains are also high in fiber and healthy proteins, and also contain some essential fatty acids (the Omegas 3, 6 & 9), and some important micronutrients. Adding whole grains to your diet will help you get off the bread, nachos, and deserts, especially if you add to them some delicious spicing and cook them in interesting ways that you love. I can personally attest to the fact that adding whole grains to my meal (in moderation) curves down my need for desert, and causes me to lose the urge to raid the munchies cabinet an hour after the meal (which is exactly what I do if I don't eat whole grains). And by the way, here is an example of the difference in glycemic load between processed grains and wholesome grains: if you look at Appendix B, three-quarters of a cup of white rice has a glycemic load of 43—pretty darn high; while the same amount of brown rice has a glycemic load of 16—nice and moderate. That's a huge difference: white rice will make you fat; brown rice of the same amount will actually help you lose weight. Isn't that wild?

Quinoa should have a section on its own, for beyond low GI carbs, quinoa, like soy and hemp, contains complete proteins, which makes it a super food for vegetarian and vegan eaters. For that reason, and because of how lean they are, quinoa, soy, and hemp seeds are excluded from any moderation requirements—you can eat them in unlimited amounts.

For the rest of the grains, the reason we are adding those in moderation is that as wonderful as whole grains are, the number of available carbohydrates grams per portion that they contain is still high. That is, they are dense in carbohydrate content, and thus have a higher glycemic load relatively to vegetables. So the bottom line with whole grains is: they are very good for you, and contain loads of important macro and micronutrients. But they are still rich in carbs and calories, and therefore can easily tilt the caloric intake-to-expenditure balance in the wrong direction, if we overindulge in them.

Nuts & Seeds ~

Nuts and seeds contain a lot of protein as well as healthy essential fatty acids. Consuming plenty of nuts and seeds will satisfy your body's need for essential fatty acid, as well as some of your body's protein needs, and therefore help you reduce the amount of saturated fats you crave.

However, even healthy essential fatty acids can still be stored in your body as fat if you eat excessive amount if them, and therefore tilt your caloric intake-to-expenditure balance towards the heavy side, which if you need to lose weight, you don't want to do.

However, when I say add nuts and seed, I do not mean sitting in front of TV and going down on a barrel of oil-roasted salty peanuts, and I don't mean stuffing your face with peanut butter. Firstly, peanuts contain much Omega-6 fatty acid, which most people already get plenty of. What I do mean is: Add a few almonds or hazelnuts (monounsaturated omega-9) either as snacks, salads and breakfast, for example. Add some walnuts and oats (omega-3) to your yogurt, cereal, salads, and other foods. But don't sit and eat a mountain of candied nuts. That is where the moderation comes in.

Are Potatoes the Enemy?

Potatoes are, of course, not a diet food. And we are not, in any way, shape, or form, adding potatoes in this diet. But potatoes are not altogether bad for you, as long as you don't fry them or overindulge in them. In fact, potatoes have plenty of potassium, iron, and other minerals, and are pretty lean in fat content, if you eat them in moderation. Boiled or steamed potatoes have a lower glycemic index than roasted potatoes. But even boiled potatoes are loaded with available carbs, and have a high glycemic index, which makes their glycemic load very high, even in moderation. Yams and sweet potatoes have a slightly lower glycemic index (not by much though) but are still high in their available carb grams, which brings their glycemic load to values above 20—too high for a weight loss diet.

Still, I love potatoes, and so do a lot of other people. And since the Zohar Kindness Diet aims not to deprive you of anything that you really like, if you crave potatoes, have them in moderation. I like boiling equal amounts of potatoes and cauliflower, and then mashing them together with just a bit of olive oil. It makes for wonderful mashed potatoes, and the introduction of cauliflower into it, not only adds a gentle texture, but also lowers the concentration of carbs—the average glycemic load per cup. I'll give you a few more ideas like that in Appendix A. And of course, if you don't have to lose weight, you can eat more potatoes. Use your inner wisdom to decide how much potatoes you should indulge in.

As you will see when we talk about the proportion of nutrients on your plate, all foods that you add from this category need to be added *after* you have added at least double their amount (by volume) of vegetables or fruit. So if you've added a healthy snack containing half a cup of almonds, for example, than you first need to add at least a cup of watermelon, oranges, or carrots. And all of this addition should be within the limits of what you are *genuinely* hungry to eat, without your stomach exploding. In other words, if you've added the almonds and the watermelon, than you may not be hungry to eat the grilled-cheese sandwich with bacon that you were originally planning to eat. You may still decide to eat a lean meal a couple of hours later. But now you have more time to plan your meal according to kindness-to-self principles.

Foods to Kindly Wean Yourself Off of:

The foods in this category are the foods that we are not adding in the Zohar Kindness diet.

There are some foods that, even if you don't need to loose any weight, you should avoid like the plague, because they are very harmful to your body. Those are:

- ☯ Processed foods, foods with lots of additives, preservatives, foods coloring, and other harmful unpronounceable chemical ingredients
- ☯ Foods containing high-fructose corn syrup and any kind of hydrogenated fats
- ☯ Artificial sweeteners (which actually increase appetite & cravings[24])
- ☯ Foods containing excessive salt and preservatives, which cause a high blood pressure, and a greater strain on your heart, arteries, kidneys and brain, and can lead to heart attack, strokes, dementia, or kidney disease.

Others are foods that if you want to be healthy, you should reduce, and if you want to lose weight, you should kindly wean yourself off of. Those are:

- ☯ Saturated fats
- ☯ Fatty animal proteins (like rib-eye steaks, for example), which are high in cholesterol and can cause arterial plaque to build up.
- ☯ High glycemic index (low grade) carbohydrates
- ☯ Calorie-dense foods, like fried foods, butter, and the like
- ☯ Sugar, which is a fast way to accumulate many calories without noticing it, as well as suppress your immune system, upset the mineral balance in your body, damage cells and tissue, increase inflammation in the body, raise triglycerides, lower HDL cholesterol (the good kind that protects against heart disease), and cause anxiety and a whole array of other health problems.[25]

All of those are things that you should gradually aim to reduce your dependency on, and eventually wean yourself off of completely. But notice I didn't say that you are to deprive yourself, or go cold turkey off of those foods. Your internal wisdom will naturally guide you on how much of those ingredients you still need at each point during your shift into the kindness diet and lifestyle.

I mean, there is nothing wrong with occasionally indulging in some pasta (in moderation), so you don't feel deprived. I sometimes make yummy homemade pasta in "cream" sauce. But when I make the "creamy" pasta, I replace the cream with low-fat milk, and I have half a cup of homemade pasta (which has a lower GI) with at least a cup-and-a-half of organic baby-broccoli, tomatoes, mushrooms, and maybe a few walnuts; I add plenty of organic fresh herbs and spices so that I don't miss the cream or the extra pasta; and for protein, I add a couple of turkey sausages (see picture in Meal Examples later this chapter). It still makes a delicious pasta meal that is very satisfying, and makes me feel like I'm indulging, but at the same time, I'm still eating lots of vegetables and lean protein, very little of the high glycemic indexed pasta, and very little fat (since it's not really a cream sauce, it's a low fat milk sauce, thickened with just a little bit of flour — see recipe in Appendix A).

The point is: As you add to your diet essential fatty acids (Omega 3, & 9 from nuts), your craving for butter and other saturated fats will naturally wean down; as you load up on legumes, especially soybeans, your cravings for fatty animal proteins will wind down on its own; as you add seeds and whole grains, your craving for high glycemic index carbs will wane down; as you add vegetables that are lovingly and yummily prepared, your level of satisfaction from the food will increase, and you will naturally need less calories; and as you add fruit (low glycemic index carbs), your sweet tooth will wean itself off. This work!

What to Add if You Crave Sweets

Speaking of a sweet tooth, if you need a little something sweet at the end of a meal, you're not alone. Beyond our subconscious association of sugar with rewards, which usually forms during our childhood, physiologically speaking, sugar also promote the body's secretion of serotonin, which elevates the moods, and causes an overall good feeling. However, sugar is addictive just like a drug, and can send not only your pancreas and blood insulin on a rollercoaster ride, but also your moods. When your blood sugar levels are high, lots of glucose gets to the brain, which orders the secretion of lots of serotonin, which in turn gives you a 'high.' But an hour later, when your blood sugar level goes down, the body is no longer secreting as much serotonin, and you lose your 'high,' which sends your moods and energy levels to plummet down, which in turn causes you to crave more sugars, and the cycle repeats again.

However, depriving yourself of your 'fix' can have extensive psychological effect that may cause you to crave it even more. So deprivation is not the right way to wean yourself off of a sugar addiction. But there is a solution that works like a charm:

The first step of this solution is to make sure that you are eating wholesome, balanced and nurturing meals, with plenty of complex carbs, essential fatty acids, and lean protein. Whole grains like are an excellent source of complex—low glycemic index complex carbs, which you'll find satisfying. And the more satisfying, balanced, and naturally healthy your meal is, the less you'll crave sweets after the meal.

Step two is to replace what you are used to eating for desert with one or two teaspoon of organic raw honey, or chew on honeycomb that you buy at the farmers' market. Honey is plenty sweet, but has glycemic index of 50 (half the GI of sugar), and has that creamy feeling in your mouth that you get when eating a creamy sweet desert. And with this method, because you're flooding your taste buds with lots of sweetness all at once, one or two teaspoons are very satisfying.

You can also bake and prepare deserts for yourself using agave nectar, or stevia, and use gradually less and less sweetening, as your dependency on sugar winds down. In Appendix A, I have given recipes for low-fat, low glycemic index deserts, sweetened mostly with fruit, with just a little bit of honey, such as pumpkin pie, chocolate mousse, and muffins that you'll find extremely satisfying to your sweet tooth.

Step three is to be satisfied with eating unsweetened dried fruit to give you your sweet 'fix.' I usually eat two or three carob almonds for desert after a meal. These organic almonds covered with unsweetened carob are pretty delicious. They are not without calories of course. But they are better than going down on a tub of ice cream. Or lately, I've gotten in a habit of decoratively arranging a large plate with prunes, figs, dates, goji berries, and almonds, and keeping it available on my coffee table (covered in cellophane). So after a meal, when I naturally reach for the sweets, the plate is "calling" me, and I usually end up just eating a couple of figs stuffed with almonds, instead of the decadent desert I was planning on eating. The thing to remember is that dried fruit, although they are high in fiber and low in their glycemic index, because the water has dried out of them, the concentration of available carbs in them are higher, and therefore their glycemic loads are higher. So moderation, please.

Step four is to satisfy your sweet tooth with fresh fruit.

What to Add if You Crave Salty Carbs

Many people crave pretzels, nachos, and other salty carbs. I hate to sound like a broken record here, but if you allow yourself to eat plenty of low GI, complex carbs, you will crave less of the junk-food carbs. So if an hour after the meal you crave nachos, than hold off on the nachos for a while you experiment with my method: cook for yourself a pot of wholesome rice, for example, salted with pink Himalayan salt (which contain many micronutrients that our bodies need). Have half a cup of brown and wild rice, with some sesame seeds (which also contains many micronutrients that our bodies crave) sprinkled on top. Drink plenty of fresh spring water, made in your favorite method of flavoring the water (remember my water flavoring ideas?). Add some baby carrots or any vegetable that feel crunchy for you when you eat it. You may dip the carrots in some tahini (which is also made of sesame seeds), to give this snack a yummy flavor. Eat slowly, so as to give your body plenty of time to signal satiety (which takes fifteen to twenty minutes). And then see if you still want the chips or nachos. My guess is that you won't want the chips/nachos (or whatever your craving was) after this treat.

The issue with salty crunchy craving is that many times, it's actually not the carbs that the body is signaling the need for, but the salt as the body's way of replenishing its healthy minerals. I have found that using Himalayan salt, and adding some sesame seed, both of which are especially rich in minerals, helps me eat much less salty processed carbs, and also helps me use less salt in general. This is because your body is not actually craving sodium chloride (NaCl); what it's craving are other micronutrients that, in nature, are normally attached to salt. So if you actually give your body a substance that is rich with the micronutrients that it needs, it'll stop prompting you to eat more and more salt, since it would be getting its fill of the required minerals with a smaller amount.

For that reason, I make a special salt from combining sesame seeds and Himalayan salt. Using this sesame-Himalayan salt helps reduce salty carbs cravings. I've included the recipe for it in Appendix A.

Recipe Substitute Examples

In this diet, you can indulge in almost all the same foods that you used to eat, if you just alter your recipes slightly. I have included a few of my recipes in Appendix A. They are all recipes of foods that were originally very fatty, full of high GI carbs or even sugar, full of saturated fat like butter or even shortening (the worst!), but which I have modified into leaner, less sugary foods that include more complex whole grain carbs, more natural ingredients, and more fruit and vegetables. Some of the recipes included in Appendix A are specifically targeted at making your veggies more appealing. Of course, the recipes included in Appendix A were not meant to be the whole "Torah" of lean cooking; but just to give you the feel of taking an unkind recipe and turning it into kindness food.

Just to give you an idea of some of the alterations you can make to the recipes of foods you're cooking, here are just a few examples:

- Eliminate margarine and all fats that are chemically processed. Replace butter with olive oil, almond oil, hazelnut oil, which are monounsaturated fats (Omega 9), or with walnut oil, which contains Omega 3 fatty acid. I can tell you that making chocolate mousse with hazelnut oil instead of butter tastes heavenly.

- If you are baking, many dough and pie crust recipes call for using real butter, and without the saturated fat of the butter, the dough doesn't coagulate. I have found that in those cases, you can use coconut oil, which is still saturated, but has tremendous health benefits, including: helping weight loss and digestion, regulating metabolism, boosting immune system, managing cholesterol levels in the body, relieving stress, kidney problems, heart disease, high blood pressure, diabetes, preventing cancer, and improving dental quality and bone health, just to name a few. Coconut also has a monumental role in relieving migraines.

- Get a couple refillable oil-spray bottles, and use them with your healthy oil of choice for most of your needs. I have two spray bottles, one with olive oil, and one with hazelnut oil. I use them to make omelets, spray on salads and on my bread (instead of butter), grease baking pans, and many more uses. It allows you to use only a little bit of oil instead of a lot, and the little you use is more evenly distributed. You can also get a dripper bottle for olive oil. Even drops of olive oil are better than just pouring it straight out of a large bottle. And you'd be surprised how tasty the food still is with just a spray of oil.

- Of course, if you want to loose weight, you shouldn't be overindulging in cakes. But if you really want to eat cakes, than it's better that you yourself bake the cake according to kindness food principles: see if you can replace white flour with organic whole-wheat flour, preferably stone-ground, perhaps even sprouted flour. See if you can use half (or start with two-thirds of) the amount of flour, and add instead oats, carrot puree, apple puree, or other fruit in its stead. In the Bliss Muffins recipe of muffins included in Appendix A, I've replaced a third of the flour of the original recipe with oats, and another third with grated apples, which makes the muffins moist and finger-licking good.

- Still on baking – see if you can replace any white sugar used in the original recipe with organic raw honey, agave nectar, or better yet, stevia. Honey's glycemic index is about fifty, as opposed to sugar, which has a glycemic index of one hundred. Stevia is a natural sweetener that is completely calorie-free and carbs-free.

- If you are baking anything with ground meat (like lasagna or moussaka for example), I find that adding some grated celery, and small-chopped parsley and onion, not only adds to the taste of what you're making, but also increases the volume of the meat without increasing the calories, which makes it into a diet food, even if it is beef. Also, see if you can use 93%-lean beef that is grass-fed and all natural (no hormones or additives).

- If you're using eggs, like in cakes, quiches and soufflés, see if you can use only the egg whites. I make low-fat chocolate mousse and low-fat pumpkin pie, which use only egg whites and are only lightly sweetened with honey, and you'd never know the difference in taste. I also make a breakfast soufflé with only egg whites, low fat cheeses, and lots of veggies inside, that tastes much better than the fatty soufflés that you'd eat at a restaurant. All these recipes are in Appendix A.

☯ If you're using cheeses in your baking or cooking, see if you can reduce the amount of fatty cheeses. For example, making lasagna, you can use a lower fat ricotta; replace the 20%-fat beef with lean (7%) grass fed beef or even turkey for the filling; replace some of the pasta layers with slices of eggplants; use homemade pasta sheets (which has a lower GI) for the rest. You can even grate some zucchini and mix it in with the ground beef. No one will notice the zucchini, and it would make the beef more juicy and moist. And you don't have to put a thick layer of mozzarella on top. You can sprinkle just a little Parmesan on top to give it some salty taste. This lasagna will, of course, be lighter in calories, and you'll be in awe of how tasty it is, despite its low fat and low glycemic index.

These are just some examples. The recipes in Appendix A will give you more of the feel of substituting saturated fats with healthy fats, fatty proteins with lean ones, and high glycemic index carbs with lower GI ones, as well as introducing more vegetables and fruit into your recipes and meals. But Appendix A is not meant to be an elaborate cookbook, or give you all the possibilities of yummy vegetable recipes that exist. It is just meant to give you some ideas and experience with substituting healthy ingredients for unhealthy ones. Once you experiment with it a bit, and get the hang of this healthy substitution thing, use your inner wisdom guide you, and enjoy being creative in the kitchen. Getting your creative juices flowing along with your digestive ones will allow you to enjoy your fresh vegetables, fruit, beans, whole grains, nuts, and seeds even more, and along with them, enjoy the zesty health that results from eating them. Besides, sometimes getting creative in one area of your life, such as food preparation, which seems totally unrelated to prosperity or to your Ideal Lifework, will awaken your creativity in other areas that are absolutely related to your Ideal Lifepath.

From a Healing Foods Perspective

If you look at this diet from a healing foods perspective (Chapter 4), all we are really doing here is adding healing foods: the first and second categories of healing foods are tangible ingredients. But however non-tangible the third kind of healing foods may seem, it is nonetheless very real.

Now let's be specific, when we add wholesome, organic, fresh, natural, fruit, vegetables, nuts, grains, legumes, and seeds (the first category of healing foods), we are not only adding their superb nutritional value. We are also adding their high vibration as foods that are the bounty that God has given us through our Earth-mother. This increases our satisfaction from the food subtly but profoundly.

When we add natural foods that contain healing nutrients—the second category of healing foods, we are not just arbitrarily adding stuff that sounds good. We are meditating (as detailed above in the section on Kindness Diet Meditation) to seek answers from our higher consciousness on specific nutrients that are missing in our diets. After you have meditationally gotten a clue on what nutrients are missing, you can then verify this information by doing some online research, and considering if logic and science back up your meditational clue. Once you have ascertained that your meditational information is based on facts, you have three options. One is to continue indulging in the unhealthy craving and continue to gain weight; the second is to find supplements that can replace the missing nutrients; and the third is to add to your diet natural foods that can supplement your missing nutrients in the most natural way. Of course, the third option is the best, if the nutrients that you are missing are readily available in adequate quantities in natural foods. If not, than you'd have to go for option two. Spending just a little bit of time on this process will go a long way to eliminate overeating or cravings.

But as wonderful as wholesome, fresh, organic, natural foods are, and as important as getting the right nutrients is, they are not the whole story when it comes to healing foods. An equally important part of your diet are foods that are spiritually and energetically healing for you – foods that you have blessed with love, or otherwise food that is healing and nurturing for you specifically, like in my example of my grandmother's Tshulnt (stew). Another example of healing foods in this category is the organic seeded whole-wheat sourdough bread that I bake. When you think about bread in the perspective of a plain diet, bread has a higher glycemic index than whole grains, and therefore is not considered a good diet food. But this bread is special. Beyond the fact that it's organic, whole wheat (=lower glycemic index), and contains three different kinds of seeds, there is another magical secret ingredient in the bread. And I believe it is this secret ingredient that makes every person who eats my bread describe it as "Heavenly good." And that secret ingredient is reiki energy—the energy of Divine Light-Love. Before I make the dough, I energetically cleanse my living space and kitchen using the sacred reiki symbols and my prayerful intent, and I put on inspiring music. Before I kneed the dough, I draw the reiki symbols of Divine-Love and Divine-Light over my hands and over the dough, and I keep a prayerful intent in my heart that all who eats this bread will be healthy, happy, uplifted, and imbued with the highest feeling of Love and Light. As I knead the dough, I dance joyfully with Kindness Movement, envisioning putting into this dough the utmost healing energy though my reiki hands. In days when I can't visualize, than as I knead the dough, I chant: Divine Love, Light, health, happiness, prosperity... over and over, for the entire duration of the kneading process (about twenty minutes). And there has not been one person who hasn't commented on how "Divinely wonderful" this bread is, including people who are atheists! But even if you are not a reiki healer, Divine Love and Light are already inherent within you. If you just allow yourself to be in a state of joy and grace as you prepare your foods, and if you just add a little prayerful intent to your food preparation, you will be imbuing your foods with the nurturing energy of the Divine. And you will absolutely notice an increased level of satisfaction from the food, which will help you eat less of it, and stay satisfied for longer. And that subtle satiety and happiness that blessed food gives you is the real stuff of not only the Zohar Kindness Diet. The contentment, enjoyment, and high-energy that results from eating blessed foods is also the real stuff of co-Creating of prosperity from your Soul.

What to Eat

While the Zohar Kindness Diet focuses on adding healthy ingredients to your diet, setting some guidelines to follow may be beneficial for a well-balanced diet, especially for weight loss. However, I precede this with a qualifier: While these guidelines have proven effective to anyone whose ever been on a low glycemic index diet, the first focus of Zohar Kindness Diet is to be kind to yourself. If you haven't quite gotten to the point where your body is satisfied with more broccoli and less pasta, that's OK. You will get there at some point soon. So be patient, kind, and gentle with yourself, because the less judgmental you are of yourself, the sooner you'll get to the point in which you are comfortable with less fatty animal foods, less processed carbs, less saturated fats, and more veggies.

According to Dr. Weil,[26] each balanced meal should contain:

50%-60% Low Glycemic Index Carbs –

50%-60% of your caloric intake should come from low glycemic index carbs in the form of vegetables (especially green veggies), whole grains, beans, and fruits – the less processed the better. Even the same foods cooked or prepared a different way can have a different glycemic index. For example, pasta cooked 'al-dente' has a lower glycemic index than overcooked pasta; boiled potatoes have lower glycemic index than roasted; whole grain bread has lower glycemic index than white bread… The less processed and the closest a food is to its natural state, the lower its glycemic index is. Remember that the glycemic index is simply a method of ascertaining how quickly your body is going to use up this food as energy. The lower the glycemic index, the slower your body metabolizes it, and the longer the food will last in your system before you get hungry again. But you don't have to study the glycemic index/glycemic load table (Appendix B) like a bible. After a few glances at it, you'll get the gist of things, and master the skill of lowering the glycemic load of your meals – an important step to weight loss and a balanced kindness diet.

20%-30% Lean Protein –

20%-30% of your caloric intake should come from lean protein. Now here is decision time. If you eat animal flesh, than you can certainly get lean complete proteins from fish, poultry, eggs, dairy, and whey products. But *if you choose* to be vegetarian or vegan, than you will need to learn to combine protein sources in ways that give your body complete proteins—proteins that contain all eight essential amino acids. Soy, quinoa, and hemp do not have to be combined with other protein sources, because they each already contain complete proteins. Other vegetarian sources for protein require that you combine them in particular ways in order to make complete proteins (see the box below).

If you go the vegetarian route, you'll also need to find ways to replace some of the micronutrients that are predominantly abundant in red meat, such as vitamins B12, D and B2, and minerals such as calcium, iron, zinc, and iodine. So *if you choose* to go the vegetarian or vegan route, be aware of these issues. Research them properly, and then joyously prepare your meals to include a healthy variety of all the

Vegetarian Sources of Nutrients
Complete Protein:
Soy, quinoa, whey, or hemp make up complete proteins on their own. Otherwise, to make a complete protein, combine:
Beans & nuts   Brown rice & nuts
Beans & seeds   Brown rice & seeds
Beans & wheat   Brown rice & wheat
Beans & brown rice
Vitamin B12: Soy, tempeh, miso, seaweed, or supplements
Calcium: Soy, bok-choy, broccoli, kale, mustard greens, okra, beans, fruit & vegetables
Vitamin D: 15-30 min. sunlight or supplements
Iron: Soy, nuts, seeds, lentils, kidney beans, chickpeas, black-eyed peas, Swiss chard, tempeh, black beans, prunes, beet greens, tahini, peas, bulgur, raisins, watermelon, millet, bok-choy & kale
Zinc: Dried beans, sea veg., soy, nuts, peas, seeds

vegetables needed to replace those nutrients. I have included here a brief summary of the main nutrients you'll need to be mindful of getting if you go vegetarian, and which foods they are abundant in. You should still research this subject further to find out how much of each nutrient your body needs daily, and how much of its vegan source foods you need to consume in order to get it.

The bottom line is: use your considerable inner wisdom to decide on the right nutritional path for you. Some people do well with vegan diets. It makes them lighter and very energetic. Others really need and love to eat meat. While getting all the required nutrients from vegan sources is possible, if eating meat is one of your joys of life, then consider that continuing to enjoy it in moderation may be the kinder way to go. As beautiful as this whole vegan idea sounds, nothing is loftier or more right for you than unique and wise path shown to you by your Soul. And nutrition is no different than any other aspect of life: the wisdom of your Soul will always guide you to the way that best serves your highest Lifepath.

10%-20% Healthy Fats –

10%-20% of your caloric intake should come from healthy fats, preferably monounsaturated (Omega 9) and Omega-3 fatty acids. Omega-9 (monounsaturated fat) is found in almonds, hazelnuts, and olive oil. Some omega-3 rich foods are fish, beans, oats, and walnuts. Use these delicious oil as a way to bring out the flavor in your foods, or as whole nuts, which also contain some healthy proteins.

How to Translate Caloric Intake to Volume of Foods on Your Plate:

In a couple of minutes, we are going to dump all formulas, and I'll give you a graphic plate composition that will be easy to remember, and satisfying to eat. But just in case you are one of those people who need scientific proof for everything, let's go through a couple of example computations that would help explain why the plate composition that I suggest in the following section indeed makes scientific sense. If the science of it bores you, or if you're not interested in the science, than skip my example computations, and go onto the section on Plate Composition & Orientation.

I have chosen two people for our example. First, let's calculate the people's ideal weight of our example people, by plugging in the parameters of the examples into Formula #1 (detailed earlier in this chapter):

Example #1:
Gender: Woman
Age: 35
Height: 5'7" (~67")
Activity Level: moderately active
Current Weight: 180 lbs.
Ideal Weight: 133 lbs. (113 lbs. to 153 lbs.)

Example #2:
Gender: Man
Age: 40
Height: 5'9" (70")
Activity Level: sedentary
Current Weight: 200 lbs.
Ideal Weight: 144 lbs. (130 lbs. to 159 lbs.)

Next let's plug in some of the data presented above into formula #3, to find out these people's basal metabolic rate—how many calories you should ingest a day. However, the BMR calculated formula #3 is not the number of calories that one should eat to lose weight, but the number of calories one would eat if he or she just wanted to sustain weight. To lose weight, one must eat less than their BMR. Most diet experts suggest that that if you have to lose a lot of weight, you should shoot for losing 10% of your current body weight first, and then recalculate once you get there. So when using formula #3, I'm going to calculate it plugging in 90% of the people's current weight:

Example #1:
90% of current weight: 162 lbs.
BMR (Formula #3): 2,103 cal/day

Example #2:
90% of current weight: 180 lbs.
BMR (Formula #3): 2,182 cal/day

Notice, though, that I did not arbitrarily say, "oh, if you want to lose weight, you should restrict yourself to 800 to 1000 calories per day" or whatever the ridiculously low number of calories that many diets advocate per day. All I did was plug into the formula a weight that is ten percent less than the person's current weight, so that the weight loss is very gradual and gentle, and the person doesn't feel hungry or deprived. If we weren't about to dump all formulas in a couple of minutes, than the idea would be that the person keeps periodically calculating the formula according to 90% of his or her current weight, until he/she gets to the desired weight. But as I've said, we're not going to be counting calories in this diet. And if we are not counting calories, than so far all these computations are doing is helping us understand the reasoning behind how combine the food on our plates *by volume.*

So For simplicity's sake, let's round both examples to an average requirement of 2,000 calories a day. Now if you follow doctor Weil's recommendation of deriving 50% of your daily caloric intake from low glycemic load carbs, 30% from lean protein, and 20% from healthy fats, than in our example of a 2,000 daily calorie diet: 1000 daily calories would come from low GI carbs; 600 daily calories would come from lean protein, and 400 daily calories would essential fatty acids. Now let's see how that translates to volume, while satisfying your needs.

<u>Protein ~</u>

The first macronutrient that we should explore is protein. Lately, amongst vegan and vegetarian loftier-than-thou circles, it has become very "in" to downplay the importance of protein, and to claim that the minute amount of proteins that are present in leafy vegetables is enough. While it is true that eating too much protein can cause some health problems, it is also true that too little protein can cause health issues too. As it relates to diet, when you don't get enough protein, than after a meal, you find yourself raiding the munchies cabinets and going down on all the ice cream and treats that you can find in the fridge, which is, of course, counterproductive to a weight loss diet.

The Institute of Medicine[27] actually recommends consuming a daily number of protein grams equal to 0.8 of a gram per each kilogram of bodyweight. That's about 0.37 grams of protein per pound of body weight. And if you're physically active, you should consume more proteins a day. This means that the people of both of the above examples should be getting about net 60-65 grams of proteins per day. Proteins release four calories per gram, which in our example, equates to about 250 calories per day from net protein grams. But protein is not the only thing adding to the caloric value of protein-rich foods. When you get your protein from animal products, than despite being rich in complete protein, more than half their calories actually come from fat. And when it comes to vegetarian sources, such as beans and whole grains, more than half of their caloric value comes from the carbohydrates in those foods. So it makes sense that if the protein needs of the people in our example release 250 calories, than the whole foods that contain those proteins should amount to about 600 calories.

Now, what does that mean in terms of a meal? Well, let's say that the average person should consume about three main meals and two healthy snacks per day. And let's assume that the people of our examples are going to eat most of their proteins during the meals, and only a little of the proteins from snacks. In that case, they each consume 18-20 grams of proteins in each meal, and the remaining proteins in the form of a snack.

Examples of sources of protein are:

- ☯ 1 egg –7 grams; 2 eggs – 14 grams of protein
- ☯ ½ cup of dry oats – 6 grams of protein
- ☯ 1 cup of milk – 8 grams of protein
- ☯ 8 ounces of yogurt – 11 grams of protein
- ☯ ¼ cup of soy nuts – 8 grams of protein
- ☯ 1 cup of chopped chicken (140 grams/~5 oz.) – 35 grams protein – (→ 7 protein g per oz.)
- ☯ Average fish filet (122 grams/4.3 oz. total) – 23 grams of protein (→ 5.3 protein g/oz.)
- ☯ A 3-ounce piece of beef has about 21 grams of protein (→ 7 protein g/oz.)
- ☯ 1 cup of quinoa contains 8 grams of complete protein
- ☯ 1 cup of cooked beans has about 15 grams of protein
- ☯ 1 cup of wholesome brown rice (195 total grams) – 5 grams

From this list, you can see that most of us don't get enough protein at breakfast, which is probably why we walk around slightly hungry throughout the morning. But even if they only got 10 grams of protein at breakfast, let say that the people in our example will get the remaining 50+ protein grams at lunch and dinner. As you can see, it's enough to have about three or four ounces of chicken with your salad at lunch, which provide about 21-28 grams of protein, respectively. The story is the same if your protein source is beef—only three to four ounces of lean beef provide you with the 21-28 grams of protein that you'd need per meal (depending on how much protein you ate for breakfast). If you're being good and getting your protein from fish, you'll need four or five ounces of fish to supply you with 22-27 grams of lean protein. But three to four ounces of chicken or beef, or even five ounces of fish, only take about a quarter of your plate, not half your plate, as we've been raised up to believe.

Even if your protein source is soybeans or half a cup of soy nuts spread over your salad, if we measured it in how much of your plate's volume it should take, than it should only take about a quarter of the plate. If you are eating a grains and beans combination to get your complete protein from a vegan source, than a cup of wholesome rice and a cup of beans, which together should give you about 20 grams of complete protein, would indeed take half your plate, but at the same time, they should count for both the protein and the low glycemic-index carbs. So conceptually, you can say that they each take a quarter of your plate's space.

Fats –

Fats do not need to occupy any volume on your plate. Since fats are extremely dense in calories (they release 9 calories per gram, as opposed to protein and carbs, which release only 4 calories per gram). So the amount, in volume, of the essential fatty acids 9 and 3 that you'll be having should be negligible. If all of the fat in your diet came from olive oil, than you should consume about 10 teaspoons of olive oil per day. Of course in a kindness diet, you'll introduce fat in a bunch of fun ways: You'll sprinkle some healthy oils on your veggies; some of your fat will come from cheeses that you'll add to your steamed veggies, and from yogurt you have as snacks; some of it will come from the nuts that you'll add in moderation; and of course, if you decide to eat animal protein, those contain plenty of fats. The point here is: we're not allocating any special room on your plate for fats.

Carbs ~

Now we get to carbs. The people in our example each need to consume 1000 calories a day from carbohydrate-rich foods. Now if they load up on rice, for example, than a cup of even brown rice, which is a diet-recommended food, contains about 43 grams of available carbohydrates, and releases 212 calories. If they each ate two cups of rice each meal, that would not necessarily fill up enough volume in their stomach and intestines to make them feel satiated. Plus two cups of rice release about 425 calories, and if they ate that as the main carb source, would amount to at least 1275 calories per day—over the recommended amount of calories from carbs for the people in our example. Thus, eating only carb-dense food would eliminate any room for fruit, vegetables, snacks, healthy deserts, or any other kind food from your diet. If instead, our example people eat only one cup of brown rice or other whole grain (which, again, takes only about a quarter of your plate), they'd be able to indulge in almost unlimited amounts of yummily prepared veggie, eat fewer calories, and at the same time, be more satiated, and feel much lighter than if they were to eat the more heavily starched meal.

For example, three cups of broccoli only contain 12 net grams of carbohydrates, and have a very low glycemic index, and therefore a negligibly low glycemic load. And sprinkling on it some olive oil, garlic, fresh ground pepper, some fresh savory herbs, and even some salt, will not add an exorbitant amount of fat to the meal, and will make it yummy and satisfying. Another example is: three cups of salad, including lettuce, carrots, and tomatoes, contain less than 15 grams of net carbs, and increases the volume (fiber & water) and therefore the satiety that you derive from the meal, as well as introduces many healing nutrients into your food. And a salad can be made fun in many different ways (as we'll explore together in Appendix A). Two tablespoons of dressing may mean about two teaspoons of healthy oil added to your caloric intake, but increases your enjoyment of your meal exponentially. And since you have to have some essential fatty acids in your diet (20%) anyway, a little bit of the right oils on your veggies never hurt no one.

Plate Composition & Orientation:

So now let's dump all the numbers and formulas from here on. Based on the above discussion (and backed up by www.ChooseMyPlate.gov), here is the magical plate composition that will help you lost weight, while enjoying your food, and feeling satiated—nutritional kindness-to-self:

- ½ of Your Plate (by volume) – should be loaded with tasty, lovingly prepared vegetables or fruit – to increase volume of food, your satiety from the food, and its micronutrient content
- ¼ of Your Plate (by volume) – should contain complex carbohydrates of low glycemic index, such as whole grains
- ¼ of Your Plate (by volume) – should contain lean protein, such as beans, soy, fish, chicken breast, egg whites, etc.

Bad Plate Composition:

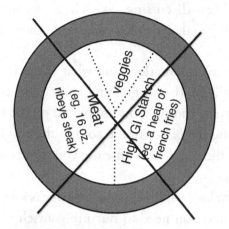

Good Plate Composition:

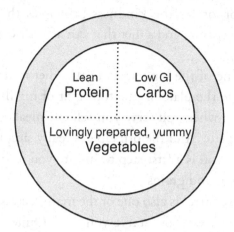

Breakfast Examples:

Notice that in both of these examples, the veggies/fruit take up half the plate, the bread is single slice of whole grain, organic bread that I homebake, and the organic eggs only take 1/4 of the plate. On the right, the omlet is made with just a spray of hazelnut oil.

Lunch Ideas:

Notice that even though these lunches is are salad-based, I did include 2 kabobs and even some pasta on left dish, and smoked salmon rolls with veggies & hummus for the right salad.

Dinner Ideas:

Typical Zohar Kindness Diet Dinner

The typical dinner on the left includes: half a plate of green cauliflower topped with low-fat chipotle-ranch dressing I made, 1/4 plate of quinoa, and salmon with garlic & herbs grilled on a plank.

In the pasta dinner on the right, I put only 1/2 a cup of homemade pasta; the sausage is a lean turkey-sausage; & I did add a whole package of baby-broccoli.

Pasta & Sausage Dinner

What it boils down to is: This plate composition allows you to dump all of these overly scientific percentages and formulas; and concentrate on the volumes of food on your plate, which incorporates the kindness principles that we've been discussing, as well as the most balanced nutrition, and a diet that can affect weight loss (if you desire to lose weight) in the most natural way.

Now, one of the big secrets to this diet is also the plate's orientation, and what to eat first. If you notice the plate on the top right of my illustration here, the veggies and fruit are placed closer to you when you serve yourself the meal, and the carbs and proteins are placed on the far side of the plate. And the principle is really simple: twisting the plate around so that the veggies are closer to you is a first step to inspire you to fill up on the veggies first, before you move over to the protein and grains.

Portion control is also one of the main secrets to weight loss. But in this diet, no one is saying to you, "Don't eat," or "starve yourself." Quite the contrary: you need to nurture yourself well on all levels. But if you want to lose weight, you should plug portion control into your diet. To lose weight, you should aim to eat about 80%-90% of what you originally thought you were going to be hungry to eat. But to facilitate kindness-to-self and make sure that you do not feel deprived, this is done in two ways: First, as we already discussed, you should increase the number of meals in your day, so that each meal is a smaller meal. As this adjustment into smaller meals, your stomach will shrink, and you will be satiated with less food. Secondly, always put on your plate less carbs and proteins than you initially think you want to eat, but reserve the option to eat more of them later. One of the reasons that many people are obese is that we load up our plates much beyond our capacity to eat. Most of us are so emotionally and spiritually deprived that we are constantly in a state of hunger, which channels towards food. On top of that, our lives are usually so hectic, that we sometimes skip meals, and by the time we get to each meal, we are quite literally starved, and so we load up our plates even more. And usually, we become full after only a fraction of what's on our plates, but feel obligated to finish it. It's that "be a good girl/boy, and finish everything off your plate" voice still speaking inside our subconscious. I mean, on a conscious level, you know that if after all these yummy veggies you still want more chicken or more rice, you can always get up and serve yourself more, so there is no reason to overload your plate on the first serving. Because for some reason, once the food is on your plate, you usually feel obligated to finish it. So don't put it all on your plate, and don't put yourself in a position to feel obligated to finish. Take comfort in knowing that there is plenty where that came from, just as there is more of anything and everything that you need in your life, ready to come to you through your Infinite Funnel of Abundance.

Of course, as you lose some weight, if you wanted to continue to lose weight, than you'd need to keep reducing the portions of your proteins and carbs again to about 90% of what your new appetite guides you to eat. But that's not going to be a problem, first because your stomach will have shrunk some by then, second because you'll be able to fill up that gap with vegetables, and thirdly because your new habit of adding healthy snacks will naturally keep your appetite lower than before.

Now let's not be shy, let's talk about bread! If your inner kindness meter has instructed you to eat bread, than consider what works best for you in terms of swaying yourself away from filling up on the bread and motivating you to load up on the veggies and complex carbs first. One method is to put the bread away and hidden in the kitchen, as an "out of site, out of mind" kind of a thing. However, putting the bread away may make some people feel deprived. And if this is the case, above all, do not deprive yourself, and don't perpetuate a subconscious mentality of lack. If putting the bread away would make you feel deprived, than by all means, put it on the table in plain view. For some people, actually holding the bread at hand helps them feel more comfortable eating it last. This availability of bread can actually work to turn off the Neanderthal-craving (discussed earlier), since having the bread readily available on a regular basis can eventually convince the subconscious that no starvation is impending, and therefore there is no need to load up on carbs and store them as fat. Use your inner wisdom to decide which method works best for you. But either way, if you are indulging in some bread once in a while, make it whole wheat, seeded, and preferably sprouted bread, since these breads have the lowest glycemic index and the highest amount of nutrients. And either way, you should try and save the bread for last, in order to give yourself a chance to learn to enjoy some fabulous vegetables and whole grains.

Where To Start

I know that the amount of information given in these two chapters about nutrition can be a little overwhelming, and can leave you wondering where to start your Zohar Kindness Diet. Remember that all this information is given as a background—as the basis of which to base your nutritional decisions—but that your actual nutritional decisions should be guided by your inner wisdom. So the first step in starting this diet is to do a Kindness Diet Meditation, to help you tune into some important information from your subconscious that would help your nutritional decisions. You can repeat the meditation every time you are faced with a nutritional decision; just change the questions that you ask to what you need to know at that time.

Next, a good place to start actually practicing the Kindness Diet is to add some of the nurturing lifestyle items listed above. So as a first step, add some good quality sleep; increase the amount of water that you drink; and add a meditation or another practice that would help you reduce your daily stress levels. Go with that for a few days, and see how you feel. Does that reduce your cravings? Do you feel more energetic?

Then add your hour of Me Time each day, if you haven't already; find a quiet nature place, and do a few minutes of deep breathing during that time. Moon-Breaths if you are unwinding in the afternoon; Sun-Breaths if it's in the morning, and you need to get going; Grounding Breaths if it's during your lunch hour (all these breaths were covered in Chapter 2 of *Seven Stages to co-Creating Prosperity From Your Soul*). Monitor how this deep breathing is affecting your readiness states and how you feel. You may find that doing a Nurturing Meditation (Chapter 5 of *Seven Stages to co-Creating Prosperity From Your Soul*) daily helps you feel very nurtured, and therefore helps reduce cravings, especially if you do it in the afternoon and evening hours, when we are most apt to munch on anything and everything. So sleep, hydration, deep breathing, Me Time, and meditation are the best places to start the Zohar Kindness Diet.

The next stage, you may want to start bringing into your life the Joyful Physical Activity of your choice. But again, don't make it a frontal attack on the gym. It doesn't have to be a five-mile run at seven miles-per-hour. It can be a fifteen-minute Nature Walk to start with. Then you can increase it to thirty minutes, an hour, or longer if you wish. Or it can even be jumping on the trampoline with your young ones... anything that makes you happy and joyous and is physical. One point I want to make with regards to your Joyful Physical Activity is put yourself first. When you wake up in the morning, there is always a point before which you are still in a daydream of all the joyful things you wish to do today, and after which you feel yourself getting sucked into doing "responsible, productive" things. It is the point of switch after which you get lost in this "productivity" mode, and forget to do your personal practices and your Joyful Physical Activity. So get in a habit of catching yourself during that morning switch-point, and not allowing yourself to get sucked in. At that point, remind yourself that your first duty and responsibility is to yourself and your health. Even your duty as a parent should come after your responsibility to your health, since you need to be healthy and happy in order to be able to care for your kids or other loved ones. Now, I'm not saying that your Joyful Physical Activity needs to necessarily be in the morning. But it is in the morning that you plan your day, and calculate when you're going to stake out time for your Me Time and your time for Joyful Physical Activity. There may be additional switching points throughout your day. For example, the point in the afternoon at which you snap out of your mode of responsibility to your boss, and tune into your responsibility to yourself. And for that one, you can set an alarm on your cellphone with a beautiful ringtone, and put some kind words to yourself – like "Go enjoy, gorgeous!" or "Yay! This is my Me Time," or "I'm fabulous and I deserve a beach-walk." The point is, be aware of those points of switching gears, and consciously make them work in your favor.

The next step is to start experimenting with fresh organic vegetables and fruit. Eat them raw, steam them, sauté them, experiment with some of the recipes given in Appendix A, or even look online for some yummy ways to cook vegetables. Even if you don't intend to become vegetarian, vegetarian websites usually have fantastic cooking tips and recipes that may help you prepare your veggies in fabulous ways. Just experiment and have fun with it. Be generous with savory herbs, spices, and condiments, as they enhance the taste. See if you can prepare/cook them yummy enough to enjoy eating half a plateful of them, and if you can manage to make your veggies in such a delicious way that would make you crave them.

Next, start experimenting with adding some whole grains instead of potatoes, and some fish, chicken, or other lean protein instead of your fatty rib-eye steak. Don't think of what you are reducing. Just have fun adding the kind foods that you are adding, and experiment with recipes that are fun and easy to make, and give you pleasure eating them.

Once you start feeling comfortable with preparing/cooking your vegetables in delicious ways, replacing the fatty proteins with lean ones, and high GI carbs with low GI ones, you can be more mindful of the plate composition and orientations mentioned above. That is, see if you can add even more veggies, and wane down the amount of carbohydrates and proteins rich food… until you get to a plate composition and orientation that feels the kindest to you.

Since this diet is about being kind to yourself, nourishing yourself on all levels is very important. Since the aim is to wean yourself off of unhealthy foods *in a natural and kind way*, the last thing you want to do is start it with self-deprivation. So reducing the foods mentioned in the Foods To Kindly Wean Yourself Off Of section above is actually the last thing that will happen in this diet. Actually, that reduction will happen automatically and naturally as you follow all the other steps mentioned here.

One more thing I'd like to mention in the spirit of kindness-to-self: the Zohar Kindness Diet is a "one day at a time" kind of a thing. Meaning, if on one particular day you veered from your diet and indulged in say, steak, French fries, and a hot-fudge Sunday, don't spend the rest of your week beating yourself up over it. In fact, don't beat yourself up at all, as you don't want the stress of guilt (releasing of cortisol in your body) to cause you to keep overeating for as long as you fuss about it. You also don't want your vibrational resonance to shift to the negative, since you don't want to start magnetizing low vibrational things into your life.

Also, there have been studies[28] in which groups of overweight people with similar health issues were given decadent creamy deserts to eat. The people in the test group were told to fully enjoy and indulge in the deserts with no guilt (they were told these deserts were good for them), and the control group people were warned about the health risks of eating the deserts. The results showed that indulging in the same creamy-sugary deserts without guilt helped support a healthy immune and cardiac systems and produced better health, whereas worrying and feeling guilty over the same deserts caused cardiac problems, immune problems, and an array of other health issues. So if on a particular day your inner guidance instructs you to indulge, then keep reciting to yourself the mantra: "I'm fabulous and worth every indulgence in life!"

Of course, if this binging keeps happening, you may need to meditate and ask your Higher Self what's going on, so that you can learn to provide your body-temple with the appropriate nutrients from healthier sources. But the most important thing is not to fret about it, and to just let it go. After all, tomorrow is another day, right? So on the day of the binge, just enjoy it, and don't ingest any guilt with it. The next day, wipe the slate clean—wake up as if nothing happened, and go back to nurturing yourself with fabulous fresh, whole foods, and with all the "I'm fabulous" practices that you now know.

Kindness Stars Diet Log

Now don't get too alarmed about the word "log" here. We are not going to be counting calories, bad no-no points, or keeping a log of beat ourselves up over our daily diet "sins." Not by any means. I mean, if on a given day you have already decided to indulge in, say a whole pizza tray with fatty sausage on top, and ice cream for desert, and you are already committed to eating it to the point that you've not only ordered the foods, but your digestive juices are also already going, than what good would it do to write down these calories? What – to beat yourself up about it? That is not the way of the Zohar Kindness Diet, and you shouldn't live your days in the dread of how things would reflect in your diet log or in your end-of-week-weighing. Depriving yourself, judging yourself, or counting calories take the joy out of the experience of eating, and do not contribute anything to your overall wellbeing, your health, or even diet goals. The real results of the Zohar Kindness Diet come from incorporating kindness practices into your eating habits, in order to adjust your taste buds and restore your original affinity to nature-based foods, which are naturally more nurturing and balancing, and at the same time lower in caloric density.

All that being said, some people find that keeping a log that documents the changes actually help to encourage them to stick with a diet. If you are one of those people that need to keep a log in order to motivate yourself, than the log that I recommend keeping is not one that documents the unhealthy and unkind things you ingest each day, but the opposite: it should be a log that documents how kind you were to yourself each day. You should give yourself reward stars for each kind thing you do for yourself. Essentially, we're using the carrot instead of stick here. If you decide to keep this log, than each evening, document the things you did to show kindness to yourself. This Kindness Stars Diet Log should not be a log that you dread writing. This log would have you actually looking forward to writing each evening how kind you were to yourself that day. Beyond the multidimensional benefits that a walk, a swim, or another Joyful Physical Activity being you, logging it in your Kindness Starts Diet Log should make you feel good about yourself at the end of a day. It may put you in a state of grace and a healthy self-love. In the same way, logging that you've added many veggies, fruit and other kind foods would energize you with the feeling that you're doing something fabulous for yourself because you *are* fabulous. This log is a constant reminder that your first responsibility is to yourself. And it feels good to remember that.

Rather than counting points or calories for what you do eat, actually rewarding yourself with a star for each kind component you add to your diet and lifestyle each day is a better motivator to keep being kind to yourself.

I have constructed this log such that for each day you can give yourself five stars: Some stars are for letting go of unkind things, and other stars are for adding kind things. Here are the kindness things that are grouped into each star:

- ★ Added at least 5-6 cups of veggies and fruit per day, and some moderate amounts of whole grains and lean proteins
- ★ Let go of some unkind foods
- ★ Added Me Time, a Joyful Physical Activity, and meditation
- ★ Got adequate sleep, and didn't deprive yourself of anything
- ★ Let go of stress, guilt, and self-judgment

Since there are five possible stars for each day, a perfect score for the week would be thirty-five stars. Beyond the reward of losing weight and feeling lighter and freer within your body-temple, you could decide that when you have a week in which you've accumulated thirty-five stars, you would reward yourself with something, say a little gift you've been wanting to buy yourself, or a nice trip to a spot that recharges you. The point is not to judge ourselves or take on no-no points for fattening foods, but to reward ourselves with stars and gifts for eating kind food and for practicing kindness-to-self principles.

A page of the Kindness Stars Diet Log, as well as a title page, and Kindness Diet Guidelines flip cards, are given in Appendix C. You are welcome to copy them, cut them, and bind them into a little diet-log booklet. You can also make any changes to them that you feel guided to make, so they can best serve your needs.

If on a particular day, you sit in front of that log puzzled as to what to write, because you feel like you haven't added anything kind, that is an opportunity to add compassion and understanding towards yourself. In the beginning, you can give yourself half a star per day just for adding a pear and an apple, or if for example you've only added one tomato to your otherwise calorie-dense dinner. As your diet progresses, you'll be able to give yourself a full star for adding lots of yummy veggies each day. In the same way, even if you feel like you haven't really let go of anything unhealthy today, at least let go of self-judgment, so you can at least earn one star for letting go of self-judgment and the stress that stems from it. As you color that star in, own it! Really let go of any self-judgment regarding what you ate today, and know that tomorrow is another day – tomorrow, a fresh new opportunity to eat kindly shines on you.

Peer Support

You can absolutely do this diet on your own, in the privacy of your secret chamber, unbeknownst to any of your friends or relatives. But letting your friends and relatives know that you are doing this diet may help earn their support. In social gatherings, when sharing meals together, or even in restaurants, you will be surprised by how respectful and compassionate people get when you share with them your diet goals, or even just mention that you are on a diet. Ten thousand years ago, people used to socialize by sitting together around the bonfire telling stories. But even then, they probably did so over a meal, sharing the bounty of a hunt. In our culture today, much of our socializing still revolves around meals. And it is helpful if people know not to stick the white bread and the butter right in front of your face, and not to shove more potatoes and heavy cream sauce into your plate with an excited "eat Johnny eat!"

Beyond that, if you have any close friends or family members that are like-minded and are also on a diet, it is helpful to establish a good feedback and support system with them. For example, my best friend and I made a pact that whenever one of us loses another ten pounds, the other one would give them a reiki treatment. And we agreed that when one of us reaches their desired goal, the other one would buy them an outfit at a clothing store that we both like. We also talk every day, and give each other support and advise, reminding each other to add healthy foods and nurturing practices to our lives, and reminding each other to be kind to ourselves. Now, if you don't have that much to lose, you can make that pact for every five pounds you lose, or for the entire goal. And if you are doing this diet just to introduce healthy practices into your life, but you don't actually need to lose weight, than you may establish a different reward system with your best friend, measured by levels of vitality you each feel, the freedom of your spirit within your body-vessel, your readiness to reclaim your Ideal Lifepath, and any other personal goals you want to reach. The point is: buddying up with a friend to encourage each other is in itself a kindness practice, and may help your diet goals tremendously.

Kindness & Food

Kindness to yourself in food means having all the choices at hand, giving yourself permission to do whatever feels right, and knowing that everything in moderation is OK, and that there is a balance that is perfect for you, in food as in everything else in life. And the only one certified to decide what that balance is, is your Soul Self – reachable through your inner wisdom.

Within this balance, it's OK to eat rib eye steak, potatoes and chocolate mousse… once in a blue moon! But eating a bucket of chocolate mousse every day may not constitute being kind to yourself, since it probably does not support the feeling of freedom that you wish to have in your body-temple. Use your inner kindness meter to guide you on when to indulge old habits, and when to push yourself to eat healthier foods. Some people know themselves well enough to know that they cannot handle just one tablespoon of chocolate mousse; they have to have the whole bucket, which means they are better off not having any at all. Others' knowledge of themselves dictates that they must allow themselves <u>small</u> indulgences in order to not feel deprived. You need to decide on the practice that would be most effective for you to drive you to be nutritiously kind to yourself.

But remember that kindness is a tri-faceted thing. For example, a beef craving could be a signal to intake more iron or vitamin B12; a French fries craving could be the body's signal that it needs better quality sleep, or more emotional-mental nurturing; cravings could also be based on old habit patterns that no longer serve your highest wellbeing. Within the three facets of kindness-to-self, there are times in which you absolutely have to indulge yourself as part of the joy of being alive, since abstinence of anything does not necessarily bring joy or happiness; and there are on the other hand times when you must push yourself to eat healthier and make choices in life that are kinder to yourself in the bigger sense. So when is it appropriate to limit your daily enjoyment of cheeseburgers, french-fries, and milkshakes; and when is it time to push yourself to make higher-vibrational choices? When your daily enjoyment of fatty foods is infringing upon your enjoyment of feeling lightness and freedom in your body—when you realize and truly feel that daily enjoyment of these fatty foods is neither healthy not kind for you. That's when you realize that kindness-to-self is best served by pushing yourself to start eating the more Truly nurturing foods of the Zohar Kindness Diet.

If you really tune into your inner meter of kindness-to-self, it will guide you to know when to indulge and when to push yourself into healthier habits. And I dare say that once you add all the kind foods discussed here in the right balance for you, your craving for "comfort food" will wind down on their own. And you—the Divine observer within you—is the only one who really knows which route serves your highest-best good at each moment of your life.

The third facet of kindness, is: just as you have learnt in Kindness Movement to find a kinder, softer ways to move and walk, you can now learn to tune into your inner wisdom and find the happy balance that would allow you to enjoy food, and at the same time to eat only healthy, wholesome, high-vibrational foods. Food is one of life's greatest pleasures. Let's experience it as such!

In this chapter, we've talked a lot about nutrition and diet, from the perspective of a diet that infuses kindness-to-self into our nutritional habits, and adds things, rather than taking them away, in order to help our bodies each find the most perfect balance and weight for each of us. But if you really look at what we have achieved in this chapter, it wasn't just about losing weight. It was mostly about integrating kindness-to-self into all the small components of our lives, in a way that makes our bodies and whole selves balanced, light, and high-vibrational – in effect, putting all the elements of our lives into the most kind balance for each of us. So really and truly, in this chapter, we've started to integrate all the elements of our lives, and the multidimensional nurturing that we are each now giving ourselves, into that perfect balance that makes each of us each ripe to merge with our Ideal Lives of prosperity from our Souls.

In the next chapter—the final chapter—I will give you more tools that could serve your the path as a conscious co-Creator well, and help you bring into further focus your Plan of Action to merge with your Ideal Lifepath.

Chapter 6

The Bridge from Your 'Now' to Your Ideal Life

Whether you realize it or not, you and I have walked a tremendous path together in these three *Prosperity From Your Soul* books. Understanding all the metaphysical Truths relating to co-Creation that you have understood in *Prosperity From Your Soul*; intimately getting to know your beautiful Soul Self through the meditations that we've done together in *Seven Stages To co-Creating Prosperity From Your Soul*; and shifting your lifestyle and body-temple into the Ideal-you, which we've begun to do in this book – are no small feats.

In this chapter, we reiterate some things, and string them together into bigger understandings that will help you safely cross the bridge from your 'now' reality to your Ideal one.

Taking Inspired Action While Reading Universal Road Signs

Okay, so you have a dream. At the initial point in which you had that dream, it may have seemed as unobtainable as a pipedream. But then when you read *Prosperity From Your Soul*, you understood the principles of the co-Creative process, and understood that your earnest-most desires are not pipedreams—that you are actually meant to co-Create and manifest into your life all the things that your heart Truly desires. Hopefully, those understandings helped you shift your perspective on your dream, so that you could energetically hold space for it to come true one day. Then, you while reading *Seven Stages to co-Creating Prosperity From Your Soul*, you meditationally saw your Ideal Lifeplan clearly—a meditational internal experience that felt so real, that it proved to you the reality of its existence, at least on the ethereal plain. As you saw meditational-internal proof of your Ideal Life, your newfound belief in its reality helped shift your energetic vibration into a resonance that attracts it. At the end of *Seven Stages to co-Creating Prosperity From Your Soul*, you also received from your Soul some directives on the initial steps that would lead you to reclaim your Ideal Life of prosperity.

But remember how raw and incomplete your initial Plan was when you first meditationally perceived it? Although you were unsure how these meditationally perceived steps were going to assist you in merging with your Ideal Life, if you trusted your Soul's inspiration and followed it with action—taking some of the steps that your Soul guided you to take while anchoring kindness-to-self and joy into your lifestyle and body-temple—more inspired steps probably came to you, and you added them to your inspired To Do list, until eventually, your inspired To Do list—now inspired not only by your meditations, but also beefed up by some new ideas, and backed up by some synchronistic events and likeminded people that you've met—started to resemble a real Plan of Action that is doable, and presents a path that could logically lead to the fulfillment of your dream. It was the action that you started to take—on faith—that gave an extra oomph to your manifestation wagon, and moved it just a little further each day towards your Ideal Life of prosperity.

And now that you've started to implement some of the practices suggested this book, you've probably seen things gradually and subtly starting to change. For as you shifted your daily schedule into one that leaves room in it for exciting new things, it created an energetic vacuum, into which the Universe *can* now start pouring Its Infinite abundance. And as you shifted yourself more and more towards the Ideal-you, your lifestyle into a lifestyle of joy, and your body-temple into a state of vitality and health, you brought yourself into a high vibration that resonates with, and therefore attracts, all the prosperity intended for you.

As the conscious co-Creator that you now are, some things are worth reiterating: The action that you take towards manifesting your Ideal Life always needs to be inspired by your Soul-Light and dipped in joy, which means that before taking any action, you must first reclaim your Balance of Grace. In other words, make sure that any action you are about to take is never a knee-jerk re-action (which builds more karma and co-Create all that you don't want to manifest), and never an action taken out of fear, but an action that comes from a centered and peaceful place of knowing your Soul-Light, being strengthened by It, acting as the Ideal-you, knowing that you are perfectly capable of achieving everything that your Soul has set out for you to do, and taking sure steps in which every action, thought, and feeling just feel right in every fiber of your being, making you more joyous and alive. That is the idea of "inspired action" – it means action that is not only inspired by, but that is a direct extension to your Soul's Will, which should be evident by the joy that you feel, as the common denominator between the will of your here-now self and that of your Soul Self. The result is an all-around vibrational resonance that just has to magnetize success, abundance, love, happiness, health… and all the positive things that you wish for.

As you take all that inspired action, you should always be listening for signs from the Universe. That is an integral part of walking the path of a conscious co-Creator. As we have discussed, the Universe and your Soul Self are constantly sending you signs all the time. Signs that you are already good at listening to are the Joy Meter and the God Meter (see Chapter 7 of *Prosperity From Your Soul*), and the multidimensional signs that your Soul is constantly giving you (see in Chapter 1 of *Seven Stages of co-Creating Prosperity From Your Soul*). To restate things briefly, what is pro-life, pro-happiness, brings joy, creates more love in the world, feels right, and resonates harmoniously with every fiber of your being, is of God, and reflects a decision that is inline with your Soul Self.

The Universe too (your Divine Creator) is constantly giving you signs. If you take a certain step, and all doors just seem to close in your face, than you are not following your Ideal Lifepath. On the other hand, when you take a step/path, and all doors just magically open before you—you seem to be meeting all the right people who love you and support your goals; and unexplainable lucky "coincidences" just keep happening to you, effortlessly carrying you towards the fulfillment of your goals, dreams and deepest yearnings—than you are indeed in the auspicious synchronistic flow of the Universe, connected to the Infinite Funnel of Abundance, and co-Creating your Ideal Lifepath.

However, even if you are at a point where all doors just slam in your face, that still doesn't mean that you have somehow lost God's favor or anything. It just means that you need to go back to the drawing board, so to speak—you need to redo some of the meditations of *Seven Stages to co-Creating Prosperity From Your Soul*, especially the meditations of Chapters 6 and 7, get a little more inspired, go deeper into Soul consciousness, and get from your Soul a clearer vision of your Ideal Lifeplan. Assuming that in Chapters 3 and 4 of *Seven Stages to co-Creating Prosperity From Your Soul*, you have done a thorough job of clearing all blockages from your path, if you come to a point where doors close in your face, it's either because it wasn't yet time to walk the new path that you've envisioned (since all evens in your life have to be auspiciously synchronized with the mosaic of everyone else's lives); you may have partnered with the wrong people; the place may be wrong; or it's possible that you just haven't quite tuned into the full extent of your highest Lifepath yet—maybe you have tuned into an impression of it, but you need to go back in, and ask your Soul for more clarity on the details.

I had experienced something like that with my aviation career. In 1994, I went to live in Israel, where I was trying to pursue my aviation career. Despite my US pilot and flight instructor licenses, and despite my vast international aviation experience at the time, all doors were slammed shut in my face. And although Israel is a beautiful country with weather and landscape very similar to California, my underlying feeling was of dissatisfaction with the place, like I wasn't where I was supposed to be in the grander scheme of things. Even without the bad breaks that I was catching with my career, I just wasn't happy there. I used to cry every night and ask my ex-boyfriend (with whom I was sharing my life at the time), "Please take me home to America." After three years, I went back to the States, where lo and behold, doors were opening for me again. I was closer to where I needed to be for the time being. Now in retrospect, I realize that although I eventually became a captain in a major airline (which was what I thought I wanted), my aviation career successes in were not so easily flowing, but were hard earned. It wasn't until I "accidentally" stumbled across reiki that I really started to merge with my Ideal Lifepath: Reiki not only uplifted me, but also restored my Original Self, and showed me my life's purpose. As I started to shift my life focus from an aviation career to a spiritual lifepath, and especially when I fully embraced my spiritual calling and started to teach workshops, doors indeed started opening for me, and gifts started landing regularly in my lap. I'm not suggesting that everyone should devote their lives to spiritual pursuit. It's just that for me personally, that is my True calling, which took me some years to realize. Even after I had tuned into my True calling, and was already a reiki master who had been teaching workshops for years, I was still afraid to leave my airline job to pursue my spiritual calling, and so I was moonlighting my activities of working in a spa, seeing reiki clients, and teaching spiritual workshops. It took another push from the Universe, in the form of debilitating migraines, to get me to quit the airline job, soon after which I started receiving (channeling) the spiritual knowledge contained in this book series, and two fantastic new modalities that I bring forth as I teach spiritual retreats. I now understand that the difficulties in my aviation career were not punishments, but instead, were actually gifts from the Universe, to help redirect me towards my True Ideal Lifepath. Now that I am closer to living my Ideal Lifepath, I feel fulfilled teaching spiritual workshops and retreats, however humble they may be, because every time I serve as the instrument that helps someone reach their Divine potential, or even just awaken to it, my heart sings with joy. Since I've been following my True path, synchronistic opportunities just keep finding me, as if to let me know that the Universe is still supporting me in every way. And that is as the Universe is designed to work for you.

When you are on the Ideal Lifepath, auspicious synchronistic events keep finding you, which seem like lucky coincidence. You just "coincidentally" meet people who offer their help, and who just "happens to" have expertise in areas you need advise on at that point; you stumble upon one opportunity after another "just by chance;" you just "happen to" get a killer deal on a business space for a fraction of what you budgeted for in your business plan… things just happen for you that let you know very clearly that the Universe is behind you, and that you are on the right path.

How the Infinite Funnel of Abundance Meets Your Lifepath

However, don't be disappointed if the grand lottery prize doesn't show up at your doorstep tomorrow morning. First of, winning the lottery is not necessarily a valid co-Creative goal, since money—in and of itself—is not a valid manifestation goal. Wanting to accumulate money for its own sake only fuels the fear of not having enough, and is therefore not supportive of prosperity from your Soul. On the other hand, money to co-Create specific endeavors that are inline with your Ideal Lifeplan would absolutely manifest as the means to empower you to reach those goals.

The way that the Infinite Funnel of Abundance usually shows up in one's life is gradually and continuously. And that's not necessarily a bad thing, because if you think about it, there is nothing more valuable than having the assurance that God is always with you, and that you'll always be provided for in a way that best serves your journey on Earth. I mean, billion-dollar companies go under all the time; and many people have lost their fortunes through life's ups and downs. But what if you had one magical gold credit card that is ethereal and therefore can never be stolen or taken away from you, and its credit limit were truly Infinite? Wouldn't that be preferable to lottery winnings? The only two limitations of this magical credit card are that it doesn't always give you the money in large chunks; and doesn't give you what you think you want, but what You Truly want—what your Soul wants for you, which serves your highest purpose. Once you've tuned into what your Soul truly wants for you, it's like you've said the ultimate "open sesame" command, and all Universal resources, including money, are at your disposal—your magical-Universal credit card would give you the specific resources you need, when you need them. Wouldn't a magical credit card like that be the ultimate "it" thing in the manifestation of prosperity? Essentially, that is what prosperity from your Soul is like: all you have to do is align your here-now will with the Will of your Soul, and act accordingly—energetically vibrate-feel in resonance with your Soul

Self, and take some inspired action towards making the vision of your Plan come true—and then Infinite resources from the Divine synchronistically and auspiciously come into your life.

Synchronicities, though, do not necessarily have to come in the form of a million dollars dropping into your lap like thunder on a bright summer day. They *can* be, if that serves your Soul's purpose at that point in your life. But more often than not, synchronistic events are not grandiose. It is the subtle synchronistic events that show up in your life steadily, that gently help guide it along the auspicious flow of the Universe. A synchronistic event could be as subtle as hearing a particular song on the radio that springs a well of creative ideas out of you, which if you follow through on, would eventually lead to monetary prosperity; it could be talking to people, or even overhearing people talk about something that inspires you to think about a new avenues in your professional career; it could be meeting likeminded people who share your vision, and are meant to become part of your Ideal Life Plan, even if you don't initially know how; or it could be synchronistically bumping into the philanthropic investors that would make your dream a reality. To drive your life steadily and harmoniously towards your Ideal Lifepath, synchronicities need to keep happening frequently. Once in a while, you may have a grandiose synchronistic event, but it is the smaller, subtler synchronicities that *keep* driving your life *steadily* towards and through your Ideal Lifepath.

Given the steady flow of synchronicities needed to drive your life towards your Ideal Life, your shift towards the higher energetic vibration that resonates with the prosperity you seek should not be a temporary thing. So the changes that you've made while reading this book, which facilitate this shift to a lighter vibration, should also not be temporary. It's not that you vacate room in your schedule for some Me Time and Joyful Physical Activity for a month, and afterwards you resume being a stressed out workaholic at a job you hate. And it's not that you eat healthily and nourish your whole self for a couple of month, and then you go back to eating processed junk food after that. To co-Create the life of a conscious co-Creator, and to stay in the auspicious synchronistic flow of the Universe, you *always* need to make time to enjoy your life; you *always* need to balance your daily activities in a manner that is kind to yourself; you *always* need to get adequate sleep; you *always* need to eat healthily; and you *always* need nourish your whole self. Making these changes permanent will help you stay in the auspicious synchronistic flow of the Universe, which will continue to precipitate gifts into your lap.

Joy as a Prerequisite

I know that we've already talked a lot about joy throughout this book series, but it's worth reiterating from a new perspective. Joy is a direct extension of Love; and Divine Love is the only energy, substance, and force in existence. It IS the very essence of the Creator, the process of Creation, and that which is Created. Quantum physicists may call it the "Unified Field," or they may talk about strings of energy as the "substance" that makes up all the forces and particles of our multiverse, but the bigger Truth here is that every universe in existence, and every particle and force within it, are composed from the energy of Divine Love. Because of that, all abundance comes from Divine Love. Although Divine Love is different from human love, the messenger that can help deliver to you the True Abundance of Divine Love is joy, which is the vibration that bridges from the Heavenly to the earthly.

To be clear, we are not talking about the temporary enjoyment of overindulging in unhealthy foods, or of getting back at someone. These kinds of temporary enjoyments don't come from the Soul or from our Heavenly Selves, but from our lower human selves. Therefore they satisfy only the crust of who we are, but not the very core of our True Selves. And those kinds of indulgences of our lower selves are usually regretted later, or even during the event at some deep level of oneself. Conversely, the kind of joy that bridges between the Infinite Abundance of the Soul and physical manifestation is deep inner joy that resonates musically through every fiber of our beings, and bursts out as the True joy of life, love, happiness, and kindness to oneself and others.

Sadly, though, our societal values for efficiency and quantifiable achievements make most of us forget how to self-soothe with simple techniques that should be basic to all human beings; we forget to take little nature walks, smell the flowers and just take in the fragrance of life; we forget to listen to the song of the birds; and we forget to just take the time to really enjoy all the precious little moments that make life worth living. We forget that the True essence of success is not to be in a constant do-do-do achievement mode, but to find the Balance of Grace. True success is not measured by the size of your investment portfolio, but in how fulfilled and happy you feel with your life. Sure, True success should include all the resources, including monetary resources, to fulfill all of your needs and do the things that you want to do. But to Truly be successful, you need to remember what is truly important in life – to enjoy it! I mean, isn't that what we all live for – to love and enjoy life in all of its precious moments?

It's not that 'I act, therefore I exist,' and it's not even that "I think therefore I exist" (humbly). At the level of the Soul, there is no separation or differentiation between thoughts and feelings. It's all one vibration of our True essence. And since feelings bring through Soul's energetic vibration much more potently than thought, it would be more accurate to say, "I feel, therefore I exist." And since the True essence of the Soul is Love and joy, it would be even more accurate to say: "I feel joy, therefore I exist," or "I am blissful, therefore I exist."

The point is: you need to live not out of duty, but out of joy. So as you anchor your Plan into reality and as you take all that inspired action, keep in mind that life is about experiencing Love and joy. Don't stress yourself out to finish or achieve anything. Whatever becomes part of your Success Calendar (discussed below) should be dipped in joy.

Your Manifestation Journal

In *Prosperity From Your Soul,* I suggested that you start a Freedom Journal, in which you write every day how you would spend that day if you had absolute freedom to do whatever you want—if money, obligations, circumstances, and physical limitations were not present. At that early stage of our path together, this Freedom Journal served the purpose of getting your creative juices going, opening up to all that might be possible for you, and vibrationally getting you to connect with the joys of whom you Truly are—your Soul Self. It was a way to affirm, at least internally, your freedom and joy, and to start creating a vibrational mutual resonance with the riches of manifestations of your Soul. And writing a Freedom Journal is still a great idea.

But since you've started to write your Freedom Journal, many changes have occurred in you: you've actually tuned into the Ideal Lifeplan of all-inclusive prosperity that is meant for you; you've started to ground the vibration of that plan into lightness within your body-temple and a lifestyle joy; and you've actually started to take some preliminary steps towards reclaiming a life that is unbound by limitations. Whether you realize it or not, you are now at a state of accelerated manifestation. The very fact that you've made contact with your radiant Soul (in *Seven Stages to co-Creating Prosperity From Your Soul*), and have learnt to live a life that is inspired by Its Light, has accelerated your vibration, and has shifted you into a state of existence in which what you think-feel manifests quicker and more powerfully. And as you continue to take steps inspired by your Soul while setting your vision free and maintaining the Balance of Grace, the wagon of manifestations in your life will start going quicker and quicker.

From this stage of your path on, every kindness practice that you introduce into your body-temple will produce a subtle shift towards becoming an even more conscious co-Creator, and every day in which you live in a vibration of a conscious co-Creator, anchoring the Light of your Soul into your daily lifestyle, will bring to you more Soul-inspired ideas and more auspicious synchronicities.

Given all these changes and the acceleration of manifestation, it may be useful for you now to start a personal journal, in which you would record daily kindnesses that you've shown yourself, creative ideas that came to you, nightly dreams that you feel were directives form your Soul to help you along your path, supportive people you've met who might end up playing important roles in manifesting your Ideal Life, shifts in your perception and inner feeling (which may foster more creative ideas and shift your energetic vibration, respectively), lucky "coincidences" that somehow plug into the Universe's plan to make your dream come true even if you don't yet know how, and anything else related to your new path as a conscious co-Creator of your life. Recording acts of kindness-to-self and their positive productive outcomes will encourage you to keep being kind to yourself. And documenting actual changes as they happen is a way of keeping your hand on the pulse, so to speak. Because the changes usually happen subtly, your ability to feel encouraged by them takes awareness. It's kind of like seeing the kids of your distant friends grow. The parents of these kids don't really notice them growing because they see them every day. You, who only see them once in a while, have a better perspective to really notice how the kids have grown since you've last seen them. This journal can help realize, with the perspective of time (looking back at your journal once in a while) how your little ideas, small actions, and subtle synchronicities, are actually driving the wagon of your life towards your Ideal. It's like those videos that actively demonstrate the process of a flower growing: To produce them, the photographer actually takes a bunch of still pictures of the flower at set time intervals, and then combines them into a video that shows the flower growing very quickly from a seed, to sprouting roots and a stem, to growing leaves and flower buds, to full bloom, to wilting – all in a matter of seconds of film. The viewer can then see and understand the entire process in a short viewing. But the understanding derived from those films would not be possible if the photographer didn't take periodic shots of the flower's growth. Likewise, your bigger 'aha' moments, relating to where you are along your path and how to understand your Soul's messages, could not happen if you don't snap periodic shots of your thoughts-feeling and of the flow of synchronicity in your life. You may be getting plenty of auspicious synchronicities from the Universe, but if you don't stop to acknowledge them you might miss their significance; and if you don't make a note in your in your Manifestation Journal, you're likely to forget how the events/thoughts/feelings reinforce your new path. And if enough time goes by without breathing new life into your new path, it's possible that you'd go back to a mundane existence of not consciously being aware what it is that you're co-Creating into your life.

So this Manifestation Journal keeps your awareness focused on your new path, and is therefore a great manifestation tool.

The style of your journal almost doesn't matter. It could be nothing more than bulletins, meant to trigger more complete memories of those events, thoughts, and feelings. It could be in essay style—something that comes from a deep thought. My favorite style is automatic writing, which helps bring things out of your subconscious, and if done meditationally, could help bring messages from your Soul. The important thing is that it is a style that works well for you.

Your Success Calendar

Richard Bach, author of *Jonathan Livingston Seagull*, *Illusions*, and many other wonderful books, once wrote: "The difference between a dream and a goal is a deadline." For our purposes, it means that even if you've had crystal-clear visions of your Ideal Life, wonderful ideas on how to bring it about, and tremendous synchronicity to assist you, and even if you have already started to cautiously take some of the steps of your Plan of Action, and are apt at reading the road signs that the Universe is giving you, you could still dillydally with the execution of your Plan for years, before you fully move forward with it, unless you put your visions and ideas into some kind of a timeframe. Putting it into a timeframe helps shift your ethereal dream into an obtainable goal.

And since free will is a fundamental law of Creation, the Universe's assistance in manifesting your Ideal Life, including the big synchronistic events, depends to a large extent on your action. It's true that some delays in manifestation could be happening because of the necessity to wait to synchronistically coordinate your Ideal Lifepath with the mosaic of the lives of everyone else involved, at the right timing. But your action, to a large extent, is what moves the wagon of manifestation (additional creative ideas coming to you, meeting of the right people to assist your plan, synchronicities, and gifts from the Universe to manifest your wishes) forward towards your Ideal Life. So if you're dillydallying, it's not moving forward.

To give an example from my own life, I was the queen of procrastinating and dillydallying before I received insight about this Success Calendar. In 2002, I had the idea of co-Creating *Soul Path Retreat*—a spiritual retreat in which people would learn to connect with the health, happiness, and True abundance of their Soul Selves. But it was only an ethereal idea, which I thought of as a pipedream. Then in 2009, when I started receiving dictation channeling the information for this book series, first of all, I had no idea that it was going to amount to three books. I felt compelled to continue to channel the information, but I had no ego involved with

Zohar Love

publishing it, and I didn't see how it would be related to Soul Path Retreat. Along with channeling of the information for the books, I was Guided to found Rezossage—the unique holistic massage modality, and RezoDance—healing movement modality that also helps manifestation. Still, in my mind, all of these things were pieces of a puzzle I did not know how to put together.

The initial auspicious To Do list that I derived from my initial Meditation to Devise A Plan of Action (see *Seven Stages to co-Creating Prosperity From Your Soul*) included only things that had no relation to teaching spiritual retreats or publishing books. For instance, one item on my initial To Do list was learning Italian, since I felt drawn to that language. Three of years later, when I repeated the meditation, it dawned on me that as the first stage to fulfilling my dream, I would be teaching retreats in existing resort locations, many of which are located in Spanish speaking countries. And as I started to learn Spanish, I realized how much easier it was for me to learn it after having learnt some Italian. So the little "indulgent" hobby of learning Italian, unbeknownst to me at the initial stage, actually played a part in my Plan to merge with my Ideal Life. In the same way, in the initial stages, I didn't know how many of the small steps that I was guided to take plugged into my Ideal Lifeplan. But as things unfolded over time, they were actually turned out to be leading steps towards the overall Plan of my Ideal Life.

After a few years of following the initial steps of my auspicious, meditationally derived To Do list, when I repeated Meditation to Devise A Plan of Action, I received a detailed, three-stage plan to merge my dream into reality. I was told, though, to expect that I may not have to follow all the steps, because at some point in the middle, when the fabric of the Universe is aligned with the auspicious perfect timing in the mosaics of the lives of everyone involved, the right investors and business people (all of whom had to be spiritual, well-intentioned, and high-vibrational) would find me. I was given the three steps to appease my "logical" skeptical here-now mind, so that I *can* actually get into vibrational resonance with the reality in which my dream is manifested. Stage one was to teach retreats in existing resort locations who specialize in hosting spiritual retreats; stage two was to open a small location in which I would teach not only retreats, but also Rezossage and RezoDance; stage three is when the investors find me and we build a resort location in which to teach, and teaching others to become teachers of these retreats and modalities, so as to spread the gifts that were Given to me by Source wider. But even with all of these clear visions from my Soul, and the logical steps that I was meditationally given, I still hesitated to move forward.

Then, a few months still later, I repeated the meditation again during the New Year's, when I usually do my three-day cleansing and deep meditation. At that time, I actually received a detailed A-B-C of how all the components of the information that I've received fit together, and in what order I should finish them. But despite all of these clarities, I still dillydallied. So the following New Year's meditation brought with it even more clarity: I was Guided to plug all of the tasks that I had received into a calendar called the Success Calendar.

As you can tell from my example, it took me quite a few years to trust the visions I was receiving from my Soul, and to believe that the resources I needed to manifest it were going to be there for me when I needed them. I am hoping, though, that this book series and my sharing with you the example of my path so far, would speed up *your* path to success, so that it doesn't

154

take you quite that long to co-Create your dream. One thing that can help shorten the time that it takes you to get to a mature stage in your Plan is the Success Calendar.

And the idea of the Success Calendar is simple: Once your auspicious To Do list has beefed up into a real Plan, it's time to put a timeframe on it. Especially if you are afraid to move forward with your plan, you need to go into a meditative mode and ask yourself: If your Plan is indeed inspired by your Soul, as verified by the deep harmonious feeling inside you, than what is it that is keeping you from going forward? After you remove fear, or maybe as part of removing fear, dividing your Plan into smaller goals will make it seem more obtainable.

In my case, Success Calendar was what got me to stop procrastinating and start finishing all the tasks that were meditationally given to me by my wise Soul and my Spirit Guide. Once I expressed my Plan in terms of twelve smaller, more doable tasks (one for each month) this year, and then twelve doable goals for next year, after which I hoped that the Universe would meet me halfway and help me achieve the rest, everything seemed more doable and achievable.

So once you get to a point along your path from where the bridge between the 'now' and the Ideal (see Chapter 8 of Prosperity From Your Soul) is in view, you may benefit greatly from dividing the tasks of your Plan into smaller doable goals. First ask yourself: What is realistic for you to achieve this year? What is realistic for you to achieve next year? And if you follow through on all these smaller tasks, will it lead you towards the manifestation of your dream? Where along this Plan are you anticipating the Universe to meet you and assist you in a bigger way?

When you've meditationally received answers to these questions, which you feel are indeed inspired by your Soul, than you have something to work with. Take the list of tasks that you've meditationally got as realistic for you to achieve this year, which would lead to the manifestation of your Ideal Lifepath, and divide them into twelve smaller steps, one for each month. Until now, all this planning that we've done was inspired and meditational. Now comes the time for your logical side to shine: Buy yourself a monthly/weekly planner, copy the tasks of each month into the monthly side. Then logically divide the monthly goals into weekly and daily tasks. I know it may sound pretty simplistic, but this Success Calendar is actually a great tool to taking your ethereal dreams off the pedestal and making them into obtainable goals, and at the same time, focusing you to follow through on those goals, all of which will help you get to the rendezvous point where the Universe is meeting you halfway to manifest the rest of your Plan for you.

However, when I say logically, I mean, keeping joy in mind. You are only human. And you are probably already busy, working, and fulfilling the regular tasks of your life. Perhaps the word task, to describe the To Do items of your Plan, is misleading, because you don't want these tasks to become chores. You want them to be things that you do out of joy, as that is the only way to magnetize True success into your life. So if on a particular day, you anticipate having time to complete some of the To Do things of your Plan to merge with your Ideal Life, don't bombard the planer of that day with a gazillion tasks. Add to it just a couple of tasks that you feel like you can achieve leisurely and joyfully. And write everything down with a pencil, so that if you don't end up achieving some of the things you had set yourself up to do, you can erase them without feeling bad about not completing them. You can always pencil those tasks in another day. After a while, you'll learn how to spread the tasks such that, within the new balanced lifestyle that you have established, and with the assistance of your new lighter, freer, and healthier body that you now have (or are on your way to having), the new tasks would just be a joyful addition to your days.

Then, as you continue walking this path of a very conscious co-Creator, the synchronicities that keep finding you will increase their auspiciousness, and plug better and more profoundly into fulfilling your dream, until at some point, you'll realize you are actually walking across the bridge from your old 'now' to your Ideal Lifepath of all-inclusive, and very blissful prosperity – from your Soul.

The Influence of Soul-Communication on Prosperity

As the conscious co-Creator that you now are, your communications with the people in your life, whether that's your boss, your employees, your spouse, your parents, your friends, your children, or just people you meet at the supermarket, should also be based in Truth. Recall from *Prosperity From Your Soul* that in Soul communications, your here-now self is only a channel to communicate your Soul's Truth to the people with whom you are communicating. You essentially put your human ego aside, and communicate from a place that is inspired by, and is a direct extension of your Soul. And the words that you speak always feel right to the very core. Soul communications always takes into account the highest wellbeing of everyone involved, and is always the most harmonious. Because Soul communications originate from the Soul, it draws on Soul wisdom. And since most of your Soul resides in the Heavenly realm even during your lifetime, It's wisdom draws on the Divine's all-knowingness, which knows no time, or any other limits, and is therefore in a perfect position to guide you towards the most auspicious future outcome of any situation. Not a bad play, when you are trying to manifest prosperity into your life, ha?

However, let's distinguish here. Spitting out the absolute whole truth at all times is a tough way to live, especially at work situations, or in communications with some of the people in your life who are less evolved. And that's not necessarily Soul Communications. Soul-Communications, or True Communications, doesn't necessarily require you to spill your guts, or to reveal your whole hand. It simply requires that what you say is a direct extension of what your Soul guides you to communicate. And your Soul will usually guide you to communicate the specific aspect of the Whole Truth that is kindest to everyone involved, presents the highest vibrational view of the situation, and would lead to the most harmonious and auspicious resolution. If you could always communicate in a way that yields such fantastic results, why not do it?

Besides the all-knowingness aspect, there are other valid reasons why it is in your highest-best interest to speak your Soul's Truth. Remember that your words have certain co-Creative powers. So it isn't productive for you to tell your boss, "I can't work overtime today because I'm not feeling well" if it isn't true, since you don't want to co-Create illness for yourself. You can, instead, say something like, "I am committed to being a good employee, but I have some pressing personal matters to attend to today." Don't tell the telemarketer, "I'm too poor to buy what you're offering," if it isn't true, since you don't want to co-Create lack in your life. You can say, "I am not interested in buying what you're offering, but I wish you success on your path." I once told a telemarketer that if he gives me his home telephone number, I would call him back at home later.

Of course, the poor young man got very confused and said that he couldn't give me his home phone number, because it wasn't ok to call him at home. So I said, "than why did you think it was ok *for you to call me* at my home?"

Anyway, the best response, with a telemarketer or otherwise, is of course to take a few Zohar Breaths (see Chapter 2 of *Seven Stages to co-Creating Prosperity From Your Soul*), tune into your Soul's wisdom, and see what It guides you to say. You'll find that speaking your inspired Truth makes everything so much simpler in the long run, and yields the best results when it comes to co-Creating your Ideal Lifepath.

Your Soul-Group's Assistance in co-Creating Your Ideal Lifepath:

One of the most precious gifts that were given to you in this lifetime is the closeness that you share with the members of your Soul-group, especially when it comes to co-Creating your most inspired Lifepath, because the members of your Soul-group will always support your highest Lifepath. Some of them may walk a parallel path to yours, while others will walk a path that is harmoniously intertwined with yours.

So when you get inspired ideas on how to positively change your life, don't bounce them off of people who are always skeptical and tell you that you can't. Instead, bounce them off the people in your life that always support your greatness—the ones who believe in you and empower you. It may even be helpful to have your close Soul brothers/sisters read this *Prosperity From your Soul* book series at the same time with you, so you could bounce off of each other insights about how these concepts touch your lives, and support one another on your new paths. The point is: share your new path with people who help you see your True Self more clearly—the people who always leave you feeling optimistic and wonderful.

To be clear: The true support of the members of your Soul-group is very different from the people who "lay it thick" in a phony and untruthful way, or people who sugarcoat things in order to push their own selfish agendas on you. No, the True support that you get from the members of your Soul-group *feels* profoundly different, since it comes from their deep love for you. As you describe your new vision, or the steps you took along your new enlightened path, your soulmates will actually tune into the Light in your vision, and hold it dear within their hearts and prayers, because they want with all of their hearts for you to succeed and be happy. The way you know the difference is that when the phony sugarcoaters react to your telling them your vision, their words make you cringe, create a knot in the pit of your stomach, and make you want to disengage from the conversation. These negative responses that you feel are real, and are triggered by your spiritual Truth Hearing ability (see Chapter 1 of *Seven Stages to co-Creating Prosperity From Your Soul*). In contrast, when your Soul sisters/brothers converse with you about your vision, their words play the inner string of your heart so harmoniously that it resonates musically throughout your entire being.

I cannot tell you how powerful it is to walk the path of life alongside the enlightened Souls of one's Soul-group. I have had many occasions in which my Soul brother or sister healed my migraines, and elevated me into a vibration of bliss, just by the sound of their voices, and the love I "heard" in it. In fact, this book series would not have materialized without the support and encouragements of my Soul brothers and sisters.

Daily Manifestation Practices

Since the stresses of life are not miraculously going to stop just because you've had a few good meditations, as you go along the daily routine while shifting your life into a more Ideal one, it becomes extra important to do little things that remind you of joy; remind you to let go and let God; remind youself that you are blessed; and keep bringing yourself back, throughout each day, into the Balance of Grace.

Of course, everyone is different in what restores the bliss for him/her. But any symbolic act that you do with prayerful intent harnesses the power of your free will to bring to you the blessings of that intent. So when you visualize Divine Light around you, by the power of free will that was Given to you, you really are calling upon more Light to surround you. And if you visualize a funnel of Divine Light and Abundance flowing into you and your surroundings, well that connects you with the Infinite Funnel of Abundance. If you affirm, "I am abundant and happy" over and over, to the point that you start tuning into that feeling, you, quite literally, make it true for you. So while your everyday symbolic acts that you choose may be different than mine, here are just a few examples of manifestation practices that have helped me tremendously over the years:

- ☯ If I go on a Nature Walk at times in which I am extremely stressed, and worried about my finances or other basic existential concerns, it is hard for me to concentrate on the visualizations that facilitate the healing energy exchange with the elements of nature. So what I do in those cases is I start silently chanting to myself positive affirmations, such as: "I am as bountiful as there are green leafs around me," "My financial resources are as plentiful as the grains of sand on this beach," "I am as radiant with health as these plants are," "I am as cheerful as the flowers are around me," "I am as powerful as this ocean that I see," "I am as grounded and peaceful as this tree…" You get the idea of these affirmations. As I walk and keep affirming these truths to myself, I deeply look at each element of nature that I wish to borrow the strength or blessing of, and I do my best to feel a oneness with it. Of course, after a while, the stress and fear leave me, and I start feeling more balanced. And when I get back to the mundane after this healing walk, things usually start looking up in the circumstances of my life. So I know that this is a tremendous manifestation practice.
- ☯ Before taking a shower, I usually bless the shower with reiki energy, envisioning that as the water of the shower wash my physical body, the Divine Light would wash away stress and negativity, and shower me with Divine Abundance, flowing easily into your life. Then as I take the shower, I close my eyes, take a few deeper breaths, and try to have an internal experience of being imbued with the Divine Light I requested.
- ☯ I do the same thing when I'm swimming… I envision myself swimming into the Infinite Funnel of Abundance, and integrating that Light into myself.

- ☯ You can bless your food with almost any positive intent. I usually reiki my food extensively and draw the sacred reiki symbols on the food before ingesting it. But even if you are not yet a reiki practitioner, the idea is to imbue the food with all the positive things that you want to bring into your life, and then as you eat it, envision that you are internalizing the blessing.

- ☯ Bless the clothes you wear with the intent that they would carry you to your most auspicious Lifepath. For example, I wear white clothes when I want to manifest calmness and pureness; I wear bright green clothes when I want to co-Create lightness and health; I wear more upscale sophisticated clothes when I want to become one with the feeling and vibration of abundance. As I get dressed, I consciously imbue the clothes with my manifestation intent of the day (and the reiki symbols).

- ☯ If you have an event that you are nervous about, like arguing on the phone with your health insurance company, an important presentation at work, or a test for example, meditate in advance and envision that event engulfed by a bubble of Divine white Light. See yourself peacefully winning. You'd be surprised at how calm and peaceful you'll be when the event actually comes, and how successful the results would be.

I know that these practices may seem silly at first. But remember how much faster (instantaneous) manifestation is in the spiritual realm, versus how relatively slow they are in the physical. These manifestation practices, as well as other practices that you come up with, actually help you tune into the positive vibration of the manifestations at the etheric level—they help you have an Internal Experience of them through your visualizations, intents, and feelings. As you say those prayers and visualize whatever you're guided to visualize, you get your internal environment to momentarily experience living the reality of your prayers, in effect creating an attractive mutual resonance with the object of your visualization. Essentially, these prayers become mini little Internal Experience meditations. The symbolic acts that you do while having these Internal Experiences help bring the vibration of your intents into something that's anchored in the physical reality, even if the act is not yet depositing a million dollars into your bank account. And the more intentful your prayerful visualizations and symbolic acts are, the more potent a manifestation tool they become.

Conclusion

There are many approaches to manifestation of abundance in one's life, some of which we have explored in this book series. But the truest form of abundance is the Infinite kind—the kind that comes from the Divine! It is the deep inner knowledge that no matter your current circumstances, the Universe would always support you, Love you, and provide for you everything that you need to fulfill your ultimate dream. And that is an assurance that is much stronger than having a few millions of dollars in the bank. For the assurance of Divine Love and readiness to provide for you is your never-ending magical credit card that is ethereal, yet more real than any other human assurance. That is what the Infinite Funnel of Abundance is – a Source of Light, health, abundance, love, happiness, freedom, beauty, radiance, joy, and Grace that is as Infinite and never-ending as God is. And the best thing you can do to stay connected to Her-His Infinite favor is to keep living a life of joy, peace, love, and heart-centeredness, guided by the wisdom, and basking in the brilliant radiance of your Soul.

As I write these lines, I feel like you and I have walked a great path together, even if we haven't physically met. Throughout these understandings, meditations, and changes, I feel like you are the reason for whom the Divine has given me these wisdoms—for your benefit. So I am grateful to both you the Divine for allowing me to be the conduit for all this information. And I feel like somehow this path has brought us closer to our core of Oneness. For as I write these lines, I am, with all my heart, rooting for you to win, find your Soul Self, and integrate all of Its blessings into your life. And I somehow feel like you—my reader—are with me too, rooting for me to integrate all of this wisdom into a life of all-inclusive prosperity.

Further Guidance...

In the near future, I will start offering a number of lovingly guided retreat courses that provide you with extra guidance as you to go through the steps of this book series, as well as give extra empowerment to your manifestation goals. The first course is called **"Level 1 Prosperity From Your Soul."** The processes of the retreat course are empowered by daily practice of RezoDance—a free-form meditational healing movement, which is a fabulous manifestation tool; and you will also receive a reiki Shoden training, which will strengthen your ability to tap into Universal energies.

To learn more about programs offered, check out my website: www.SoulPathReteat.com. If you need further guidance, you may contact me at: Zohar@SoulPathRetreat.com. I am always here to serve your highest purpose in any way that I can.

Afterwards

When I first started to be awakened at 3am to take dictation from the Divine, I had no idea that this automatic writing would result in three books about how to co-Create an auspicious life. But with all of the esoteric concepts, Soul-searching meditations, and profound lifestyle and health changes that we've gone through together, the one thing I really want you to take with you is how Truly fabulous you are, and how uniquely precious all of you is to God, to yourSelf, and to all of humanity. You are here on Earth to do what only you, and nobody else can do: be authentically you – in all the radiance of Whom you represent.

So do engage in these processes passed along to you in this book series. Do look for your radiant Soul to shine your way through life. And go out into the world with confidence and zest of one who is joyfully ready for all of the blessings that life has to offer, which your Creator wishes to experience through you.

It is my sincerest heartfelt wish that this book series will, in some way, help you reclaim a life that dwells in the brightest Light of your Soul—a life that is guided by Divine Intelligence, and blessed with health, abundance, Love, Light, happiness, freedom, joy, peace, and the Balance of Grace. I am with you at heart as you go thorough these processes of reclaiming your True Self. And I pray, with everything that I am, that as all of us around the globe reclaim our Soul Selves, we can all just learn to love each other, and study no more war.

With love & gratitude,
Zohar Love.

Appendix A

Kindness Recipes

The recipes included in this appendix are not meant to be a complete cookbook, but just to give you some ideas on how to make your vegetables yummier, and how to substitute kind food ingredients for unkind ones—i.e., lower fat, healthier fats, lower carbs, lower glycemic index, more wholesome ingredients. Kindness Diet foods should be fun, relatively easy to make (or if they involve extensive preparation, than it's a preparation that you only do once in a while, because the food has a long shelf/fridge/freezer life), and most importantly they should teach you to prepare kindness foods yummily. Once you got the point—once your kitchen creative sense is awakened—you should be able to take any recipe or cooking idea, switch some of the ingredients, and make it lean, low glycemic load, wholesome food.

Recipes That Make Veggies Much More Fun

Balsamic Vinaigrette Salad Dressing:

I have to share with you that during my entire childhood and adolescent I did not like salads or veggies. What turned me onto salads was when I discovered blue cheese creamy dressing. Over the years, I discovered that a dressing does not have to be heavily creamy to be tasty, and liven up your salad with rich flavor.

   This balsamic vinaigrette is a very delicious homemade recipe that I've developed—one that has been raved over by all of my guests—which gives a simple salad literally new life:

40% of a cup balsamic vinegar
60% of a cup olive oil (preferably organic, extra virgin, first cold pressed)
1-2 tsp. organic raw honey (from your local farmer's market) or authentic raw maple syrup
1-3 pinches of Himalayan salt (or natural sea salt)
1-4 pinches of fresh ground pepper
1-1½ tsp. of pesto (see recipe below)
2-3 pinches of Herbs of Provence

And the beauty of it is – it can last almost forever without refrigeration. Just mix the ingredients in a jar or a dressing bottle, close and shake the jar/bottle, e presto – the dressing is made.

Pesto:

Homemade pesto is something you should always have in your refrigerator. It is good for so many uses: Added to flavor your salad dressing; as a bread spread to spice up something bland like tofu for example; added to meatloaf, Italian style eggplant, or to any Italian style dish.

Just a couple of notes here: Traditional Italian pesto also has parmesan cheese mixed into the paste. I prefer to leave the parmesan cheese out, so that the pesto lasts longer in the fridge. You can always add fresh Parmigiano Reggiano cheese to the final recipe to which you're adding the pesto, which will taste much fresher and more flavorful. Also, original Italian peso uses pine nuts. I use walnuts simply because they contain acid omega-3, which reduces your cholesterol and is very healthy for you, and nobody—not even an Italian chef—can tell the difference in taste between pine nuts and walnuts in the pesto.

Ingredients –

Basil – 1 package (about 1½-2 cups by volume)
Garlic – 1 large head, or 1½ small heads
Walnuts – a fistful
Olive oil – a few tablespoons
Himalayan or sea salt, and fresh ground pepper – as needed
And – if you have access to other fresh herbs like savory, thyme, or oregano, throw a handful of these in too.

How To Make –

Clean the basil. Peal the garlic. Throw into a food processor the whole basil, the peeled garlic cloves, and the rest of the ingredients. Chop until it's all pasty.

It's better to start with less walnuts & olive oil. You can always add some later. If the combination is too watery, add walnuts. If it's too solid, add olive oil. Add salt & pepper as needed. This pesto can stay in your refrigerator for quite a few months.

Low-Fat Vegan Aioli Dressing/Sauce:

A few years back, I discovered the creamy, rich, and wonderful flavor of the aioli dressing when I worked in a spa that was adjacent a restaurant called Wolfgang Puck. I immediately got hooked on their Chicken Aioli Pocket, and continued to frequent the restaurant for a while… until one day I decided that it couldn't be that complicated to make this aioli dressing at home. After reviewing a few online recipes, and making a few tries, I came up with my own version of the aioli dressing. I decided to use low fat vegan mayo for the simple reason that it lasts longer, and can serve a wider variety of people. I'm sure you'll find it tasty even if you are a meat eater.

This aioli recipe can be used as a salad dressing, in which case you may want to dilute it with a bit more water, as a dip, in which case you'll want to have it fairly thick, or as a sauce for cooked vegetables and dishes.

Ingredients –

1¼ cup organic low fat Veganaise (I like vegan mayo better, simply because it has a farther expiration date, and doesn't contain raw eggs like regular mayo does. But you can definitely make this dressing/sauce with real mayo if you prefer it.)
3 teaspoons Dijon mustard
Juice from ½ large lemon
2-3 tablespoon of olive oil
5 large garlic cloves
Dash of Himalayan salt
Dash of freshly ground pepper
¼-½ cup natural spring water

Preparation –

In a blender or a food processor, mix all the ingredients into a light-creamy homogenous mix. If you don't have a blender or a food processor, you can absolutely mix it all by hand. But then you have to press the garlic with a garlic-press, and mix pretty thoroughly. I made it by hand for quite a few months before I decided to use a blender.

Add the water slowly to achieve the consistency that you like. Pastier consistency works well as a topping for fish, chicken, etc., or as a dip for vegetables like celery, carrot, and cucumber sticks. More watery consistency works much better as a salad dressing. Taste and enjoy as you mix the ingredients, to make sure the taste is to your liking. If the taste is too spicy or strong, add Vegenaise, and a bit of olive oil.

As you mix and prepare the ingredients together, don't forget to put on inspirational music, and do some Kindness Movement to imbue joy and freedom into the aioli sauce that you are making…

Chill in the refrigerator for a couple of hours to let the sauce absorb all the tastes better.

Health Benefits –

Soy Oil (contained in vegan mayo) contains essential fatty acids Omega 6 & 3.
Soy Protein (contained in vegan mayo) is a complete protein.
Apple Cider Vinegar (contained in vegan mayo) can help heartburn, improve bowl regularity, and break down fats so the body can utilize them instead of storing them.
Olive Oil – Mono-unsaturated fat reduces cholesterol
Mustard –anti-inflammatory (selenium & magnesium), helps prevent gastrointestinal cancer (phytonutrients).
Garlic – helps cardiovascular health and cholesterol reduction, antifungal, antibiotics, and many other benefits…

Lemon – lowers blood pressure, raises HDL (good) cholesterol, antioxidant & helps fight infections.

Himalayan salt – promotes healthy pH balance in cells, balanced blood sugar, vascular health, respiratory health, and bone strength. Also helps absorption of food in the GI tract & regulate sleep.

Low Fat Chipotle-Ranch Dressing:

I find that this chipotle-ranch dressing/dip makes veggies much yummier. With this dip, even something as simple as steamed cauliflower becomes very tasty, and makes me want to eat heaps of it.

Ingredients –

¾ cup organic low fat Veganaise (or regular mayo if you prefer)
2-3 tablespoons low fat goat milk yogurt (or low fat sour cream)
1-2 chipotle peppers in adobo sauce
2 large garlic cloves
1 tablespoon of chopped onion
½ tablespoon of chopped chives
¼ cup of chopped Italian parsley (or if you wish to make it spicier, use cilantro instead)
Black pepper – to taste (about ½ teaspoon)
Sea salt – to taste (about ½ teaspoon)
Paprika – to taste (about ¼ teaspoon)
Chili powder – to taste (about ¼ teaspoon)
A pinch of cayenne – if you wish to make it even spicier
About ¼ cup of spring water – to dilute it into a dressing.

How to Make –

Put all the ingredients into a food processor, and chop/blend them there until it becomes a sauce. Add the water to dilute it to the right dressing consistency last.

Tai-Peanut Salad Dressing:

The first time I actually made this dressing, my first response upon tasting it was: "Oh, my God! This yummy thing came out of my kitchen?" That day, I intended to eat only a little bit of salad, and had designs on a large juicy hamburger and some potatoes. But once I tasted the salad with that dressing, I had to go down on a large bowl of salad with this dressing, and after that, I could only eat a very small lean hamburger with maybe a tablespoon of cauliflower mashed potatoes (recipe below). So this is an example of the Zohar Kindness Diet at its finest: add just a couple of tablespoons of yummy dressing, and transform the entire meal from unkind to kind…

2 tablespoons creamy peanut butter
1 tablespoon rice vinegar
2 tablespoons of raw honey
1½ teaspoons soy sauce
¾ teaspoon fine ground Himalayan salt
1 pinch of cayenne pepper
1 tablespoon hazelnut oil
1 teaspoons spring water

Preparation ~

The preparation is easy… Just whisk together the peanut butter, vinegar, honey and soy sauce. Add the salt and cayenne, and mix it in. Add the oil and then water as needed to make the consistency you like. Some people like their salad dressing more watery, so it can be well mixed with the salad. Other people like it pastier like a dip. So if you see that the consistency is already pretty watery (after adding the vinegar, honey, soy sauce and oil), than don't add any water. Enjoy!

Himalayan-Sesame Salt:

A couple of years ago, I used to have cravings for sesame pretzels, which ruined my diet, until I discovered that my cravings were actually for the sesame, not the low-grade carbs. A simple online research revealed the many health benefits of sesame, and its contribution to a healthy mineral balance in the body. During the same period, I also used to load up on simple iodized salt, until I discovered that if I give my body the minerals it's really cravings (not necessarily NaCl), the salt and sesame cravings will stop. So I developed this recipe, which I use instead of table salt in almost all my food. Later, I discovered that a macrobiotic-vegan restaurant in Santa Monica, California called Real Food Daily also use a similar sesame salt for the same purposes I mentioned, albeit they use regular sea-salt instead of Himalayan salt, and their ingredients proportions are, not doubt, different.

Besides the health benefits of this special salt, you'll be in awe of how much it spikes the flavor of a simple salad, steamed vegetables, and many other dishes.

Ingredients ~

There are only two ingredients you need to get for this recipe:
Organic raw non-hulled sesame seed
Fine-ground Himalayan salt

I usually order non-hulled organic raw sesame seeds online (www.herbco.com, www.iherb.com) by the pound, and exponentially cheaper than at the supermarket or the health food store.

Roasting it is easy… When you get the package, empty the entire pound into a wok or a large frying pan. The pan or wok should be dry: no water, no oil. Stove-cook the seeds on medium heat, and occasionally stir them to allow even roasting. After a few minutes (3-5), the color of the seeds will probably not change noticeably. But you'll start to smell the wonderful aroma of roasted sesame. That's when the seeds are roasted. Turn off the stove, and let it cool down. Then, if the package you got the sesame in is re-zippable, you can put the roasted and cooled sesame seeds into the same package. Otherwise just find a jar or ziplock bag, and store the roasted sesame seeds in the refrigerator.

To Prepare Himalayan-Sesame Salt –

Grind ⅓ of a cup of sesame seed in a coffee grinder. Than, in a small bowl mix it with 1 cup of the unground sesame seed that you've roasted & stored. Add 3-5 tablespoons of Himalayan salt. Mix everything so the ingredients are fairly uniformly distributed.

Pour some of it into an empty spice shaker that you've cleaned and dried for this purpose. You can also use parmesan-shaker, but those don't have a cap. I like putting using something with a cap, so as to seal the flavor lemon of the sesame.

Store the rest in a ziplock bag in the refrigerator.

Health Benefits –

Sesame seed – rich in many minerals, including copper, magnesium & calcium. Copper is known to reduce some of the pain and swelling of rheumatoid arthritis. Magnesium supports vascular and respirator health, not to mention helps prevent migraines. Calcium helps prevent colon cancer, osteoporosis, migraine, and PMS.

Himalayan salt has tons of health benefits, including – regulating water content in the body; helping balance cell pH; promoting blood-sugar health; helping absorption of food particles in the digestive trace; supporting respirator & sinus health; regulating sleep; supporting bone health; promoting vascular health; and even supporting your libido, according to some online resources (http://products.mercola.com/himalayan-salt/).

Tahini Recipe:

Tahini is one food item that can absolutely make vegetables fun. If you make it as a thick pasty dip, than dipping celery, carrot, and cucumber sticks in it will give you motivation to eat your veggies, just because the dip is so good. I literally have tahini cravings, and it drives me to eat more raw veggies every time. If you dilute some of the tahini with more water—to the point that it has a more watery consistency, it can absolutely serve as a salad dressing.

Ingredients –

1 cup – raw Tahini paste, which is just sesame paste, preferably organic non-hulled
⅓-½ cup – water – depending on the consistency you want
½ head of garlic (at least!), preferably organic
½-¾ cup of chopped parsley (preferably organic Italian parsley)
Juice from ½-1 organic Lemon

3-4 pinches of Himalayan or sea salt – according to your taste
5-7 pinches of Fresh ground pepper – according to your taste
A tiny touch of cayene pepper
1-3 teaspoons of olive oil

How to make –

Put all the ingredients in the food processor and mix. It should come out flavorful & pasty. If it comes out too watery, add raw Tahini. If it comes out too pasty add either water or lemon juice, depending on the taste. It should have enough garlic, parsley, salt & pepper to make it very richly flavorful.

Health Benefits –

Tahini is very healthy for you. Since it's made out of sesame seed, it has plenty of protein and iron. Sesame seeds are also a great source of manganese, copper (relieves rheumatoid arthritis), calcium (helps prevent colon cancer, osteoporosis, migraine & PMS), magnesium (supports vascular & respiratory health & prevents migraines), phosphorus, vitamin B1, zinc (helps bone mineral density) & fiber, all of which are important to our health. Sesame also has two unique substances called Sesamin & Sesamolin, which lower cholesterol, increase vitamin E, and prevent high blood pressure.

Homemade Hummus:

Hummus is another one of those dips that, in moderation (it is not calorie-free), can make your veggies much more fun.

Ingredients –

About 1½ cups of organic dry garbanzo beans – to yield at least 2 cups of cooked ones.
1 cup of raw tahini paste (just the non-spiced raw sesame paste)
¾ a cup of fresh water
10 garlic cloves
3 teaspoons of fresh squeezed lemon
About 1 teaspoon of Himalayan or sea salt
About 2 teaspoons of fresh ground pepper
4 tablespoons of olive oil
An almost unnoticeably tiny sprinkle of cayenne or chili pepper

Pre-Preparation Soaking & Cooking –

The day before you plan to make the hummus, soak the dry garbanzo beans in water overnight, such that the beans are covered by at least three inches of water. If you change the water every few hours, it will reduce the gaseous effects of the hummus.

The next day, pour out the soaking water, and cook the beans in fresh water for a few hours until the beans are soft. If you own a pressure-pot, the cooking time is reduced to about 1 hour.

<u>Preparation</u> –

Preparation is easy. Just put all the ingredients in a food processor, and mix.

Notice that after soaking and cooking, the 1½ cup of garbanzo beans that you've started with is now at least 2½ cups. You need 2 cups of cooked garbanzo beans to make the hummus. Leave the rest aside, in case you've added too much water or too much tahini, and need to add some garbanzo bean to even out the recipe. Any remaining cooked garbanzo beans are good for a few things: you can sprinkle salt, pepper, and a little paprika on them and serve them warm as a snack. If you have a lot of extra, you can put it in a Ziploc bag and freeze it for next hummus batch. Or you can add them to a salad, or any veggie recipe to spice it up and give it an oomph of fun and flavor.

After you first mix the ingredients in the food processor, stop and taste. If the mixture tastes too bland, add salt and pepper. You might also consider adding a clove or two of garlic. If the mixture is too dry and hard to blend, add some water. If you've added plenty of salt, pepper, and garlic, and the flavor is still not jumping at you… and you feel like something is missing, it's probably a little lemon. Squeeze some more lemon and taste. If it's not too lemony, you can add some of the garbanzo beans you've set on the side, and some raw tahini.

If you've come up with gigantic amounts of hummus that neither you nor your family can finish in a while, no worries. Put the access in a freezable container, and freeze it. I like to put about a pint in the fridge, and put the rest in pint-size freezable containers in the freezer. That way, I can defrost only one pint at a time, and have fresh hummus for a while.

Mediterranean Eggplant Dip:

This eggplant dip is one of the most wonderful additions to vegetable. It's wonderful because it adds very few calories to your meal, and at the same time adds tons of flavor, and quite literally makes you want to eat your vegetables. Steamed broccoli, cauliflower, or asparagus are no longer boring when you put this eggplant dip on top. And since the dip has very few calories, you can add heaps of it to your meal.

<u>Ingredients</u> –

2-3 large eggplants
5-6 large garlic cloves (or more…)
2-3 tablespoons light mayonnaise (I like to use low-fat vegan mayo- it stays fresh longer)
Sea salt & fresh ground pepper – as required for taste

Instead of mayo, you can also use some of the Tahini sip you've made in the recipe above, which gives it more of a Mediterranean taste.

How To Make –

Use a fork to gently punch some holes through the eggplants. Barbeque the eggplants whole on the smallest flame possible for at least 30-45 minutes. During the cooking, turn them around at least once, so that they are done on all sides. The eggplants should get very soft, but not shrink much in size. If the peal gets overly dry, and the eggplants start shrinking in size, they are overdone.

Turn off the grill, and leave the eggplants to cool down in the still warm grill. That way they can continue to soften as they stand and cool down along with the grill. Let them cool down until you can touch them.

Don't forget to bless your space, your kitchen, and your hands with Divine Light-Love. Take a few deep breaths, do a few Kindness Movement, so that you feel freedom in your body and can imbue the food with high vibrational loving energy as you prepare it.

With your (cleansed) hands, break open each eggplant, and scoop the soft insides into a bowl. Crush the garlic into the mixture. Add the mayo, salt, and pepper into the mix. Now use a fork in one hand to mash the eggplants into a dip, and a knife in your other hand to cut any remaining long strips of eggplants. Taste it to see if more spices or mayo are needed. Cool down in the refrigerator.

Health Benefits –

Eggplants contain the compounds that has been shown to be strong antioxidants, protect cell membrane from damage, lower blood cholesterol while relaxing the walls of blood vessels & improving blood flow.

Homemade Marinara Sauce:

Ingredients –

7 large fresh organic tomatoes
2 tablespoons extra virgin olive oil
1 large onion
4 cloves of garlic
3 tablespoons of pesto
About ½ a cup of fresh organic Italian parsley
3-4 small branches of organic fresh oregano (or 2 teaspoons of dry oregano)
10 branches of fresh thyme
1 cup white wine
At least ½-1 teaspoon Himalayan or sea salt
At least 1 a teaspoon of fresh ground black pepper

Preparation –

Cut the tomatoes to quarters, and place them on a baking sheet lined with non-stick parchment paper (or a greased one), and roast them in the oven for about 10 minutes at 450°F. Then, allow the tomatoes to slightly cool. Once they are cool enough to touch, strip the skins right off the tomatoes.

While the tomatoes are roasting and then cooling, chop the parsley and the onion small. Mince the garlic real small. Strip the thyme and oregano leaves off the stems. Throw away the stems and wash the leaves in a small strainer. The thyme leaves are fine in their original size.

Don't forget to bless your space and put on inspiring music before you cook, and to do some Kindness Movement as you cook. If you are a reiki practitioner, mentally project or draw the Divine-Light and the Love symbols on your hands before touching the tomatoes. Otherwise, just envision Divine Light coming into your crown with every deep inhalation, being amplified at your heart center, and projecting out of the palms of your hands as you touch the tomatoes.

Peal the tomato skin off the tomato-quarters, and transfer them into a bowl. Crush-mash the tomatoes with your blessed hands. You can assist the process using a potato masher. Cut any remaining large chunks of tomatoes.

In a wok or a saucer pan, heat the olive oil in medium heat. Add the onion until yellow-translucent. Add the minced garlic and sauté for another minute. Add the chopped basil, parsley, oregano & thyme and let it get oiled and mixed with the onion and garlic for just a moment. Add the pesto, and mix in. Add the wine, mix it with the rest of the herbs, and let it come to a boiling. Let the mix simmer for a few minutes until the wine is reduced to half-a-cup. Now add the crushed tomatoes. Add the salt and pepper. Let the mixture simmer for about 2 hours at low heat.

Salads Don't Have to Be Boring

Here are some salad ideas, just to emphasize that salads don't have to be boring. I like to use different kinds of organic lettuce and leaf-mixes, and add to them ingredients that would add many different flavors and textures. For example, nuts add a crunchy texture to the salad, not to mention some healthy essential fatty acids (if it's the right nut), and some protein. Crumbles of feta, blue cheese, or even shaves of parmesano regioano add a salty flavor, as well as some complete protein. And a couple of tablespoons of Grapes, strawberries, candied cranberries, or even candied pecans add a sweet flavor that compliments the saltiness of the cheese, and offsets any pungent (spicy) flavored vegetable, which in turn will help you want to eat more salad. Not to say that any salad should be macrobiotically balanced to the 't'. I just find that it tastes better when the salad has different flavors and textures, which are balanced right.

Here are just a few suggestions and ideas for salads in which the different flavors and textures are balanced just right. Once you experiment with these salads and adapt them to your taste, you'll get the hang of it, and will want to keep creatively inventing more salads with a variety of flavors and textures that are balanced just right for you.

Vegetarian Health Bowl:

Organic spring mix, chopped tomatoes, chopped Persian cucumbers (they are more flavorful and can be eaten with the peal), carrot peels, organic grapes, almonds, and feta cheese. To give the salad a vegan source of complete protein, add some quinoa. If you want to make this salad non-vegetarian, it tastes great with cubes/chunks of grilled chicken in it.

Goes well with both the Vegan Aioli and the balsamic vinaigrette dressings above.

Spinach-Me Salad:

Organic baby spinach leafs, Gorgonzola, candied cranberries, and candied pecans

This goes well with balsamic vinaigrette dressing above.

Omega-3 Salad:

Organic spring mix, cherry tomatoes, walnuts, small pieces of smoked salmon, organic strawberries.

Goes well with Balsamic vinaigrette dressing above

Vegan Arugula Bliss:

Organic arugula, tiny carrot cubes, chopped tomatoes, candied cranberries, roasted salted soy nuts, avocado pieces.

This one can actually be just dressed with just olive oil, lemon, salt & pepper.

Asian Salad:

Strips of cabbage, carrot strips, peanut chips, canned (sweet) clementine pieces, salty cracker stripes (the Asian kind). For protein, add cubes of grilled chicken, or baked tofu cubes.

This salad is fantastic with the Tai-Peanut dressing above.

Israeli Salad:

Cucumbers and tomatoes chopped into small (less than ¼") cubes, small chopped Italian (or actually, it's Israeli-) parsley, and some small chopped onion. I myself do not like raw onion, so I make this salad with just cucumbers, tomatoes, and parsley, chopped small.

Traditionally, we do not put a real dressing—in the traditional sense—on this salad, but just dress it with a pinch of sea salt, some fresh ground pepper, a fresh squeeze of lemon, and some extra virgin olive oil. It is simple and yummy.

Tabouli Salad:

Ingredients ~

½ cup bulgur

¼ cup water

3-5 diced organic tomatoes

1 cup minced fresh parsley leaves

⅓ cup minced fresh peppermint leaves

2 garlic cloves (traditional tabouli is made with ½ a cup of chopped onion. I personally do not like fresh uncooked onion. So I've substituted garlic, and the recipe came out very good. If you like fresh onion, than add some fresh chopped onion to your liking.)

2-3 tablespoons extra virgin olive oil

2-3 tablespoons lemon juice, or to taste

3-4 pinches of Himalayan or sea salt

2-3 pinches of fresh ground pepper

Preparation ~

Pouring the water over the bulgur and letting it sit for a while makes the bulgur soft, as it absorbs the water. The original recipe called for ½ a cup of water, and waiting 20 minutes. And if you intend to eat/serve all of the tabouli within 1-3 hours of making it, than do that. In my experience, pouring only ¼ cup (instead of ½ a cup) of water over the ½-cup of bulgur, and waiting less time for absorption, will allow the bulgur to absorb the extra liquids coming out of the chopped tomatoes, thereby prolonging the freshness of the salad. That is why store-bought tabouli salad is soggy and watery by the time you eat it. This homemade tabouli will stay fresh for longer, since the half-dry bulgur will absorb the extra liquid in the tomatoes, and keep everything fresh longer.

So onto the bowl where the bulgur has absorbed the water, add the chopped tomatoes, parsley, mint, and press the garlic. Add salt, pepper, fresh-squeezed lemon, and olive oil to your liking. Bless the food with your intents, serve, and enjoy!

Health Benefits ~

Bulgur – is high in protein, low in fat and glycemic index, and contain potassium and iron.

Garlic – is a strong natural antibiotic, and helps manage blood pressure and cholesterol levels.

Parsley – has tons of vitamin C, lots of vitamin A (which is known for its vision benefits & can reduce risk of diabetes and atherosclerosis), and also some manganese, calcium, potassium, and antioxidants (flavonoids). Eaten aw, parsley is known to cleanse the blood, aid in digestion, and assist removing kidney stones.

Mint leaves – I can personally attest to their function in reducing headache, and their calming affect. In fact, I also make cold mint tea by just adding boiling water to fresh mint leaves, letting it soak for a while, and then chilling it. And it helps reduce my migraine pain, as well as calms me down every time. I found out online that peppermint also helps digestion, reduces nausea, reduces fever, and contains lots of important micronutrients, such as manganese, iron, magnesium, calcium, folate, potassium, vitamins A & C, and also the cholesterol-reducing omega-3.

Tomatocs – great source for vitamins C, A (antioxidants) & K, for folate and potassium, and for some important phytonutrients. Tomato skins has a nutrient called lycopene, which can improve bone mass, and reduce the risk of several types of cancers.

Lemon Juice – obviously has vitamin C, which is the best known immune booster and antioxidant. But it also helps cleanse the liver, assist digestion, relieve asthma and sore throat, and contains flavonoids (antioxidants), which helps fight fever.

Olive oil – is the most famous monounsaturated (omega-9) oil, which helps reduce the total cholesterol.

All these salads are obviously just examples – to give you an idea of how to add more flavors and textures to balance the tastes and enjoyment of the salad. Also, notice that with the exception of Israeli salad, I've added to each salad a source of protein, such as either a cheese, grilled chicken, soy or other nuts, or quinoa. And as you experiment with these and other salad ideas, notice how much fuller you feel after eating the salad when you balance all the macronutrients… that is – you get the oils in the dressings, log GI carbs in the vegetables themselves, and if you've added a grain, such as brown rice or quinoa, than you've also added some starchy carbs in a very balanced way. So if you add chicken chunks, some fun cheese, soy nuts, or even quinoa, you've also added some complete protein to the salad, which can make it a very satisfying complete meal.

Soups:

Soups are a fantastic diet food (lots of water & volume in the food make them very filling) that can tastes rich, even creamy, and be low in calories at the same time. I actually like to eat a large bowl of soup as a complete dinner. And you can make almost any combination vegetables that you have in your fridge, which are about to wilt down, into a wonderful thick and filling soup.

I always like to chop the vegetables and roots real small when I'm preparing the soup for two reasons: one is that when the roots and veggies are chopped small, they have more surface contact with the water (or milk if it is milk based), and thus are able to give more flavor to the broth. The second reason is that if you have large chunks or a whole celery root in your plate, you're not very likely to eat it. But if you have a few small cubes of celery roots, mixed in with small chunks of parsley root, turnip, potatoes and other vegetables, than all the root-cubes really look like cubes of potatoes, and you're more likely to eat them. And those roots have a great flavor and many health benefits.

Another point about soups that I'd like to make is: I usually make a large pot of soup when I have free time. After I've eaten a bowl of it for dinner, once it cools down, I divide the soup into many 2½-cup plastic containers, and freeze them. Then when I make a different soup I do the same. My freezer is always rich with soups and other yummy homemade dishes. So when I'm tired or just not in the mood to cook, but very much in the mood for a hot home cooked meal, it's easy to take it out of the freezer and warm it up. You just run some warm water over the closed container, then open it and separate the frozen soup from the container, put the frozen soup-block in a pan with a few tablespoons of water, and warm it on low heat until it boils.

Here are the three soups that I've become famous for amongst my friends and family members…

Low-Fat Creamy Tomato-Basil:

Most soups that proclaim to be creamy use heavy whipping cream or half-and-half to achieve the creaminess. In this recipe, I've achieved creaminess by adding some potatoes and other vegetables, and blending it in the food processor after it is cooked. The soup is more orange than red in color because of it. But it is very yummy… and low-fat, I might add!

Ingredients –

4 tablespoons of extra virgin olive oil, preferably organic
½ a large onion or 1 small onion, preferably organic
5 large garlic cloves, preferably organic
7 large tomatoes, preferably organic
7 large basil leaves, preferably organic
2 small to medium potatoes, preferably organic
2 carrots, preferably organic
1 large parsley root, preferably organic
3 stalks of celery, preferably organic
About 10 stalks of parsley, preferably organic
About 3 cups of low fat milk (I prefer low fat goat milk)
Several dashes of Himalayan or sea salt, to your taste
Fresh ground pepper to your taste

Preparation –

Chop the onions and garlic. Mince the garlic. Chop the basil into fairly small strips. Chop the tomatoes and the rest of the vegetables into medium-small cubes, and the parsley into small pieces.

In a pot, sauté the onion on low heat until golden-transparent. Add the garlic and sauté for another minutes or so. Add the basil and blend it all for a few seconds so that the olive oil absorbs the flavor and aroma of the onion, garlic, and basil. Than add the tomato chunks, and sauté them for a few extra minutes while blending, until they begin to juice a little. Add the rest of the vegetables. Blend for a few seconds. Then add the milk. If the milk doesn't quite cover the vegetables, add some more, or add some water. There should be enough liquid in the pot to cover the chopped vegetables, plus ¼-½ an inch. Add salt and pepper, boil it, and let it simmer for 30-45 minutes.

When the vegetables are very soft, and the mixture smells and tastes good, turn off the stove. Let it cool for a few minutes. Then transfer the soup into a blender or a food processor, and blend/mix it until it's a creamy paste. If your food processor/blender is small, you can transfer a little bit at a time.

Ladle into a soup bowl, garnish with a few fresh parsley leaves that you left aside for that purpose, and serve with joy.

Vegan Vegetable Soup:

<u>Ingredients</u> ~

1 large onion
7 garlic cloves
2 tablespoons of extra virgin olive oil
1 package of Italian parsley
2 large parsley roots
1 celery root
1 rutabaga root or orange beet root
3-5 large carrots
Optional: about an inch of fresh ginger root
Also optional: 1 package of organic hard tofu + 3-5 tablespoons of soy sauce
3 medium potatoes
1-2 teaspoons of Himalayan or sea salt

<u>Preparation</u> ~

Chop the onion, garlic, and parsley into tiny pieces. Chop the rest of the vegetables into cubes no more than the size of your fingertip. If you're adding ginger root, chop that into tiny pieces too. If this soup is going to be a complete meal for you, than you should add the tofu, in which case, one of the first things you should do is cut the tofu into cubes, add the soy sauce to it, and let it absorb the flavor of the soy sauce.

Sauté the onion with olive oil for a few minutes until golden-transparent. Add the garlic and sauté for another minute. If you're adding ginger root, sauté that also with the onion and garlic for a minute or two, so that the olive oil would absorb its taste too. Add the parsley and other vegetables, and blend in so that everything is mixed in with the sautéed onion and garlic olive oil. Add water to cover the vegetables, plus 1 inch, and let it boil.

If you're adding tofu, than in a frying pan (separate from the soup pot), put a little bit of olive oil and fry the tofu until it is brown, crisp, and yummy to eat on its own. Than add that to the soup, which should be almost boiling by now. Add salt and pepper to the soup. Reduce the heat, and let it simmer for at least an hour, maybe more, until the vegetables are very soft, and the water in the soup tastes flavorful.

Meatball & Potato Stew-Soup:

This recipe is the my crown jewel of recipes… it is the most healing food that I can share with you. I have no idea why, but this soup actually heals my migraines, soothes me, and makes me feel nurtured and beloved. And the funny thing is that it is not a recipe that I've learnt from my grandma or that has any nurturing childhood memory for me. It's a recipe that has somehow evolved over the years through experimentation in the kitchen, just like you'll probably take my basic ideas, change them to suit your taste and needs, and let them evolve into your own wonderful creations.

Ingredients –

2 lbs. ground organic lean beef, hormones & additives-free, all natural
2 large organic onions
2 large packages (which is at least 2-3 cups) of organic Italian parsley
1½ organic garlic heads
5-6 large zucchini
2-3 organic large parsley root
1 organic celery root
4 large organic carrots
4-5 stalks of organic celery
3 medium organic potatoes
1-2 cups of organic Brussels sprouts (baby cabbages)
About 1 cup's worth of organic cauliflower
Optional: 3 fresh organic corns on a cob
About 4 teaspoons of extra virgin olive oil
A dash of cumin
2 dashes of allspice
3-4 bay leaves
About 3-4 teaspoons of fresh ground pepper
About 3-5 teaspoon of Himalayan or sea salt

Preparation –

Now before you prepare this soup, you absolutely have to make sure that you cleanse and bless your space as you've learnt to do in Chapter 10 in the section on Clearing & Protection. And it is essential that you do "Safta's Pre-Cooking Meditation" I've detailed in Chapter 4. If you are a reiki practitioner, you know what to do to add Divine Love-energy into your cooking. Now the preparation…

Chop the garlic, onion, and parsley into tiny pieces. It is actually better to do this in the food processor. Just chop the garlic and onion separate from the parsley, and make sure that they do not become a liquid—that the pieces are actually minced pieces of onion & garlic, and tiny leaf-pieces of parsley.

In a bowl, put the beef and make a receptive indentation in it. Put into it half of the minced onion & garlic, and half of the parsley. Add the cumin, allspice, 1½ teaspoon of the fresh ground pepper, and about 1-1½ teaspoons of the salt. Use your pure intent to bless your hands with Divine Love-Light, and knead it all into a uniform mix. Knead the meat into medium-small meatballs, humming songs and chants that make your heart sing. Make sure that you mentally thank the animal for its sacrifice, aim to release it (and the meat) from any energy of suffering, and imbue the meat with Divine Love-Light that will be palpable to all who eat it. Set the meatballs in the fridge while you chop the veggies.

Chop the rest of the roots and vegetables into cubes of ½"- ¾" size. If you're adding corns, use a knife to cut-shave the corn kernels from the cobs. All of this chopping will take a while. So make sure there is some uplifting music in the background, and do plenty of Kindness Movements for yourself, so that you keep your body free and relaxed, and your spirits high.

Now, in a huge pot, sauté the other half of the minced onion-garlic with about half of the olive oil for a few minutes, until the onion looks transparent. Add the vegetables and root cubes, and mix for a few seconds so that they all have a little coat of the garlic-onion olive oil. Add water to cover the vegetables + about 2 inches, and bring to a boil. This should take a while.

While you're waiting for the soup-water to boil, fry the meatballs in a separate frying pan. Use only about 1-2 teaspoons of olive oil, and don't cook them all the way. You are just trying to brown them on the outside some, so that they become cohesive and not crumble in the soup.

Once the water is boiling, add the browned meatballs, lower the heat, and let it simmer for at least 1½ hour. Once the water boils, add the bay leaves. Halfway through the cooking, add the salt and pepper to your liking. Remember that the amount of salt and pepper that I gave above are just approximate. I don't know how salty or spicy you like your soup. So it's better to put less than the amount I've written, taste the soup, and then add more according to your taste.

Pumpkin Ginger Soup

Ingredients –

1 large organic onion
3 tbsp. organic coconut oil
1 medium/semi-large size organic pumpkin
3 huge organic carrots
4 small (or 2-3 large) organic sweet potatoes
3-4 stalks of organic celery
2 cans (about 2 cups) of organic natural coconut milk
2" of organic fresh ginger root
Sea-salt & fresh pepper as needed for personal taste
Cinnamon – about 1 tsp.
Nutmeg – about ½ a tsp.
2-3 tbsp. organic raw honey
Pumpkin seeds & cinnamon for decoration

Preparation –

Bless your space, relax the body with Kindness Movement, and put on some uplifting music before you start cooking.

Chop the pumpkin into cubes, and then peal each cube using a knife and cutting board, and preferably cutting gloves to protect your hands from getting cut. Cut the celery, and then peal and cut the carrots and sweet potatoes into cubes. Place the reiki symbols on your hands, and then use your hands to reiki the ingredients while you blend all the cubes in a bowl.

Chop the onion into small pieces. Then, in a medium size pot (about 4 quarts), melt the coconut oil, add the onion pieces, and sauté the onion until transparent-yellow.

Add the pumpkin, carrots, sweet potatoes and celery cubes, and let them sauté for about a minute. Then mix everything, so that the vegetables get coated with the melted coconut oil, and well mixed with the transparent-golden onion pieces.

Add the coconut milk, and as much water as would just cover the vegetables. The amount of vegetables that you have should pretty much fill the pot. The water and coconut milk just fills the spaces in between the vegetable cubes. So if you pot is bigger, than you need to multiply the amount of vegetables.

Grate the ginger (no need to peal), and add it to the soup. Add the cinnamon and nutmeg. The amount of cinnamon and nutmeg that I've written is approximate. You'll need to eyeball how much of them is enough for you. Add salt and pepper to your taste. And let it all cook for a while, until the vegetables are soft. You can stick a fork in them to check that they are soft.

When the vegetables are soft, transfer a portion of the soup at a time to your blender, and blend everything until the entire soup is a creamy mash. Add enough honey to achieve a taste that is salty yet sweet & to your liking.

Ladle the soup into bowls, decorate with cinnamon & pumpkin seeds, and lovingly serve it to your guests.

Low-Fat Clam Chowder Recipe:

Ingredients –

1 cup of minced organic onion
2 large organic garlic cloves
3 tablespoons of extra virgin olive oil
1 cup of diced organic celery
2 cups of small-cubed organic potatoes
1 cup of diced organic carrots
1 cup of chopped organic Italian parsley
3 (6.5 oz.) cans of clams
3-4 cups of low-fat milk
1 tablespoon of organic fresh thyme leaves (stripped from the stems)
2 bay leaves
4-5 drops of Worcestershire sauce
Himalayan or sea salt – to taste (about 1-2 teaspoons)
Fresh black pepper – to taste
3-4 tablespoons of organic unbleached flour
Vegan bacon bits for decoration

<u>Preparation ~</u>

Chop/mince the garlic and onion real small. Put the olive oil in the pot where you're going to cook the soup. Add to it the minced onion and garlic. Cover, and let it stand (so that the olive oil can absorb the taste and aroma of the onions and garlic) with the fire turned off, while you chop the rest of the veggies. Then chop the rest of the veggies into small cubes. Open the cans of clams, and cut the clams into quarters. Save the liquids.

Turn on the stove on medium-to-low heat, and start sautéing the garlic and onion. When the onion turns transparent, add the diced/cubed celery, carrots, and potatoes. Let the veggies sauté with the olive oil, garlic and onion for a minute or two, while stirring it occasionally. Then add the cut clams to the sautéing veggies, and stir some. Let that sauté for another minute.

Add the milk, Italian parsley, and the liquids from 1-2 of the clam cans. Add the thyme and the bay leaves. Stir everything. Increase the heat until it boils. Make sure the milk doesn't overspill. Then reduce the heat again, and let it cook for about 20-25 minutes. While it's cooking, add salt, pepper, and the Worcestershire sauce to taste.

When the veggies are soft, put the flour in a small bowl, then add half a ladle of the boiling soup liquids at a time into the four bowl, and stir. Stir very well, so that the flour and liquids in the bowl become uniform. Initially they'll become a paste, and then a more liquidy cream. At that point, add it back into the soup and stir well. Fish the soup for chunks of flour that are unblended; then crush them and blend back into the soup liquids. Do this until the soup has no flour chunks, but its liquids are creamy.

Serve the soup with vegan bacon bits on top. You can add regular bacon bits, but the vegan ones are leaner, and are pretty tasty.

Veggie-Loaded Recipes

This section by no means includes all the main dishes you can have in the Zohar Kindness Diet. Rather, it includes just a few recipes of dishes I regularly make, which will give you a better idea of how to replace unkind ingredients with kind ones, while retaining the indulgent flavor of the original recipe, and perhaps even improving it. You see, now that I'm used to kindness foods, trying to eat unkind foods makes me feel nauseated, heavy, and in most cases unfulfilled (digestively). And as you'll see, there is nothing wrong with indulging in yummy foods, even deserts.

First, since vegetables is the main food that you'll be adding to your plate as part of the Zohar Kindness Diet, I'd like to give you a few veggie recipes just to impress upon you that vegetables are not boring, and can actually be extremely tasty. Pay more attention here not to which vegetables I named in each recipe, but more to the method of preparation.

Italian Style Grilled Vegetables:

This dish is extremely easy to make. In the ingredients, you can replace the vegetables with any other, or use just whichever vegetables from this list that you happen to have in your fridge. For the Zohar Kindness Diet, use an amount of these vegetables that will cover half the plate and amount to at least two cups of vegetables for each person.

<u>Ingredients</u> –

Large Portobello mushrooms
Zucchini
Carrots
Onion
Eggplant
Tomato
Radicchio
Balsamic Vinaigrette dressing you made from the recipe above
Optional: a teaspoon or two or the pesto you made
Optional: A touch of Toscana, Swiss, or parmesan cheese to melt on top

<u>Preparation</u> –

Wash and slice the vegetables into slices. If you're including tomato and radicchio, than cut them in half of quarter. Pour a little of the vinaigrette dressing into a small bowl, and using a brush, brush some vinaigrette on each slice of vegetables. For radicchio, place it on a plate with the open (cut) part facing up, and pour a couple of tablespoons of the dressing into in between the layers of the radicchio. If you're grilling Portobello mushrooms, you should place them on the plate and on the grill face up, and put the dressing in them. Tomatoes could use a teaspoon or two of pesto spread on the cut part. Let everything sit for a while (30 minutes if you're not in a rush to eat) while you prepare some of your other meal items.

Then, place the vegetables into one of those nets that are made for barbequing fish or veggies, and grill them in medium heat for a few (probably not more than 5) minutes on each side. Sticking a fork inside, the veggies should be soft inside and browned on the outside. Carrots should be halfway soft and halfway crunchy. You can add a little more dressing once you're done grilling. Or instead, you can place a few thin slices of cheese on top of the veggies in the last 1-2 minutes of grilling. The cheese will melt, and add wonderful flavor to the veggies, while adding minimal fat calories (unless you're drowning the veggies in cheese, which you shouldn't, because it'll take away from the wonderful flavor of the veggies).

Grill-Steamed Savory Veggies:

This is one of the quickest, easiest, and at the same time yummiest ways to prepare vegetables.

<u>Ingredients Per Person</u> –

2 cups of: baby broccoli, asparagus, cauliflower or any other vegetable
2-3 cloves of garlic
Dash of Himalayan salt

Fresh ground pepper

½ a teaspoon Herbs De Provence

½ a teaspoon of extra virgin olive oil

1+ tablespoon of water

Optional: 2-3 branches of fresh oregano, thyme, or other savory herb you currently have

Optional: Teaspoon of pesto

Preparation –

Wash the vegetables, and lay them wet in a sheet of aluminum foil big enough to wrap around them. Mince the garlic and sprinkle it on top. Add the salt, pepper, and Herbs De Provence, If you have any fresh herbs that you're adding to the recipe, wash them and strip the leaves off the stems. Throw the stems away and sprinkle the leaves on the veggies. If you're adding pesto, put it on top of the vegetables.

Now, bless your hands with loving intent. Add the olive oil and water to the vegetables. And with your blessed hands, blend everything so that the spices, herbs, oil, pesto and water will be evenly distributed amongst the vegetables.

Fold the aluminum foil in half, folding/closing everything inside it, and where the two edges of foil meet at the top, fold those edges two or three times in to completely seal the vegetable mix in. Fold the side edges of the foil too at least twice. You want to make sure that the liquids are trapped in and can create steam, because if the liquids leak out, than the veggies will be too dry.

If you're turning on the barbeque to grill fish, chicken, or other stuff, you can throw the sealed aluminum foil with the veggies in an area of the grill that is not too hot. If you're barbequing this alone, do so in medium flame. Otherwise, bake it in the oven at about 325°F. Baking/grilling time here is about 3 minutes on each side, meaning that after 3 minutes you turn the whole aluminum foil package over and grill it for another 3 minutes.

When you get the package out of the grill, be careful. Hot steam will be escaping out of the package. So don't stick your nose right in there and burn yourself. And use some utensils to open it.

Sautéed Spinach:

This is a recipe you'll probably find in just about any Italian restaurant. It is very tasty, and is actually surprisingly easy to make at home.

Ingredients For Each Person –

4+ cups of fresh organic baby spinach leaves

1-2 teaspoon of extra virgin olive oil

3+ cloves of organic garlic

Dash or two of Himalayan or sea salt

Optional: 2 tablespoons of home roasted organic sesame seeds

Wash the spinach and dry it thoroughly. If you have one of those lettuce spinners that dry the leaves with centrifugal force, that's best to use. Otherwise put it in a strainer, and shake the strainer up and down quite a few times to drain all the water out. If there is any water left in the spinach when you cook, it'll make the recipe too soggy. So it's very important to drain all the water. After you shake the strainer quite a few times, turn the leaves over, pat them with dry paper towel, and then shake the strainer some more… if you have a little bit of time before the meal, you can either wrap the spinach in a clean dry towel and let them dry for a while, or you can leave them in the strainer to let all the water drip out.

Mince the garlic into real small pieces, or press it. In a wok, sauté the garlic in the olive oil for about a minute in medium heat. Add the spinach, and sauté it while stirring. DO NOT add salt yet. You're looking for the spinach to get warm and become kind of a glossy beautiful green, not get soggy. The spinach will reduce in volume as it cooks. Cooking time is no more than 2 minutes. Once you've turned off the heat, add the salt and sesame seeds, and serve.

Baked Cheesy Veggies:

I came up with this recipe quite recently, one evening when I was looking for a fresh new non-boring ways to cook asparagus. So in the ingredients, I've named specifically asparagus as the vegetable that's being cooked. But this recipe works quite well for baby broccoli, and many other vegetables. By adding the cheeses, it's true I've added a few fat-calories. But I figured – the number of fat-grams added is minimal, compared to the added flavor, and the nurturing feeling that cheese gives us all…

Ingredients for Each Person ~

1 package (which is about 1 lb.) of asparagus
2-3 teaspoons of ricotta cheese
2-3 garlic cloves
3 tablespoons of spring water
1-2 teaspoons of Parmigiano Regiano cheese
Dash of Himalayan or sea salt
Fresh ground pepper
Optional: Italian spices or Herbs De Provence
Optional: a few drops of extra virgin olive oil

Method of Preparation ~

Wash the asparagus (or other veggie you're using). Mince the garlic, or crush it in a garlic press. Lay the asparagus in a baking dish just big enough to lay the asparagus stalks. You can use a Pyrex or an aluminum dish. I usually just use aluminum foil, and bend its edge-corners together to create a dish just big enough to lay the asparagus stalks. Then add the minced garlic, spring water, and ricotta. If you're adding Italian spice mix or Herbs De Provence, this is the time to sprinkle them on top.

Bless your hands with intents to conduct through them and imbue the food with Divine Light-Love. Then use your blessed hands to gently and lovingly blend all the food ingredients so that the little cheese that you've used is spread all over the dish. If it's not enough, add a few drops of olive oil. But usually the water that you've added will help the cheese spread evenly through the dish. Sprinkle the Parmesan cheese on top.

Cover the dish with another sheet of aluminum foil (sorry mother-Nature), and bake it at 325°F for about 15-20 minutes.

Eggplants in a Wok:

If you've got some eggplants, and you're lazy, but feel like indulging a bit, this is your recipe…

Ingredients ~

Eggplant
½-1 teaspoon of extra olive oil
2-4 cloves of Garlic
4 branches of fresh thyme or a few dashes of Herbs De Provence
Dash or two of Himalayan salt

Method of preparation ~

Wash and cut the eggplants into slices, and then cut each slice into cubes. Put some salt on the eggplants and use your hands to gently spread the salt all over the eggplant cubes. Put it aside and let it absorb the salt while you deal with the thyme and garlic. Mince the garlic or crush it in a garlic-press. Wash the thyme and strip the leaves away from the stems.

In a wok, sauté the garlic with the olive oil in low-medium heat for a minute or two. Add the salted eggplants, and the thyme, and/or Herbs De Provence. Sauté/fry the eggplants on low-medium heat until they extract some liquids and are soft, and slightly browned.

Eggplant Salad:

The core of this recipe (without the bell peppers) was passed onto him by his mother, and is an old Tripoli recipe. He added to it bell peppers, which he makes in a pretty unique way.

Ingredients ~

3 large eggplants
3 dashes of Himalayan or sea salt
2-3 teaspoons of extra virgin olive oil
1 yellow bell pepper
1 red bell pepper

4 garlic cloves
1 package of 7 stalks of chives
½ a cup of cilantro or Italian parsley
A few dashes of fresh ground pepper
2-3 tablespoons of white wine or white balsamic vinegar
2-3 teaspoons of extra virgin olive oil

<u>Preparation</u> ~

Wash and slice the eggplants into slices. Rub the salt on both sides of each slice, and set the eggplant slices aside in a covered strainer for a few hours. This will allow the eggplants to absorb the salty taste, and also to juice out some access liquids without over drying.

Then, bake the bell peppers whole at 350-400°F until they are soft, and golden-brown, but not burnt. Once the bell peppers are out of the oven, put them in a Tupperware or closed Pyrex dish, close the lid tightly, and wrap the dish in a towel to lock in the steam, for at least a ½-hour or an hour.

At some point later that day, after the eggplants have absorbed the salt and dried some, and after the bell peppers have softened in the towel-wrapped Tupperware, it's time to start frying or baking the eggplants. If you're frying/sautéing them, than drip just a little bit of olive oil into the frying pan. If you want to bake the eggplants, than brush or spray them with a thin coat of olive oil, and then bake them at about 300°F for 15-20 minutes. You might try both ways, and see which ones you like best. The eggplants should be fried/baked until they are soft and golden in color. Then let the eggplants cool.

Meanwhile, open up the bell pepper Tupperware, and peel the thin skin off of them. It should peel off real easily at this point. Cut out the seeds, and cut the peppers into strips. Mince the garlic or crush it in a garlic press. Wash and cut the chives and cilantro (or parsley).

Once the eggplants have cooled some, place them in a large bowl or a Pyrex dish. I've actually seen Eli arrange them nicely in a 9"x12" Pyrex dish. Then add the strips of peeled-skinned bell peppers. Sprinkle the chives, cilantro (or parsley), and garlic evenly on the eggplants and peppers. Grind fresh pepper over everything. Drip the vinegar and olive oil over everything evenly. Chill in the refrigerator or eat warm

Vegetable and tofu stir-fry:

This stir-fry tastes wonderful over a little bit of brown-and-wild rice, and makes a complete meal. When I haven't made this recipe for a while, I actually crave it, which I can't decide if it's because of how wonderful it tastes or because it is so rich with kindness food ingredients. Either way, try it and you'll see for yourself.

<u>Ingredients</u> ~

1 package of hard or semi-hard organic tofu
2-4 carrots
2-3 stalks of celery

1+ cup of cabbage or Brussels sprouts
2 cups of bean sprouts
Optional: mushrooms (any kind you feel inspired to use, that is available fresh)
1 small onion
2-3 teaspoons of extra virgin olive oil (or substitute sesame oil if you want an Asian taste)
7-10 garlic cloves
Ginger root – about the length of your thumb
6-7 teaspoons of low-sodium soy sauce (with no MSG and no unpronounceable ingredients!)
Optional: 2-3 tablespoons of home-roasted sesame seeds
Optional: 3-4 tablespoons of pine nuts

Preparation ~

First, cut the tofu into small squares, and place them in a bowl. Drip on top of them about 3 teaspoons of the soy sauce, such that the soy sauce would be distributed evenly over the tofu squares. Small-grate a little bit of the ginger root, and press 1-2 garlic cloves onto the tofu. Set it aside to absorb the tastes. Mid way through the process of washing and chopping the vegetables, gently blend the tofu so that the soy sauce, ginger & garlic are again distributed evenly around it.

In a large strainer, wash and chop the carrots, celery, and cabbage (or Brussels sprouts) either into thin slices or strips that look good to your creative senses. Wash the bean sprouts and blend it into the other veggies in the strainer. Chop the onion however small you want it. Mince the garlic real small. Wash and cut the ginger root into tiny strips the size of matches.

In a wok, start sautéing the onion for a couple of minutes. Add the minced garlic and strips of ginger, and sauté for 2-3 more minutes. Add the veggie mix from your strainer—the carrots, bean sprouts, cabbage strips, celery, and mushrooms. Let it all sauté, while mixing it every once in a while.

Meanwhile in a separate frying pan, use about 1 teaspoon of olive oil (or sesame oil if that's what you're using) to fry the tofu. Add to the frying pan all the soy sauce, garlic and ginger that it was sautéed in. Fry it on medium-high flame until the liquids have burnt off and the tofu is browned and flavorful. Add those to the wok.

When the vegetables in the wok start softening, secreting fluids, and reducing, add soy sauce to salt it to your liking. The vegetables should not become overly soggy. Cook them only until they are half-soft, but retain a little bit of their original crunchiness. After you turn off the stove is the time to add pine nuts, sesame seeds, or both, if you're going to add them.

Zohar's Fabu-Soufflé:

Soufflé is a food that most people definitely associate with lots of calories and lots of fat-grams. The original soufflé recipe does call for ½ a cup of butter, 2 cups of Gouda, cheddar or other full-fat cheese, plus the parmesan that goes on top, not to mention full eggs (not just egg whites). Doing the Zohar Kindness Diet means that you do not deprive yourself of indulgent recipes, provided you can make the alterations to render them kinder to yourself. Here, the alterations I've made was to use hazelnut oil (omega-9) instead of butter, and use less of it; use only the egg whites; spike the recipe with lots of baby spinach, mushrooms, and parsley; use low-fat cheese; and reduce the amount of cheese in the recipe. The soufflé still tastes pretty heavenly, and after I've gotten used to eating leaner foods, it is much easier on the stomach to digest. So here it is:

Ingredients –

5 tablespoons hazelnut oil
1 good size organic onion
5 cloves of organic garlic
1 cup of organic baby spinach
½ cup of mushrooms
5 tablespoons flour
½ cup chopped organic Italian parsley
1¼-cup low fat milk
½ cup of grated low-fat feta
⅓ cup of parmigiano reggiano cheese
5 eggs whites
Himalayan or sea salt – as needed
Fresh ground pepper – as needed
1 tablespoon of Herbs De Provence spice

Making The Soufflé –

Chop the onion small. Press-crush the garlic. In a large frying pan or a wok, sauté the onion and garlic until golden. Add the spinach, and sauté it while stirring for only a minute. Than add the mushrooms and sauté until soft. Add the flour mix it into the veggies, so that it's evenly distributed, and slightly absorbed by the juices of the vegetables. Then add the milk and stir it in so that it's uniform, meaning – there are no moguls or chunks of flower. Add the parsley and mix it in. Add salt, pepper, and the Herbs De Provence, and mix them in. Turn off the stove and let the mixture cool some.

Grate the cheeses and set them aside. Oil a 9"x9" baking Pyrex or several smaller individual baking dishes, and set aside.

Separate the eggs, and set the yokes aside. With a mixer, beat the egg whites with a dash of salt into hard white foam.

As for the yokes, if you want, you can add one of them to the vegetable mix after it cools down some. The rest of the yokes, you can either toss them out, or use them for something else. If you are adding any egg-yoke in, than add a few spoons of the somewhat cooled veggie mix into a little bowl containing the egg yoke, and mix it to make sure that the yoke doesn't harden from the heat of the mix. Then add the content of this little bowl into the veggie mix.

Now add the veggie mixture into the egg-white foam. Add the grated feta cheese. Now gently fold everything into a somewhat uniform mix, being careful not to break the egg-foam too much. Pour it into the oiled Pyrex dish(s). Sprinkle the Parmesan on top. And bake at 350°F for 30-35 minutes. Let it cool down some. And enjoy without guilt.

Lean Proteins

OK, so now that I've turned on your digestive juices for how yummy vegetables can be, let's talk about lean proteins. And lean proteins do not have to be as lame as they may at first sound. Here are some recipes that will help awaken your creative juices, and give you some ideas on how to eat your old favorite foods – the kind way.

Barbecued Fish – Italian Style:

My all-time favorite recipe for fish is actually pretty easy to make. When I buy fresh fish, whether it be salmon or tilapia or any other fish—whether I'm going to freeze them or eat them that day—I immediately marinate them in the herbs and spices to let them absorb the taste. So if I'm going to freeze the fish, I put them in the spice-herb mix, separate each portion by plastic wrap, and then seal the package in a Ziplock bag and freeze it. That way, when I wish to cook fish, I can just separate however many portions as there are people I'm serving dinner to, and throw the fish on the grill. Simple. And I always have pre-marinated fish in my freezer, ready to become dinner at a moment's notice.

Ingredients For Two People –

1 lb. of salmon, tilapia, red snapper, or any other fresh fish you like
4 cloves of garlic
4 little branches of fresh thyme
Optional: 2-3 branches of fresh oregano, fresh savory, and/or fresh parsley
4 dashes of Herbs De Provence (or Italian herb mix)
4 dashes of fresh ground pepper
4 small dashes of Himalayan or sea salt
2-3 teaspoons of extra virgin olive oil

Preparation –

Wash the fish, and cut them into the right portions for two people. Wash the Styrofoam/plastic tray they came in, or find a plastic tray you'd be able to freeze them in. I usually save the trays of the baby broccoli that I buy at Trader Joe's for that purpose. That way, even if I buy fresh fish at the fish market, I have a tray to let them sit in.

Into a little bowl, press the garlic cloves. Wash and strip the thyme and other fresh herbs leaves off the stems. Discard the stems and add the leaves to the little bowl. Add the Himalayan salt, fresh ground pepper, and Herbs De Provence (or Italian herbs). Mix the ingredients well.

Bless your hands with intent of Divine Love-Light. Use your hands to rub the herb-spice mix you just made on both sides of the fish. Now, if you're freezing it, than separate each portion (or each slice) using plastic wrap, and seal everything tightly in a Ziplock bag.

If you're cooking the fish the same day, you may let them stand in the herb-spice marinate for several hours. Cook the fish just a few minutes before the rest of your meal is ready to eat.

Heat up your barbeque grill in medium heat. Place the fish on the grill and barbecue them for about 3-4 minutes each side. If it's tilapia or red snapper you're grilling, those are very delicate fish, and you may need to put them in one of those rectangle grilling baskets, so that you can turn them over.

Lightly Seared Tuna:

This recipe actually works well with swordfish also, and is very yummy.

Ingredients For Each Person ~

1 filet of sashimi-quality ahi tuna
Juice form ½ an orange
½ a teaspoon of organic raw honey (preferable orange-blossom honey)
½ a teaspoon of small-grated ginger
Fresh ground pepper
1-2 garlic cloves
1 teaspoon of organic natural soy sauce
A spray of sesame oil
A tablespoon of chopped chives or lemongrass for decoration

Preparation ~

Wash the tuna, and place it in a dish in which it could be marinated and set aside for a while.

Grate the ginger real tiny – so that the grated ginger is almost like a paste. Press the garlic. Sprinkle fresh ground pepper over both sides of the tuna. Use a teaspoon (or honey dripper) to drip a tiny (the thickness of the drizzle should be thinner than a match) drizzle of honey over the fish, such that it is distributed evenly. Now rub the grated ginger and the pressed garlic into the honey to distribute everything as evenly as possible on both sides of the tuna. Drizzle the orange juice and soy sauce on both sides of the fish. Spray sesame oil, or drizzle it on both sides of the fish. Let everything sit for at least a half-hour to absorb all these wonderful flavors.

Heat up your barbecue grill in high-heat. Then spray some extra oil on the area of the grill where you're about to put the tuna. Place the tuna there, and close the grill. Depending on the tuna's thickness, you should time no more than 1-2 minutes each side. I personally think that 2 minutes would be overcooking it. If the filet is an inch-thick, about 1½ minute each side is plenty. If you want, use a knife to make an incision and check how the inside is cooked. The cooked filet should be seared-browned on the outside, but raw (completely raw) in the inner third of it. Take it out of the grill, serve, and eat immediately as it is ready. If you don't serve/eat within a few minutes, the fish that is still hot out of the oven will continue to cook in its own heat for a while, and you'll lose the wonderful sashimi-style raw part in the middle. You can decorate with chives or lemongrass on top.

Blackened Sword Fish:

This recipe is as easy as they come. You don't even have to bother too much with the spices. You can just buy a spice mix for blackened fish.

Ingredients for two filets –

2 fresh swordfish filets
4 dashes of Chef Paul's "Fish Magic"
(or if you don't have that particular spice, mix some – garlic powder, onion powder, paprika, fresh ground black pepper, Himalayan salt, chili pepper, and a touch of chayenne pepper)
1-2 teaspoons of extra virgin olive oil
Optional: a few drops of lemon

Preparation –

Wash the fish and pat them dry with a paper towel. Rub the fish with olive oil and plenty of the spice mix, so that the spice mix and olive oil are evenly distributed on the fish. You may also drip a few drops of lemon if the fish smells too "fishy" to begin with. Cover or wrap, and let the fish stand at least a ½-hour to absorb the taste or the spices.

Heat up a dry skillet on medium-high heat. Let it heat up. A good measure of if it's hot enough, which you should exercise with extreme caution, is to put your hand 1½-2 inches above the skillet (but DO NOT TOUCH IT!). After two seconds the skillet should be too hot for you to bear, and you would have to withdraw your hand away. That's when you know the skillet is hot enough for you to put the fish.

Place the fish filets in the dry skillet, and cook them for a few minutes on each side. You can make an incision to make sure the fish is cooked all the way through.

Grilled Chicken:

As you might have learnt from the salad section, I always like to have cubes of grill chicken in my freezer. What I do is, usually as I buy the fresh chicken breast, I grill them, then cut them into cubes, and freeze them in a Ziploc bag, such that I can always grab a fistful of chicken cubes, heat them up real quick, and add them to my lunch salad. So here is how I prepare the grilled chicken…

Ingredients –

1 package (1+ lb.) of organic or otherwise all natural chicken breast
3-4 cloves of garlic

7 stalks of fresh thyme

Couple of dashes of fresh ground black pepper

Dash or two or Himalayan or sea salt

Optional: instead of thyme, you can add paprika, and the chicken gets a different flavor

1 teaspoon of extra virgin olive oil

Preparation ~

Cut the chicken breast into its two halves. Cut away all access fat and ligaments. Slice each half into two thinner slices. Crush the garlic onto the chicken. Add the salt, pepper and thyme leaves (stripped off their stems), or the paprika, if you're adding paprika instead. Drip the olive oil, and rub all the spices together so that they are evenly distributed.

Barbecue in medium heat for about 4 minutes each side. The chicken should be golden, and making an incision should reveal that it's white and cooked all the way through.

Eat as the protein portion of your dinner, or cut into cubes and freeze, or sprinkle over your salad now.

Chicken-~~fried~~ Baked Steak:

OK, this chicken tastes exactly like chicken-fried steak, except that it is not actually fried. But even if you were to serve this recipe to a child—and children are usually pretty picky when it comes to food—I guarantee that the child would not know that this is not actually fried. It's that yummy. And I've also replaced the breadcrumbs with wheat germ, which is healthier and more loaded with protein and other nutrients. So here it goes…

Ingredients ~

1 package (about 1+ lb.) of organic or all natural chicken breast

1 large (or two small) egg

1 teaspoon of pesto

2 dashes of Himalayan or sea salt

About 1 teaspoon of fresh ground black pepper

¾-1 cup of organic wheat germ (you may not use it all for this chicken package)

1 teaspoon of garlic powder

1-2 teaspoons of Herbs De Provence (or Italian seasoning mix)

Spray of olive oil

Preparation –

Again, wash and cut the chicken breast into two halves. Cut away all observable access fat and all ligaments. Slice each half of the breast into two thinner slices. You may actually have more than four slices, since each half of the breast may not cut so evenly. That's OK. It's all going to be very tasty.

In a medium bowl, beat the egg. You can add a few drops of water to help break the yoke. Add the pesto, a dash of salt, and the pepper into the egg. Put all the chicken slices in it to absorb the taste, while you prep the wheat germ.

In a large flat plate, mix the wheat germ with the garlic powder and Herbs De Provence, and mix them pretty well so that the garlic powder and herbs would be evenly distributed through the wheat germ.

Line a baking sheet with parchment paper and set on one side of your working space, so that it is conveniently accessible.

Now take each slice of chicken, making sure that it is well dipped in the spiced egg, and dip it in the wheat germ mix. Turn it to the other side, and make sure that it is well covered in wheat germ. Place it on the parchment papered baking sheet.

When all the chicken is double dipped (in egg and wheat germ, along with all of their spices), spray olive oil evenly on the upper side of the chicken. Bake at 350°F until the top part is golden-brown. Then take the chicken out of the oven for a minute. Turn each piece over to its other side, spray the new upper part with olive oil, and put it back in the oven. Bake until both sides are golden-brown. It should take no more than 20-25 minutes. If you're grilling it in high-heat in order to make sure that the top side gets brown, than it'll take a lot less than 20 minutes.

Moussaka:

Moussaka is actually a Greek food, which is similar to lasagna, but with eggplant slices replacing the pasta. The original Greek moussaka recipe is with tomato sauce. I make it without tomato sauce simply because I like that better, but you may add tomato sauce to this recipe, and it'll come out pretty good.

What is new in my recipe is that besides using lean ground beef, I add veggies to the ground meat, which increases its volume, thereby reducing the number of fat-grams you eat in your dinner portion. I've also reduced the amount of cheese, and replaced all fattening cheeses with just a few sprinkles of Parmesan, which is the leanest of cheeses. But the flavor is so good that you wouldn't be able to tell all these lean alterations by tasting it… It tastes just like sinfully rich moussaka.

Ingredients ~

2 large organic eggplants
4 tablespoons of pesto
1 lb. organic or all-natural (hormone-free) lean (93% lean) ground beef
2-3 zucchini
1 package (which chops to about ⅔ of a cup) of Italian parsley
1 small to medium organic onion
¼ teaspoon cumin
½ teaspoon of salt
½-1 teaspoon of fresh ground black pepper
5 tablespoons of parmigiano reggiano cheese

3-4 tablespoons of wheat germ
Optional: dash of Italian spices or Herbs De Provence

Preparation –

Wash and grate the zucchini. Chop the onion and parsley real small. You may use a food processor on intermittent-chop cycle to chop them small but without allowing them to mash into a watery consistency. Place the beef in a large bowl. Add the chopped onion and parsley, Add the grated zucchini. Add the cumin, and some of the salt and pepper. Add about a tablespoon of pesto. Bless your hands with intent of Divine Light-Love, and use your blessed hands to knead the beef and everything into a uniform blend. Let it sit for a few minutes while you deal with the eggplants.

Oil a 9"x12" Pyrex with olive oil. Wash and slice the eggplants. Lay half of the slices in the Pyrex so that they form a layer. You may have to cut a slice or two into quarters or other shapes to fill in any voids. Sprinkle some salt and fresh ground pepper on this layer. Then, use a spatula or your pre-blessed hands to rub a thin layer of pesto.

On top of this layer, lay the beef, and use your hands to flatten it into a uniform-thickness. Place the rest of the eggplant slices you have into a uniform layer on top of the beef. Salt and pepper them slightly. Rub them again with a little bit of pesto.

On top of everything, sprinkle the Parmesan cheese as evenly as you can, and on top of it, the wheat germ. You can decorate with a sprinkle of Italian spice mix or Herbs De Provence.

Bake at 350°F for… to tell you the truth I have no idea how long I'm baking it for. It needs to be baked until the beef is cooked all the way through, the eggplants are soft, and or course the cheese will be melted on top. I estimate that I bake it for at least 30-45 minutes. As you bake the moussaka, if you periodically open the oven, you'll see the juices that the eggplants secreted flooding about half of the height of the Pyrex. When the juices reduce, and everything looks like it's cooked through, than the moussaka is ready.

Low Glycemic Load Carbs

Quinoa:

The #1 grain that's recommended is quinoa, which not only has the lowest glycemic load of all grains, but also contains a high amount of complete protein. So essentially, you're getting the complex, low glycemic-load carbs, along with the protein that you need in one fell swoop.

And quinoa is really easy to make. Multiply the amounts of ingredients by how many cups of it you wish to make. I'm including it as a recipe just to give you an idea of how to make it yummier.

Ingredients –

1 cup of dry organic quinoa
2 cups of spring water
1 teaspoon of hazelnut oil
A dash or two of Himalayan or sea salt

Wash the quinoa in a small-hole strainer, and let the water drain out. Then put the washed and drained quinoa in a pot, and turn on the stove on low to medium heat. Keep stirring the quinoa for a few minutes without adding water or any other ingredient. It helps to open up the taste of the grains.

Then add the water, turn the heat up a bit, and let it boil. Once it boils, add hazelnut oil, and as much salt as you think you'd need, reduce heat to low, cover the pot, and let it simmer for about 15 minutes, until all the water is gone.

That's it. Pretty simple, ha? And this grain is just about the best diet food you can have in your fridge. If you have some cooked quinoa in your fridge, knowing it makes a complete protein, you can add it to salads, steamed veggies, anything else – guilt-free!

Country-Style Wholesome Rice:

This wholesome country-style rice is one of the best diet foods you can have. I buy the country style organic brown and wild rice mix at Wholefoods Market by the pound. But I've actually seen similar products on iHerb.com and even at Target. What's unique about it is that it's very flavorful, very filling, and has a low glycemic index at the same time. And for the starches that you do eat as part of the Zohar Kindness Diet, this is a perfect one.

This recipe works well also with other natural whole grains. But you may have to adjust the ratio of grain to water. No biggie. I wrote the amounts for 1 cup of rice. Obviously, if you're feeding a family of 5 people, you'd multiply the amounts by however much rice you wish to make.

Ingredients –

1-2 teaspoons of extra virgin olive oil
2-3 garlic cloves
1 cup of brown and wild country rice mix
1 cup of spring water
1 cup of white wine
Pinch or two of Himalayan or sea salt (to your taste)
¼ teaspoon of Herbs of Provence

Preparation –

Wash the rice in a small-hole strainer. Mince the garlic cloves into tiny pieces, or press it. In a pot, sauté the garlic with the olive oil for a minute or two. Then add the washed and drained rice, and stir it for a moment so the rice absorbs the taste and aroma of the garlic-oil. Add wine and water, and let it boil.

Once it boils, add salt and Herbs of Provence. Reduce heat to the smallest, cover the pot, and let it simmer for 45-50 minutes, until all the liquids are gone. In case you're not used to wholesome rice – the rice should be soft but a bit grainy. Brown rice has a little more texture than white rice.

This rice is also a good source of protein. If you're eating it as part of a vegetarian/vegan meal, than to make a complete protein, you can combine it with beans of any kind, or just sprinkle some nuts or seeds. I love eating this rice with either sesame seeds or some almonds on top.

Omega-3 Gluten-Free Bread:

The number one bread that I recommend eating as part of the Zohar Kindness Diet, and one of the top low glycemic index carb you can eat is this bread. As you'll notice, there is no flour of any kind in this bread. It is entirely made of seeds, nuts and grains, the top grain being oats, flax and chia seeds, which are rich in omega-3 fatty acid. Besides the health benefits of this bread, it really is so tasty, that once I made it, I started craving it and didn't want to eat any other bread.

And the beauty of this bread preparation is: it takes less than five minutes to combine the ingredients into what would make the loaf. Then you let the mixture sit there for pretty much as long as you want, and come back and bake it whenever you have time. Fantastic: minimal effort in preparation; maximum health benefits and taste!

Ingredients –

1½ cups organic rolled oats (not instant)
1 cup organic sunflower or pumpkin seeds (sprouted seeds are healthier and crunchier)
½ cup flax seeds (whole flaxseed makes the bread more grainy and a bit crumbly; using ground flaxseed makes the bread more cohesive and softer—like a bread)
½ cup hazelnuts or almonds (whole)
2 tablespoons chia seeds
4 heaping tablespoons psyllium seed husks powder
(This is actually what keeps the bread together)
1 teaspoon of fine grain sea salt
1½ cups of warm water
3 tablespoons of coconut oil/butter
1 tablespoon of honey or maple syrup

You'll Also Need –

Either a flexible silicone loaf-pan (those are fantastic), or an aluminum loaf-pan (the disposable kind) that is flexible.

In a large bowl, combine all the dry ingredients. Stir them well so that all the nuts and seeds are evenly distributed with the psyllium and flax seed powders.

In a 2-cup glass measuring-cup, put boiling water (so you can measure 1.5 cups). Add the honey and coconut oil, and stir until the coconut oil and honey are melted and mixed in with the water. Then, add the honey-coconut-oil water to the dry ingredients, and stir well until everything is completely and uniformly wet. If you've added the liquids, and the mixture is still not wet, add some more warm water, a couple of tablespoons at a time, until all the mixture is uniformly wet.

Pour the mixture into your loaf pan. If you're using a silicone loaf pan, than there is no need to grease the pan. It's perfect without oiling the pan. If you're using a disposable aluminum loaf pan, spray it with oil, and then pour the mixture into the loaf pan.

Let the mixture stand for at least two hour, so that the oats and seeds can soak the water. Depending on your time constrains, you can let it soak all-day or overnight.

Preheat the oven to 350°F, and bake for 20 minutes. Then remove the bread from the flexible pan in one swift move, turning it upside down, so that the bread sits right on the oven rack. Bake it upside down for another 30-40 minutes. The bread is done with its bottom sounds hollow when tapped.

Let the bread cool completely before slicing. Bread can keep well in the fridge for about five days, but I like to slice it and freeze it. It toasts well. It even microwaves well, if you like microwaving.

Cauliflower Mashed Potatoes:

If you're going to have potatoes while on a diet, this is the way to have it…

Most mashed potato recipes call for boiling the potatoes, and then adding heaps of butter, or worse – all kinds of chemically derived margarines, and tons of iodized salt. This recipe is low fat and low glycemic index, and I'll just tell you how I achieve that…

So chop equal amounts of potatoes and cauliflower into a pot. If organic and fresh, the potatoes don't really have to be pealed. Just clean any 'eyes' or dark spots from the potatoes, and chop them. Cover it with water, add a dash or two of Himalayan salt, and boil for about 12 minutes until you can stick a form in the potatoes and tell that they are soft.

Then, Turn the stove off, and cover the pot almost all the way, so that you can pour the water out while keeping the potatoes and cauliflower in the pot. Add a few drops of olive oil – no more than 1-teaspoon, and mash. The cooked cauliflower is pretty watery, and will help make the mash soft. If the mix feels too dry, add some low-fat (goat) milk. Add salt if it needs it.

This mashed potato is low in fat, because instead of heaps of butter, we've just put 1 single teaspoon of (cholesterol-reducing) olive oil. It'll have a soft wonderful texture thanks to the mashed cauliflower. The potatoes have a lower glycemic index since they are boiled in water; and a low glycemic load, since half of the volume of the dish comes from cauliflower, thus it reduces the grams of available carbs to half. And I promise you won't know the difference in taste between this mashed potatoes and the butter-loaded ones.

Mediterranean Mashed Potatoes:

This another recipe for mashed potatoes, which has a little more spice, and still uses the same principles to lower the glycemic load that we've used above.

Ingredients –

3-4 medium or large potatoes
2-3 zucchini
¼-⅓ of a cup of chopped organic Italian parsley
5 large cloves of garlic
About 4 teaspoons olive oil
Himalayan or sea salt – as needed
Fresh ground pepper – as needed

How To Make –

Cleanse and bless your space and the kitchen for inspired cooking. Perform Safta's Pre-Cooking Meditation for a few minutes before you start to cook. Do a few Kindness Movements…

Wash and chop the parsley very small, and press the garlic. Place them into a small bowl. Add a little bit of Himalayan salt and fresh ground pepper. Add the olive oil and mix with a teaspoon, so that the olive oil is well mixed in with the garlic and parsley. The oil will probably almost cover the mix, but not quite. Let the mixture sit and absorb the taste. If you happen to think of wanting to make this recipe an hour or two in advance, than that's even better. Let the oil absorb the taste of the parsley and garlic for however long you have before you actually have to use it.

About 15 minutes before you want to eat, wash, peal, and cut the potatoes into cubes. Wash & cut the zucchinis into cubes. Put them into a pot with water and salt and cook for about 12-15 minutes until everything is soft. Turn the stove off, and cover the pot almost all the way, so that you can pour the water out while keeping the potatoes and zucchini in the pot. Then, mash the zucchini and potatoes, add the parsley, garlic & olive oil mix, and blend everything together.

So as you see, in this recipe too, we've added vegetables to not only lower the glycemic load, but also spike the taste of the potatoes. The zucchini, as the cauliflower in the above recipe, will also retain lots of liquids, which will make the mash soft in texture. If it's not soft enough, add low-fat milk. Add salt as needed. And enjoy in moderation.

Home-Fries Roasted Potatoes:

Now, every now and then, everyone wants comfort food in the form of home-fried potatoes. Not that I'm advocating home fried or roasted potatoes as a diet food in any way shape or form. Roasted potatoes have a high glycemic index and a high glycemic load. But if you're absolutely craving roasted or home fried potatoes, than you'd better make it this style of home-baked potatoes instead…

Ingredients –

3-4 medium potatoes
At least 4 cups of other vegetables, such as zucchini, eggplants, carrots, Brussels sprouts…
1 Large onion
3-5 garlic cloves
1 teaspoon of pesto
3-5 branches of fresh thyme
Himalayan or sea salt – as necessary
Fresh ground pepper – as necessary
A couple of dashes of Herbs of Provence
1-2 teaspoons of extra virgin olive oil
3-4 tablespoon of spring water

Preparation –

Peel the potatoes only if they are old and non-organic. Chop the potatoes and other veggies into slices. Zucchini, eggplants and carrots are great in slices because they blend in with the texture of the potatoes, and while eating you won't know the difference in taste. Brussels sprouts go very well with this recipe too, but you'll have to chop them in half instead. Chop the onion into fairly large strips, press or mince the garlic. Rinse and strip the thyme leaves off their stem.

Now line a baking pan with good quality parchment paper (I use parchment paper because of environmental reasons. If you don't have it, than line your baking pan with aluminum foil and spray some olive oil on it). Put the potatoes and vegetables into the baking pan. Add the onion, garlic, thyme, salt, pepper, Herbs of Provence, olive oil, and water. Bless your hands with intents of Divine Love-Light before you touch the food. With your blessed hands, mix all the ingredients until the potatoes are evenly spread with the vegetables and all the spices.

Cover it with aluminum foil, and bake at 350°F until the potatoes and veggies are all soft. Then, uncover, and grill it for additional time until everything is browned to your liking. At this stage, I actually like to take it out of the oven, turn things over, and put it back into the grill several times, so that all parts of the mix are browned evenly. This will give this recipe a texture and taste of home fries that are actually fried, except that it will have a lower fat content because we've used very little olive oil, and a low glycemic load because we've diluted the amount of potatoes with veggies. Enjoy in moderation, only when your inner kindness meter is telling you that it's ok to indulge today.

Homemade Pasta Ai Fungi:

You're probably surprised to see pasta with cream sauce as a diet food. But the Zohar Kindness Diet takes into account that you would crave pasta sometime in your life, and that it is not good to permanently deprive yourself of anything you desire. Thus it's better to eat small amounts of it, prepared lovingly at home where you can control the glycemic load and the amounts of fat that you add to the pasta, so that you don't crave a mountain of it later, when you're in a restaurant that drowns their pasta with real cream sauce and butter. The ingredients here are written for a portion for one person. You can multiply it by however many people you're hosting.

<u>Ingredients For Pasta Dough</u> –

½ a cup + a few fist-fulls of <u>durum</u> wheat semolina (yellowish in color)
¼ of a cup of lukewarm water
1 small pinch of Himalayan salt

<u>Pasta Preparation</u> –

Before you make the dough, bless your space, do Safta's Pre-Cooking Meditation, do a few Kindness Movements to get yourself into a relaxed body and lighthearted vibration, and bless your hands with intents to channel into the dough Divine Love-Light.

To make the dough, simply combine the ½-cup of semolina, the warm water and the salt in a small bowl, and knead it into dough. Now the pasta dough has to be kind of hard. It should be pliable not too soft, to the point that it's gets kind of hard to knead it, and you have to use a fair amount of muscles in your hands to knead it. To achieve that consistency, after you first achieve uniform dough, start adding a fistful of semolina at a time, and knead it into the dough until the dough gets to the right consistency.

Now comes the question of whom you're making the pasta for… If you're making the pasta for just yourself, and you're in a rush to eat, than just tear-make little ¼" pasta balls from it, and let them cool and dry for about 10 minutes before cooking them. If you're multiplying the recipe amount by a few because you have guests that you'd like to impress, than you should make fettuccine. Homemade fettuccine will impress the heck out of your guests, and it is pretty simple to make… Flour a dry surface with semolina, and roll the dough into a sheet. Then line up your dining table or other surface that you're not using with parchment paper, and gently move your pasta sheet onto the parchment paper. Use a simple knife to cut the sheet into strips of pasta—fettuccine. And leave the strips there for a few hours to dry a bit. After drying, the pasta will not be as dry as store-bought pasta. It'll still be fresh homemade pasta. But drying it for a few hours makes sure that the fettuccine don't stick.

Whichever form of pasta you're making, put it aside until the last few minutes before you eat. Cooking homemade pasta only takes 5 minutes to make it al dente, which not only has a chewier funner consistency, but also a much lower glycemic index! That's actually why I'm giving you a recipe of homemade pasta – because homemade pasta tends to have a much lower glycemic index.

So that's the first secret about why even pasta can be a diet food. The second secret is that if you notice, the amount of pasta that each person is having here is ¾ of a cup, including the water. So compared to dry store-bought pasta, you'll actually only be having ½ a cup of it (½ a cup of semolina). The remainder of your dish will consist of veggies.

If you're having a quick dinner on your own, than just cut some broccoli or asparagus or another veggie into small chunks (I love eating baby broccoli with pasta), and cook it for 5 minutes in water in same pot with the pasta. That means that you're going to boil water in a pot, add a dash of salt, and a few drops of olive oil. Then when the water gets to a strong boil, add the pasta balls, and the little chunks of broccoli. Let the water get back into a strong boil, and then time about 5 minutes. Drain the water out, add a few drops of olive oil, fresh ground pepper, Herbs of Provence, and any protein form you wish to add to the meal. I like grilling Trader Joe's turkey sausages on the side, and then cutting it into small pieces and adding it to the pasta. But understand that to make a complete meal, according to the Zohar Kindness Diet, which includes pasta, the proportions have to be: ¾ of a cup will come from the cooked pasta balls; 1 turkey sausage; and a whole package of baby broccoli (1 lb.) per person. If you want to have this as a vegetarian meal, you can substitute the turkey sausage with ½ a cup of feta cheese, and it'll still give you a complete protein. Or if you want to make this a vegan meal, add some walnuts, which combined with the semolina grain in the pasta, constitute a complete protein.

If you're having guests over, you can impress them better with this "cream" of mushroom sauce.

"Cream" of Mushroom Sauce Ingredients –

2-3 teaspoons of extra virgin olive oil
4-5 cloves of garlic
½ a medium onion
½ cup of shitake mushrooms
1 cup of Portobello
1 cup of oyster mushroom, or any other interesting mushrooms
1-2 lbs. of baby broccoli
2-3 cups of low fat milk (depending on how much baby broccoli you've added)
1 teaspoon of homemade pesto you've made from the recipe above
Dash or two of Himalayan or sea salt
Fresh ground pepper – to your taste
2-3 drops of Worcestershire sauce.
2 tablespoons of pine nuts
2-3 tablespoons of Parmigiano reggiano cheese
2 tablespoons of flour

Preparation –

In a restaurant, when you order pasta with cream sauce, they use heavy whipping cream, or at the very least half-and-half with a load of butter to make the sauce. Here, as you can see, I've replaced the cream with low-fat milk, and I've added the baby broccoli, which adds veggies—kind of in the back door—into this recipe. That way, you won't really notice you're eating lots of vegetables, because you'll enjoy the taste so much.

So first, chop the onion into small pieces. Mince the garlic or press it. Wash and chop the mushrooms and baby broccoli into medium-small pieces.

In a wok or a saucepan, sauté the garlic and onion with the olive oil until the onion is fairly transparent. Add the mushrooms and baby-broccoli, and let them sauté until they start getting soft. Add the salt, so that it'll allow the vegetables to start juicing. Then add enough milk to cover the vegetables, and let it boil. Once it boils, lower the flame, and let it simmer for a while, so that the veggies continue to cook in the milk, and the milk is reducing some. While it's simmering, add the pepper, pesto, and Worcestershire. After about 10-15 minutes of simmering, put the flour into a small bowl, add to it some of the warm milk from the mushroom sauce, and stir so it becomes creamy, then a more watery cream. Then add it back to the wok, and blend in real well, so that the milk becomes a little thicker. Add the Parmesan and pine nuts in the end, in the last minute of cooking.

This sauce may be just a little bit more watery than restaurant cream sauce, but tastes much better. And you can eat it guilt-free – since the majority of it is vegetables and low fat milk. The little bit of olive oil, the few nuts, and the touch of Parmesan that are in here are nothing to fret over, since you'll also be eating lots of veggies, and at the same time, you'll feel like you're actually eating a creamy pasta dinner. Now that is a perfect example of how to take a food that was originally fattening, and make it into a Kindness Diet dinner!

Homemade Whole Wheat Seeded Sourdough Bread:

Bread is not the enemy either. It is only the very rarely disciplined person who does not eat bread at all. Bread can be very enjoyable in moderation, especially this bread. So if you're going to have any bread, you'd better eat this one. This bread does several things to lower the glycemic index… First, I use only organic stone-ground whole-wheat sprouted flour, which is high in fiber and protein, and therefore lower in its glycemic load. Secondly, I add seeds to the dough. And thirdly, this bread is so dense and filling that after half a slice, you'll be totally full. You wouldn't be able to eat anything else. So here is the secret for my other most prized recipe…

To make sourdough bread, you first need to develop your starter culture. It takes a few days (about a week) to develop it…

Starter –

1 cup whole wheat flour
1 cup warm water
1 package of yeast
a few drops of organic maple syrup or honey.

Mix all those ingredients in a jar that allows more room on the top, so that when the culture bubbles, there'll be room for it to expand into. Place it in a warm place open to air. When I made my first starter culture, and whenever I'm reviving it from the fridge thereafter, I like to pick a branch of fresh rosemary, a small branch of cedar, and a branch of sage from my garden, and lay it around the jar, so that the culture could absorb the fragrance of the herbs through the air. Never let metal touch your culture. Use plastic or wooden utensils to blend it.

Feed Every 24-hours – Dump half the amount. And add ½ cup flower + ½ cup of warm water. After a few days, when the starter culture gets bubbly and have a pleasant soury smell (kind of almost like beer), it's ready.

<u>The Sponge –</u>

Pour the starter into a large bowl.

Add 1 cup of whole-wheat stone-ground flower, 1 cup of warm spring water, and 1 (large) wooden tablespoon of honey. Blend it well using a spatula until it's even, and let sit in a warm place for 1-5 hours. It's ready when it looks like sponge (and added volume) with bubbly white froth & smells kind of sour.

<u>Kneading The Dough –</u>

2½ cups of the sponge

3 flat wooden tablespoons of Himalayan salt

2 wooden tablespoons of organic raw honey

3-4 wooden tablespoons of olive oil

1 cup – flax seed, pumkin seed

2-3 cups of organic whole-wheat flower

(1 cup of sunflower seeds to put on top after making the loaf)

Measure 2½ cups of sponge into the mixing bowl. Put the rest in a clean jar, and give it a fresh feed of ½ a cup of flower & ½ a cup of warm water. Cover and refrigerate it as a future culture.

Add to the sponge that's in the bowl salt, honey and olive oil. Add the seeds. Now start adding the flower a bit at a time and knead well. Add only as much flower as it takes to make it nice flexible dough. Knead the dough for at about 20 minutes, until it becomes flexible. This is important, as the kneading process is what causes the gluten to break, and makes it pliable and flexible. As you knead, let your body loose, think positive loving thoughts, and imbue the bread with blessings of Light and Love…

Let the dough rise for several (about 12) hours until it doubles in size. I like to time everything so that I take the culture out of the fridge and revive (feed) it in the morning; I make sponge around 2-3pm, and I make the actual dough around 9-10 pm. Then the dough rises overnight. I knead it again to make loaf early in the morning when I first open my eyes, and before I'm quite ready to give up bed. Then I bake it while I'm making breakfast and showering, letting it cool while I'm out of the house, and slicing it after a few hours of cooling. If you're leaving the dough to rise overnight, than add a few drops of warm water on top and cover it with plastic to keep it moist, so that it doesn't dry out.

Now, once your dough has risen for all those hours, grease a loaf pan with hazelnut oil (which has a higher smoke point than olive oil, but is still monounsaturated). Shape our dough into a loaf and place it onto your loaf pan. Sprinkle the sunflower seeds on top. Cover it with another loaf-pan, and let it rise for another hour.

Here come the final step: Bake the bread (covered with the other loaf-pan) at 375°F for 45-55 minutes. When you're ready to take the bread out of the oven, you can stick a long match into it to check if it's done. If the match comes out gooey and web, the bread needs to be baked for a little bit longer. If the match comes out fairly dry, with no goo sticking to it, the bread is ready.

Low-Fat Deserts

OK, deserts aren't the enemy either. Again, I'm not advocating deserts as a diet food. You're better off eating a fruit, a couple of unsweetened carob-covered almonds, or even a date or two if you need something sweet at the end of a meal. But every now and then, you're going to want a real desert. When you do, you'd better have in your freezer some desert that you've prepared especially with low glycemic load for the occasion. Here are some ideas:

Apple Bliss Muffins:

These muffins are very moist in texture and very yummy in flavor. They taste just like store-bought muffins—the fatty sweet ones, except they have a very low glycemic load. Firstly, I've sweetened them with honey (instead of sugar), which has a GI of 50, and not very much honey at that. As you'll see one cup of honey makes 24 muffins. So each muffin has maybe 2 teaspoons of honey. Additionally, two thirds of the flour that the original recipe called for was replaced by organic rolled oats, and grated apple, which lower the glycemic index and load considerably. On top of that the recipe is vegan and uses homemade applesauce instead of eggs. Here it is…

Applesauce Preparation –

7-10 organic Pink Lady apples (substitute Fuji or Gala)
1 flat teaspoon (or less) of ground cinnamon
2-4 tablespoons of organic raw orange blossom honey

Peal and cut the apples into a pot. Cover with natural spring water. Boil & cook for about 15 minutes. Add the cinnamon and honey. Then let it stand and cool.

Drain some of the water into a jar, and save it as apple cider. It's delicious to drink hot or cold… Mash the rest with the apples into an applesauce.

Muffins Ingredients –

2 cups of grated organic Pink Lady or gala apples
1 cup of organic rolled oats
½ cup ground pistachio (substitute walnuts or almonds)
1 cup of organic raw orange blossom honey
5 tablespoons hazelnut oil
1 teaspoon of organic non-alcoholic vanilla flavor
1 teaspoon of organic non-alcoholic orange flavor
4 teaspoons of organic ground cinnamon
1 teaspoon of ground nutmeg
1½ cup of the applesauce you've just made
1½ cup of organic whole-wheat flour
1 cup of natural orange-mango or natural red grape juice

5 heaping teaspoons of aluminum-free cooking powder
A little extra hazelnut oil to oil the muffin trays…

<u>Preparation</u> ~

In a large bowl, mix the list of ingredients in the order that they are written… all except the additional apples. Mix them with a tablespoon, and remember to feel blissful and free within your own body as you do the preparation. Dance & sing a song of the heart as you mix & prepare the ingredients.

Then, peal and cut the additional apples into very small cubes. Add them and mix a bit more so that they are evenly distributed within the mix. Sing a happy song to yourself as you so. Reiki the mix with your highest healing-blessing intent for the people eating the muffins… Don't forget to bless yourself too…

Spray 2 muffin trays with hazelnut oil. Use two tablespoons to scoop the mix and fill out the trays.

Bake at 325°F for about 25-30 minutes. Let cool, and then serve it to your guests with love…

Once the muffins cool, I usually separate them from the baking tray, put them in a couple of large Ziploc bags, and freeze them. When I'm in need of a muffin, I microwave each muffin for about 15-20 seconds, and it's warm and deliciously moist just as it was when it first got out of the oven.

Low Fat, Low GI Chocolate Mousse:

You see, even chocolate mousse can be low-fat. I've replaced the butter with a lower amount of hazelnut oil, which is monounsaturated (omega-9, just like olive oil); reduced the amount of sweetening by much, and replaced the sugar with raw honey (which has a lower glycemic index); dispensed with the whipped cream that is usually part of the recipe; and dispensed with the egg yokes. So this is, quite literally, a very low-fat, low glycemic index chocolate mousse. And as you'll see below, chocolate has tremendous health benefits.

<u>Ingredients</u>:

1 package (9.7 oz.) of Scharffenberger Dark Unsweetened chocolate (99%)
7 tbsp. hazelnut oil
¾ cup organic orange blossom honey
1 teaspoon organic non-alcoholic orange flavor
2 teaspoons organic non-alcoholic vanilla flavor
1 teaspoon organic non-alcoholic almond flavor
Whites from 8 jumbo eggs + pinch of salt

<u>Making the Mousse</u> ~

Use a knife and a cutting board to chop the chocolate mass into as small a chunks as you can. In a double boiler, melt the chocolate. Add hazelnut oil, honey & flavors. Use this chocolate-melting time to do some Kindness Movements… Occasionally stir the blend with a wooden spoon. When all the chocolate mass has melted and the mix is uniform, take the bowl out of the water pot, and let it cool some…

Meanwhile, separate the egg whites from the yokes and discard the yokes (or save it for a different purpose). In a large bowl, beat the egg whites with a pinch of salt into a hard foam. Pour the chocolate blend onto the egg whites foam, and then gently fold everything into a uniform mix.

Pour into about 6-8 little cups. You may decorate with fresh berries & a pretty mint leaf on top.

Bless it with your loving intent. And cool thoroughly in the refrigerator for a few hours… and then serve it to your guests with delight & love…

Health Benefits –

Chocolate contains large amounts of flavonoids & phenolic, which are important antioxidants that help prevent cell damage and thus prevent heart disease, stroke & many cancers. Chocolate also contains phenylthylamine (PEA), which is the antidepressant responsible for the euphoric and aphrodisiac effects of chocolates. Theobromine contained in chocolate helps relieve drowsiness & give jitter-free stimulant.

Besides chocolate, this recipe contains hazelnut oil, which contains antidepressant compounds & heart-disease preventing monounsaturated fat.

Chocolate Covered Strawberries:

Ingredients –

12 large fresh stawberries with stems intact
6 onces of Scharffenberger Dark Unsweetened chocolate (99%)
2 tablespoons of organic raw honey
1 tablespoon of hazelnut oil

Preparation –

Rinse and dry the strawberries. Strain them thoroughly, and then let them dry completely on paper towel while you deal with the chocolate. Prepare a baking sheet lined with waxed parchment paper.

Again, use a knife and cutting-board to chop the chocolate mass into smaller chunks. Then put the chocolate chunks in the top bowl of a double boiler set over hot water. Melt the chocolate. Add the hazelnut oil and honey, stirring constantly until the chocolate melts. If necessary, add additional hazelnut oil to the chocolate to achieve desired coating consistency. Stir until the mixture is smooth, and then let it cool to lukewarm—about body temperature.

Holding each strawberry by the stem, dip into the chocolate mixture allowing the excess chocolate to drip back into the pan. Transfer the coated strawberry to the lined sheet and repeat the process.

Allow the chocolate to cool and then chill in the fridge for about 20-30 minutes until the chocolate is set.

Zohar's Low-Fat Custard

This is an example of me taking a perfectly fattening recipe, and turning it into a diet food. The original recipe was actually a crème burette recipe demonstrated to me by a famous Italian chef in a restaurant. It was, of course, made with heavy cream, using whole eggs, and lots and lots of white sugar, including the added sugar that they use a burner for to burn on top. Needless to say that I made a few changes to the original recipe. And my guests actually liked this low-fat custard better than the fattening crème Brule.

Ingredients (for 6 portions) –

2 cups low fat goat milk
2 whole vanilla beans
Whites from 5 eggs
Dash of sea salt
¾ of a cup of raw honey*
* For other healthy choices, you can may substitute with ½ a sup of agave nectar, or 3-4 tablespoons of stevia. When all else fails, you can substitute ½ a cup of natural brown sugar.

How To Make –

Warm the milk in a pot in low heat, but make sure it does **not** boil. Meanwhile, split the vanilla beans, cutting along the length of the bean, and add them to the warming cream. Keep whisking it lightly while it warms.

Separate the eggs and discard the yokes. In a large bowl, beat the egg whites with the dash of salt into stiff white foam. After the foam is hard, add the honey and beat that into the foam.

Once the cream is warm, it'll be dotted with little brown dots from the essence of the vanilla beans. Fish the vanilla bean halves out one at a time, "milk"–squeeze the rest of their essence into the milk, and toss away the shell of the beans.

Now gently pour the vanilla-flavored warm milk into the sweet egg-white foam, while continuing to whisk it.

Now pour the mixture into ceramic bowls, mixing gently every time just before pouring it into a bowl. Put the Bowls into a baking pan, and add water to surround ½ the height of the bowls. Bake at 350°F for 25 minutes. Then refrigerate for at least 4-5 hours in the to let it set.

Appendix B

Glycemic Index, Protein & Fat Tables

I've included in this appendix three tables in which I've compiled and interpolated nutritional information about common foods: The first table is analyzes the carb content, glycemic index, and glycemic load of common foods that we eat; the second table is a proteins & fat table; and the third table is a nuts & oils table.

In the first table, foods that are with white background are what I've referred to in Chapter 5 as "Main Foods to Add"—foods that you should add to your plate without limitation; foods shaded in light gray are foods that you should add to your plate in moderation; and foods shaded in darker gray are foods that you should kindly wean yourself from. Most light-gray shaded foods are healthy for you but have a moderately high glycemic load of 11-19. I've shaded in dark-gray foods that either have a very high glycemic load (20+), or are unkind foods (i.e., contains unpronounceable ingredients, saturated or trans fats, highly processed, etc.). Note that pasta, bread, sweet beverages, and breakfast cereals in light gray only because they have a moderate glycemic load. But they are not foods that should be added to your plate in any way, shape or form.

Food ↓	Glycemic Index (Glucose= 100)	Grams	Approx. Portion	Avail. Carb Grams	Approx. Glycemic Load
Vegetables: NOTE – for veggies there are no studies because of their low GI/GL. So I've taken the approx. GI from one website[3], and the GL and available carbs from another website[4]. So as a result, the values do not always match when plugged into the formula.					
Artichoke, cooked with salt, drained	15	120	1 medium	4	3
Asparagus, cooked, drained	15	90	½ cup	2	2
Broccoli	15	91	1 cup	4	3
Cauliflower	15	62	½ cup	2	1
Celery	15	101	1 cup	1	1
Carrots, chopped, raw	37	128	1 cup	8	3
Cucumber, raw	15	201	1 medium	3	1
Eggplant, cooked	15	99	1 cup	7	2
Green beans	15	110	1 cup	4	3
Lettuce & leafy salad mixes	15	36	1 cup	1	1

Parsnips	52	80	0.6 cup	8	4
Peppers, sweet, green, raw	15	149	1 cup	4	2
Snow-peas, podded, boiled	15	160	1 cup	7	5
Spinach, raw	15	30	1 cup	0	0
Tomatoes, cherry tomatoes, raw	15	149	1 cup	4	2
Zucchini	15	180	1 cup	5	2
Corn, sweet	60	150	⅔ cup	33	20
Potato, sweet	70	150	1 large	31	22
Potato, white, boiled	82	150	½ a potato	26	21
Yam	54	150	1+ cup	37	20

Fruit:

Apple	39	182	1 medium	21	5
Dates, dried	42	30	4 dates	22	9
Grapefruit	25	120	1 medium	12	3
Grapes	59	90	1 cup	14	8
Melon, cantaloupe	70	120	1 ½ cup	6	4
Orange	40	120	1 medium	10	4
Peach	42	120	1 large	12	4
Pear	38	120	1 small	11	4
Prunes, pitted	29	60	5 prunes	34	10
Strawberries	40	120	.8 cup	3	1
Watermelon	72	120	¾ cup	6	4
Banana	62	120	1 medium	26	16
Raisins	64	60	2 tbsp.	44	28

Beans:

Beans, baked, average	40	150	.6 cup	15	6
Beans, black	30	150	.6 cup	23	7
Beans, kidney	29	150	.6 cup	24	7
Beans, navy	31	150	.6 cup	29	9
Black-eyed peas	33	150	.6 cup	30	10
Chickpeas, dry	10	150	¾ cup	30	3
Chickpeas, canned in brine	38	150	.6 cup	24	9
Lentils	29	150	.7 cup	17	5
Soy beans	15	150	.6 cup	7	1
Hummus (chickpeas & sesame seeds)	6	30	2 tbsp.	0	0*

Whole Grains:					
Couscous	65	150	⅔ cup	14	9
Barley, pearled	28	150	⅘ cup	43	12
Bulgur	48	150	1 ⅛ cup	25	12
Oats, rolled, cooked	55	45	½ cup	22	13
Oats, rolled, dry	50	45	½ cup	22	11
Quinoa	53	150	⅘ cup	25	13
Rice, brown	50	150	¾ cup	32	16
Rice, wild	57	164	1 cup	32	16
Wheat germ	53	58	½ cup	23	12
Wheat kernels, whole	30	50	½ cup	37	11
Millet, steamed	68	150	⅘ cup	34	23
Rice, white	67	150	¾ cup	42	28
Cereals:					
All-Bran™	55	35	1 cup	26	14
Puffed wheat	80	30	2 cups	21	17
Special K™ (Kellogg's)	69	30	1 cup	20	14
Coco Pops™	77	30	???	26	20
Cornflakes™	93	30	2 cups	25	23
Grapenuts™	75	120	1 cup	84	63
Museli, average	66	90	⅘ cup	72	48
Raisin Bran™ (Kellogg's)	61	60	1 cup	40	24
Pastas:					
Fettuccine	32	180	⅔ cup	47	15
Spaghetti, whole wheat	42	180	⅔ cup	40	17
Homemade pasta	56	100	⅔ cup	45	25
Linguine	43	180	⅔ cup	48	21
Macaroni	47	180	⅔ cup	49	23
Semolina, durum (homemade pasta)	64	128	⅔ cup	91	58
Spaghetti, white	46	180	⅔ cup	48	22

Breads: NOTE – Even though for 1 single small slice, most breads have a glycemic load that is considered pretty low, I left all of the breads in orange & red, as breads are not really an ideal diet food that you want to add. So it's not a "Green Boxed" item (as explained in chapter 20).

Baguette, white, plain	95	30	1 small slice	16	15

Bread, barley, coarse (75% kernels)	34	30	1 small slice	21	7
Bread, white, average	71	30	1 small slice	14	10
Bread, whole grain	51	30	1 small slice	14	7
Bread, whole wheat	71	30	1 small slice	13	9
Hamburger bun	61	30	1 bun	15	9
Pita bread	68	30	⅔ of a pita	15	10
Pumpernickel bread	56	30	1 small slice	13	7
Tortilla, corn	52	50	2 tortillas	23	12
Tortilla, whole wheat	30	50	2 tortillas	27	8
Bagel, white	72	70	1 bagel	35	25
Waffles, Aunt Jemima	76	35	1 small slice	13	10

Beverages: NOTE – Despite the medium glycemic load of some sodas, I colored them all in red for the simple reason that they contain many chemical & unpronounceable ingredients, which are all unhealthy, and are therefore counterproductive to a healthy weight loss diet.

Coconut water, young, all-natural	50	250 mL	1 small cup	6	3
Grapefruit juice, red	47	250 mL	1 small cup	23	7
Tomato juice, canned	38	250 mL	1 small cup	11	4
Orange juice, unsweetened	50	250 mL	1 small cup	24	12
Smoothie- banana, strawberry & milk	44	250 mL	1 small cup	26	11
The same smoothie in twice the size…	44	16 Fl. Oz.	Large cup	52	23
Apple Juice, unsweetened, average	44	250 mL	1 small cup	68	30
Coca Cola™	63	250 mL	1 small cup	26	16
Fanta™	68	250 mL	1 small cup	34	23
Fruit punch	67	250 mL	1 small cup	29	19
Gatorade™	78	250 mL	1 small cup	15	12
Lemonade Schweppes™	54	250 mL	1 small cup	27	15
Rice milk drink, low fat,	92	250 mL	1 small cup	32	29

Crackers, Cookies & Snacks: NOTE – I left most of the crackers/cookies in orange, since their glycemic loads are medium. But remember that in the Zohar Kindness Diet, simple (high GI) carbs are not really a food that you'd want to add to your diet.

Pop corn, plain	55	20		11	6
Chips, tortilla	42	28	1 cup	18	11
Graham crackers	74	25	2 crackers	19	14
Rice cakes	82	25	2 rice cakes	21	17
Rice crisps	74	25	2 cookies	16	12
Shortbread	64	25	2 cookies	16	10

Vanilla wafers	77	25	2 small w.	18	14
Chips, potato, plain, salted	52	227	1 x 8-oz. bag	103	54

Cakes: NOTE- Despite the medium glycemic load of banana & sponge cakes, I colored all cakes in red. Notice the portion is 1 tiny slice equivalent to <u>half</u> a thin slice of bread. So if you start adding all kinds of cakes in all kinds of portions to your diet, you will gain weight!

Banana cake, made with sugar	47	60	1 tiny slice	29	14
Banana cake, made without sugar	55	60	1 tiny slice	22	12
Sponge cake	46	63	1 tiny slice	37	17
Vanilla cake with frosting	42	111	1 tiny slice	57	24

Miscellaneous & Dairy: NOTE- With full-fat milk & ice creams, the issue that makes them counterproductive to diet is not really the carbs, but the fat content. Therefore despite their low glycemic index/load, I colored them red—because of their high fat content.

Milk, skim	32	250 mL	1 small cup	13	4
Honey	61	25	1 tbsp.	20	12
Reduced fat yogurt with fruit	33	200	⅘ cup	33	11
Ice cream, regular	57	50	3 reg. tbsp.	10	6*
Ice cream, low fat	51	50	3 reg. tbsp.	13	7*
Milk, full fat	41	250 mL	1 small cup	12	5*

* The fact that these items have a low glycemic index and a low glycemic load does not mean that they are ideal diet foods. They are not calorie-free, since hummus, nuts and oils obviously have a very high fat content, even if it is healthy fat.

Proteins & Fats Table:

Most protein-rich, nuts and oils have a very low carb content. So with those foods, having low glycemic indexes/loads is not really the issue. In fact, all of the oils I've listed in the oils table have a '0' carb content, and therefore a '0' value for their glycemic load. The main issue with protein-rich foods, nuts, and oils is choosing foods with a low fat content and a high content of complete protein (which contain all 8 essential amino acids).

The second important issue with proteins is getting a higher percentage of essential fatty acids and a low percentage of saturated animal fat.

I've shaded in light gray protein sources that have a moderately high fat content, and in dark gray protein sources that have an extremely high fat content.

Protein-Rich Foods – Meats, Poultry, Dairy, Fish, Soy:						
Food ↓	Grams	Approx. Portion	Fat Grams	Type of Fat	Protein Grams	Carb Grams
Bacon, baked, fat trimmed out	8	1 slice	3	Saturated	3	0
Beef, filet mignon, grilled/baked, steak	126	4.4 oz.	12	Saturated	36	0
Beef liver, pan fried	160	5.6 oz.	8	Saturated	42	4
Beef, rib eye, fat trimmed out, grilled/ baked	236	8.3 oz.	40	Saturated	63	0
Bison, game, fat trimmed out, roasted/ cooked	340	12 oz. steak	8	Saturated	97	0
Chicken breast, roasted, no skin or skin	86	½ breast	3	Saturated	27	0
Chicken liver, pan fried	100	3.5 oz.	6	Saturated	26	1
Chicken thighs, no bones or skin	52	1 thigh	6	Saturated	13	0
Duck, no bones or skin, cooked	221	½ a duck	25	Saturated	52	0
Egg, hard boiled	50	1 large	5	Saturated	6	1
Egg whites	61	¼ cup	0	--	7	1
Goose, no bones or skin, cooked/roasted	295	¼ goose	38	Saturated	86	0
Halibut, Atlantic & Pacific, cooked	159	5.6 oz. filet	5	Omega-3	42	0
Ham	28	1 oz. slice	2	Saturated	5	1
Lamb, average, fat trimmed out, cooked	270	9.5 oz.	45	Saturated	66	0
Milk, cow, full fat	244	1 cup	8	Saturated	8	13
Milk, cow, reduced fat 2%	245	1 cup	5	Saturated	10	13
Milk, goat, low fat	240	1 cup	2.5	Saturated	8	11
Pastrami, turkey	57	2 slices	4	Saturated	9	2
Salami, Italian, pork	28	1 oz.	10	Saturated	6	0

Salmon, Atlantic, wild, cooked or dry heat	154	5.4 oz. filet	13	Omega-3	39	0
Sausage, pork, cooked	112	4 oz. link	32	Saturated	20	0
Sea Bass, cooked with mixed spices	101	2.5 oz. filet	3	Omega-3	24	3
Snapper, cooked with mixed spices	170	6 oz. filet	3	Omega-3	45	0
Sword fish, cooked or dry heat	106	3.7 oz. piece	5	Omega-3	27	0
Tempe	56	2 oz. slice	6	Omega-6	10	6
Tilapia, cooked or dry heat	140	5 oz. filet	5	Omega-3	35	0
Tofu, silken, firm	56	2 oz. slice	1	Omega-6	2	1
Tuna, yellow-fin, raw	85	1 oz. piece	1	Omega-3	20	0

Nuts & Oils Tables:

The main issue with nuts and oils is choosing ones that are higher in omega-9 (monounsaturated) and omega-3, and lower in omega-6. Also, again with nuts, you want to choose the ones that have high protein contents and which contain mostly the heart-healthy omega-3 and omega-9.

Keep in mind that both oils & nuts (since nuts contain oils) are best kept refrigerated to avoid oxidation and rancidity. With oils, I recommend that you get small drip bottles or dressing bottles with caps. Pour into these bottles only the oils you think you'll use that week, and keep them outside of refrigeration. Keep the rest of the oil in the fridge. With nuts, it's healthiest to buy them raw and keep them refrigerated. Take out of refrigeration and roast only the nuts you intend to eat that day. I sometimes just eat the nuts raw, since refrigerated nuts tend to be crisp and crunchy, just like roasted nuts.

All nuts contain essential fatty acids, with the exception of coconut oil, which contains a healthy type of saturated oil. You can choose your nuts by the ones that contain the healthiest fatty acids, such as omega-3 (flax, walnut) and omega-9 (almonds, hazelnuts, macadamia nuts, cashews, pistachios, pecans); or you can choose your nuts by the ones that have the highest protein content with the lowest fat content. And the two don't always go together. For that reason, it is hard to categorize nuts, and I did not shade the entire lines of nuts in the table. Rather, I shaded in light gray the fat column, to remind you that nuts contain lots of fat; in dark gray the fat content of specific nuts which are extremely high in fat; and I've bolded out the words "omega-9" and "Omega-3" for nut that contain them, to remind you that those are the healthy fats. I've also bolded out protein contents that are high in nuts, so you know that the nut that contain them is good for you. All nuts have a high fat content, no matter how healthy the fat is. So eat those in moderation.

As far as oils (also contained in this table), an issue that is exclusive to oils is the smoke point. Smoke point is the temperature at which the oil starts burning. The higher the smoke point of any particular oil, the less likely you are to burn it (rather than just cook it). So you always want to use oils at temperatures that are well below its smoke point, since you don't want to be creating trans-fatty acids in your home kitchen.

Notice the highest smoke point oils, which are good for cooking and baking as long as you cook/bake at temperatures below their smoke points, (from high to low) are: avocado, walnut, soy, sunflower, hazelnut, olive and canola oil. The rest of the oils should be either cooked at extremely low heat, or be eaten raw (in salads/sauces).

Also notice oils containing omega-3 are: walnut oil (expensive!) and soy oil. The main oils containing omega-9 (monounsaturated) are: olive, hazelnut, avocado, and macadamia oil. Peanut, sunflower, and to a lesser degree, sesame oil also contain some omega-9.

So of all the oils, hazelnut, avocado, and walnut oils have both high smoke points and healthy essential fatty acids.

Here is a table that combines both oils and nuts:

Food ↓	Grams	Approx. Portion	Fat Grams	Type of Fat	Protein Grams	Carb gr./GL or smoke pt.
Almonds, dry roasted, unsalted	138	1 cup	73	**Omega-9** Omega-6	**30**	27/0
Avocado oil (heat extracted)	14	1 tbsp.	14	**Omega-9**	0	520°F
Butter	14	1 tbsp.	11	Saturated	0	350°F
Cashews, dry roasted, salted	137	1 cup	63	**Omega-9** Omega-6	21	45/15
Coconut oil	14	1 tbsp.	14	Saturated **Omega-9**	0	350°F
Corn & canola oil (heat-extracted)	14	1 tbsp.	14	Omega-9 Omega-6	0	400°F
Flax seed	168	1 cup	71	**Omega-3**	31	49/0
Hazelnut oil	14	1 tbsp.	14	**Omega-9**	0	430°F
Hazelnuts, dry roasted, no salt	112	1 cup	68	**Omega-9**	16	20/0
Hemp seed	128	1 cup	48	Omega-6 **Omega-3**	**40**	12/0
Macadamia nuts, dry roasted, no salt	132	1 cup	100	**Omega-9**	10	18/0
Macadamia oil	14	1 tbsp.	14	**Omega-9**	1	389°F
Margarine	14	1 tbsp.	11	Hydrogenated!	0	
Mayonnaise	14	1 tbsp.	12	Saturated	0	
Olive oil, extra virgin	14	1 tbsp.	14	**Omega-9**	0	406°F
Peanuts, oil roasted with salt	133	1 cup	66	**Omega-9** Omega-6	35	25/0
Peanut oil	14	1 tbsp.	14	**Omega-9** Omega-6	0	320°F

Pecans	109	1 cup	78	**Omega-9** . Omega-6	10	15/0
Pistachios, dry roasted with salt	123	1 cup	57	**Omega-9** Omega-6	26	33/4
Pumpkin seed, kernels only, roasted with salt	227	1 cup	96	Omega-6	**75**	30/2
Sesame, whole, roasted/toasted	127	1 cup	59	Omega-6 **Omega-9**	23	32/0
Sesame oil, cold pressed	14	1 tbsp.	14	Omega-6 **Omega-9**	0	350°F
Shortening	13	1 tbsp.	13	Partially hydrogenated!	0	325°F
Soy oil (heat extracted)	14	1 tbsp.	14	Omega-6 **Omega-3**	0	450°F
Sunflower oil (heat extracted)	14	1 tbsp.	14	**Omega-9** Omega-6	0	440°F
Sunflower seed kernels, dry roasted, no salt	128	1 cup	64	Omega-6	**25**	31/0
Walnut oil	14	1 tbsp.	14	Omega-6 **Omega-3**	0	450°F
Walnuts, chopped	117	1 cup	76	Omega-6 **Omega-3**	18	16/0

Notes:

<u>Coconut oil</u> – even though its fat is saturated. It is a healthy type of saturated fat. So I did not highlight it in red.

<u>Mayonnaise</u> – even though it is full of saturated fat, having some mayo in moderation (a little teaspoon of mayo to give your lean protein) is not altogether bad. So I colored it in orange.

<u>Shortening & Margarine</u> – **should be avoided like a plague!**

Computations & Interpolations:

Just in case you're interested, the glycemic load formula is:

Glycemic Load = Glycemic Index × Number of Available Carb Grams/100

So in resource materials in which only the carb grams and glycemic load was given, I interpolated according to a formula that is a derivative of the above formula:

Glycemic Index = Glycemic Load x 100/ Available Carb Grams

Appendix C

Kindness Stars Diet Log

NOTE: If you choose to keep the Kindness Stars Diet Log that I suggested in Chapter 5, you are invited to copy the log that is included in this appendix and use it as your own.

Kindness Stars Diet Log

Name: _____

Goal Weight: _____ Goal Waist: _____

Lifestyle & Habit Goals: _____

Health Goals: _____

Fitness & Enhanced Physical Abilities Goals: _____

General Feeling Goals: _____

Personal Goals: _____

Starting Measurements

Starting Weight: _____

Starting Waist: _____

Starting Hip: _____

Starting Arm: _____

Starting Thy: _____

Place a picture of
Thin Me here...

(This is a picture from your youth, or even if you have to put a model's picture under your head... This is a motivational tool!)

Place another picture
of
Thin Me here...

Kindness Stars Diet Log – Week #_____

Date	Added @least 5 cups veggies & fruit	Added Joyful Physical Activity	Let Go of unkind foods	Got a good night sleep	Let go of stress &judg-ment	General feeling today	Total stars
Weight:			Waist:			Total stars	

Kindness Stars Diet Log – Week #_____

Date	Added @least 5 cups veggies & fruit	Added Joyful Physical Activity	Let Go of unkind foods	Got a good night sleep	Let go of stress &judg-ment	General feeling today	Total stars
Weight:			Waist:			Total stars	

Kindness Stars Diet Log – Week #_____

Date	Added @least 5 cups veggies & fruit	Added Joyful Physical Activity	Let Go of unkind foods	Got a good night sleep	Let go of stress &judg-ment	General feeling today	Total stars
Weight:			Waist:			Total stars	

Kindness Stars Diet Log – Week #_____

Date	Added @least 5 cups veggies & fruit	Added Joyful Physical Activity	Let Go of unkind foods	Got a good night sleep	Let go of stress &judg-ment	General feeling today	Total stars
Weight:			Waist:			Total stars	

Notes, Feelings & Impressions...

Notes, Feelings & Impressions...

Notes, Feelings & Impressions...

Notes, Feelings & Impressions...

220

Plate Composition & Orientation (By Volume):

- 50% of Your Plate - **Veggies &/or fruit**

- 25% of Your Plate - Lean proteins: soy, tempeh, hemp, beans, nuts, seeds, fish, chicken, turkey, egg whites, and low-fat dairy

- 25% of Your Plate - Low glycemic index carbs: whole grains, boiled potatoes, seeded & sprouted whole grain bread

- Oils - The oils on your plate should not take any extra volume, since they'll inevitably comprise part of your protein-rich foods. You'll also use healthy oils in cooking, dressing and preparing your veggies, proteins & carbs. Healthy oils: omega-3 (fish, oats, wheat-germ, flaxseed, walnuts, hemp), omega-9 (olive oil, hazelnuts, avocado), omega-6 (pistachios, safflower oil, hemp seeds, sunflower, flax seed) & coconut oil

Foods To Make Sure You're Getting Enough Of...

- Lean Protein - soy, whey, hemp, chicken, turkey, fish, egg-whites, low fat dairy & other vegetarian sources for complete protein
- Whole grains - brown & wild rice, quinoa, whole wheat, barley...
- Beans - all kinds

Healthy Snack Ideas:

- Carrots dipped in cottage cheese, eggplant dip, or tahini...
- Nuts & fruit
- Fruit with oats & sesame sprinkled on them
- Low-fat yogurt with berries, oats, raisins, nuts
- All natural protein bar
- Cucumber or celery wrapped in turkey cold cuts or with veggie dip

Foods To Add In Moderation:

Nuts & seeds in their natural form - flaxseed, walnuts, hazelnut, pistachios, almonds, macadamia, olive oil.
When adding grains-especially rice, be mindful of moderation...

Foods To Add Plenty Of:

- Water - _____ (wt) ÷2 = _____ oz. of water
  ÷8 = _____ cups of water a day
- Vegetables - all non starchy veggies, lovingly prepared & spiced yummily to your liking... **except** potatos, pumpkin, yams & corn
- Fruit - all fresh juicy fruit **except** juices, dried fruit & bananas
- Healing Foods - imbued with your healing intent and/or fond memories

Lifestyle Things To Add:

- Good quality sleep (8 hours a day)
- Joyful Physical activity
- Deep natural breaths
- Me-Time & Meditation
- Small healthy meals/snacks
- Time to eat relaxed meals
- Time to do things without stress
- Group/peer support
- Self-love - the "I am fabulous" mantra

If You're Going To Eat...

- Potatoes - eat yams or sweet potatoes, and boil them to lower the glycemic index. Better yet mash them with 50% cauliflower.
- Saturated Fats - make it coconut oil, which has many health benefits & helps weight loss
- Red Meat - eat organic or naturally grown lean (less than 10% fat) beef & make it a celebration in which you reward yourself!

Foods To Kindly Wean Yourself Off Of:

- Energy-dense foods with empty calories - candy, ice creams, soft drinks, pizza, beer...
- Fat, especially animal saturated fats (butter, lard, cream cheese, shortening, margarine)
- Red meat with 10%+ fat (rib-eye, lamb, pork, bacon, sausage...)
- Processed high glycemic index carbs (potatoes, French fries, chips, pasta, white breads, tortilla, croissants, donuts, etc.)
- Junk foods with many chemical unpronounceable ingredients, high fructose corn syrup, or hydrogenated fats

If You're Gonna Do The Vegetarian Thing, You Better Get Plenty of...

Complete Protein:
Soy, quinoa, whey, or hemp alone, or combine—

Beans & nuts	Brown rice & nuts
Beans & seeds	Brown rice & seeds
Beans & wheat	Brown rice & wheat
Beans & brown rice	

Per day...you need:
46-56 grams of protein;
2.4 mcg of vitamin B12;
1000-1200 mg of calcium;
10-15 mg of iron (30 if pregnant);
8-11 mg of zinc (13 if pregnant)

Vitamin B12: Supplements, meat (especially beef); in small amounts in eggs & dairy; and in minute amounts in soy, tempeh, miso, & seaweed

Calcium: Soy, bok-choy, broccoli, kale, mustard greens, okra, beans, fruit & vegetables

Vitamin D: 15-30 min. sunlight or supplements

Iron: Soy, nuts, seeds, lentils, kidney beans, chickpeas, black-eyed peas, Swiss chard, tempeh, black beans, prunes, beet greens, tahini, peas, bulgur, raisins, watermelon, millet, bok-choy & kale

Zinc: Dried beans, sea veg, soy, nuts, peas, seeds

Vitamin B2: Yogurt, soy, milk, spinach & Crimini & Shitake mushrooms

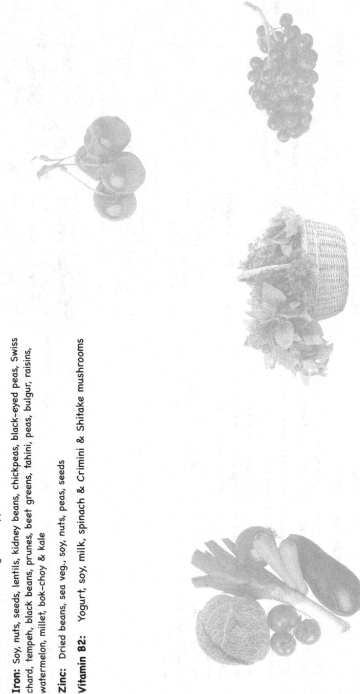

222

Bibliography

Chapter 1

[1] Yogi Bhajan, PhD. *The Aquarian Teacher*. KRI International Teacher Training in Kundalini Yoga as taught by Yogi Bhajan. Santa Cruz, NM: Kundalini Research Institute, 2007.

[2] Kaufman, Ron. "Television Addiction Identification And Self Help Guide." 2005. Jan 2014. <http://www.turnoffyourtv.com/healtheducation/addiction/addiction.html>

[3] Kubey, Robert and Mihaly Csikszentmihalyi. "Television Addiction Is No Mere Metaphor." *Scientific American*. February 2002.

[4] Beattie, Geoffrey Ph.D. and Dr. Heather Shovelton. "Making Thought Visible: The New Psychology of Body Language." *Department of Psychology, The University of Manchester*. Manchester, UK. 2003.

[5] "Boredom." Wikipedia. Dec. 2013. Jan. 2014. <http://en.wikipedia.org/wiki/Boredom>

Chapter 2

[1] "Benefits of Sleep." Division of Sleep Medicine at Harvard Medical School. Publication date unknown. Jan. 2014. <http://healthysleep.med.harvard.edu/healthy/matters/benefits-of-sleep>

[2] Balch, James F. MD, and Stengler, Mark ND. *Prescriptions For Natural Cures*. Put out by The Vitamin Shoppe. Hoboken, NJ: John Wiley & Sons, Inc., 2004.

[3] Yogi Bhajan, PhD. *The Aquarian Teacher*. KRI International Teacher Training in Kundalini Yoga as taught by Yogi Bhajan. Santa Cruz, NM: Kundalini Research Institute, 2007.

[4] Castleman, Michael. *The New Healing Herbs*. New York, NY: Rodale, Inc., 2009.

Chapter 3

[1] "Benefits Of exercise." *Georgia State University*. Publication date unknown. Jan 2014. <http://www2.gsu.edu/~wwwfit/benefits.html>

[2] Weir, Kirsten. "The Exercise Effect." *American Psychology Association*. Printed version: December 2011, Vol. 42, No. 11, page 48. Dec 2011. Jan 2014. http://www.apa.org/monitor/2011/12/exercise.aspx

[3] Reynolds, Gretchen. "When Exercise Is Too Much Of A Good Thing." *New York Times*. Mar. 2011. Jan 2014. <http://well.blogs.nytimes.com/2011/03/09/when-exercise-is-too-much-of-a-good-thing/>

[4] "Exercise In Depth Report." *New York Times*. 2008. Jan. 2014. <http://health.nytimes.com/health/guides/specialtopic/physical-activity/print.html>

[5] Laino, Charlene. Reviewed by Chang, Louise MD. "Strenuous Exercise Linked To Memory Loss." *WebMD*. 2009. Jan 2014. <http://www.webmd.com/fitness-exercise/news/20090715/strenuous-exercise-linked-to_memory-loss>

[6] Christiane Northrup, M.D. *Goddesses Never Age*. Carlsbad, CA: Hay House, Inc., 2015.

Chapter 4

1. Wade, Nicholas. "Your Body Is Younger Than You Think." New York Times. Aug. 2005. Jan 2014. <http://www.nytimes.com/2005/08/02/science/02cell.html?pagewanted=all>

2. Weil, Andrew, MD. *Eating Well For Optimum Health.* New York, NY: Random House Inc., 2000.

3. Thibodeau, Gary A. and Patton, Kevin T. *Anatomy & Physiology.* Fifth edition. St. Louise, Missouri: Mosby publishing, 2003.

4. Weil, Andrew, MD. "Q & A Library - Conjugated Linoleic Acid for Weight Loss?" *Dr. Weil's website.* Jul. 2006. Jan 2014. <http://www.drweil.com/drw/u/id/QAA400002>

5. "L-Carnitine." University of Maryland Medical Center. Jul. 2013. Jan 2014. <http://www.umm.edu/altmed/articles/carnitine-l-000291.htm>

6. Weil, Andrew, MD. "Q & A Library - The Acid, Alkaline Diet: Eating to Protect Bones?" Feb. 2011. Jan. 2014. <http://www.drweil.com/drw/u/QAA400883/The-Acid-Alkaline-Diet-Eating-to-Protect-Bones.html>

7. Loux, Renée. *The Balanced Plate.* New York, NY: Rodale Inc., 2006.

Chapter 5

1. "Overweight And Obesity In The U.S." Food Research and Addiction Center. Sources sited within the article are: Ogden, C. L., Carroll, M. D., Kit, B.K., & Flegal, K. M. (2012). Prevalence of obesity and trends in body mass index among U.S. children and adolescents, 1999-2010. *Journal of the American Medical Association*, 307(5), 483-490. Date of article publication unknown. Jan 2014. <http://frac.org/initiatives/hunger-and-obesity/obesity-in-the-us/>

2. Little, Elaine, LCDR. "Fit For Duty... Fit For Life – Drinking Water Week May 6-12, 2007." *U.S. Public Health Service Commissioned Corps.* May 2007. Jan. 2014. <http://www.care2.com/greenliving/thirsty.html>

3. Turner, Natasha, ND. "Best Times To Eat For Weight Loss." *Women's Health.* April 18 2012. Jan 2014. <http://www.womenshealthmag.com/weight-loss/best-time-to-eat>

4. Matthews, Susan E. "When To Eat To Lose Weight." *Live Science.* Nov. 30, 2012. Jan. 2014. <http://www.myhealthnewsdaily.com/2892-eat-meals.html>

5. Weil, Andrew, MD. *Eating Well For Optimum Health.* New York, NY: Random House Inc., 2000.

6. McDowell, Dimity. "Fill 'Er Up." *Runner's World.* Sep. 27 2011. Jan. 2014. <http://www.runnersworld.com/nutrition-runners/fill-er?page=single>

7. Weil, Andrew, MD. "Q & A Library – Is Liver Cleansing Dangerous?" *Dr. Andrew Weil's website.* July 2004. Jan. 2014. < http://www.drweil.com/drw/u/id/QAA326652>

8. Scott, Jennifer R. "How To Calculate Your Caloric Needs And Lose Weight." *About.com.* Nov. 12, 2013. Jan. 2014. <http://weightloss.about.com/od/eatsmart/a/blcalintake.htm>

9. Thibodeau, Gary A. and Patton, Kevin T. *Anatomy & Physiology.* Fifth edition. St. Louise, Missouri: Mosby publishing, 2003.

10. "Can Eating Fruit And Vegetables Help People To Manage Their Weight?" *National Center for Chronic Disease Prevention and Health Promotion Division of Nutrition and Physical Activity.* Date of publication unknown. Jan. 2014. <http://www.cdc.gov/nccdphp/dnpa/nutrition/pdf/rtp_practitioner_10_07.pdf>

11. Bell EA, Castellanos VH, Pelkman CL, Thorwart ML, Rolls BJ. *Energy density of foods affects energy intake in normal-weight women.* Am J Clin Nutr 1998;67:412-20.

12. Duncan KH, Bacon JA, Weinsier RL. *The effects of high and low energy density diets on satiety, energy intake, and eating time of obese and no obese subjects.* Am J Clin Nutr 1983;37:763-7.

13. Rolls BJ, Bell EA, Waugh BA. *Increasing the volume of a food by incorporating air affects satiety in men.* Am J Clin Nutr 2000;72:361- 8.

14. Rolls BJ, Bell EA, Thorwart ML. *Water incorporated into a food but not served with a food decreases energy intake in lean women.* Am J Clin Nutr 1999;70:448-55.

15. "Leptin." *Wikipedia.* Dec. 2013. Jan. 2014. <http://en.wikipedia.org/wiki/Leptin>

16 Lalonde, Bethany. "How To Raise Leptin Levels." *Living Strong.* Oct 21, 2013. Jan 2014. <http://www.livestrong.com/article/276188-how-to-raise-leptin-levels/>

17 O'connor, Anahad. "The Claim: Your Stomach Shrinks When You Eat Less." *New York Times.* Dec. 21, 2009. Jan 2014. <http://www.nytimes.com/2009/12/22/health/22real.html?_r=0>

18 "The Weight-Loss Secret You've Never Heard." *Shape.* May 2013. Apr 2015. <*http://www.shape.com/weight-loss/weight-loss-strategies/weight-loss-secret-youve-never-heard*>

19 "The top 9 Herbs for Liver Cleansing." *G.H.C. – Global Healing Center.* Aug 2013. Apr 2015. < http://www.globalhealingcenter.com/natural-health/top-9-herbs-for-liver-cleansing/>

20 "14 Foods The Cleanse The Liver." *G.H.C. – Global Healing Center.* Feb 2015. Apr 2015. < http://www.globalhealingcenter.com/natural-health/liver-cleanse-foods/>

21 "Simple Dietary Changes That Can Help Your Thyroid Naturally." *Women To Women.* 2015. Apr 2015. < https://www.womentowomen.com/thyroid-health/simple-dietary-changes-that-can-help-your-thyroid-naturally/>

22 "Weight Loss and Adrenal Stress." *Women to Women.* 2015. Apr 2015. https://www.womentowomen.com/healthy-weight/weight-loss-and-adrenal-stress-2/

23 "Top 10 Superfoods To Reduce Belly Fat." *To 10 Home Remedies.* Pub date unknown. Apr 2015. < http://www.top10homeremedies.com/superfoods/top-10-superfoods-reduce-belly-fat.html>

24 "Artificial Sweeteners May Damage Diet Efforts." *WebMD.* Jun. 30, 2004. Jan. 2014. <http://www.webmd.com/diet/news/20040630/artificial-sweeteners-damage-diet-efforts>

25 Appleton, Nancy, PhD, and Jacobs G.N. "141 Reasons Sugar Ruins Your Health." *Nancy Appleton Books Health Club.* Publication date unknown. Jan. 2014. <http://nancyappleton.com/141-reasons-sugar-ruins-your-health/>

26 Weil, Andrew, MD. *Eating Well For Optimum Health.* New York, NY: Random House Inc., 2000.

27 "Dietary Reference Intakes – Macronutrients." (page 4, remark a.) Institute of Medicine. 2005. Apr 2015. <https://www.iom.edu/~/media/Files/Activity%20Files/Nutrition/DRIs/DRI_Macronutrients.pdf>

28 "Guilt Bad For Your Health." *BBC News.* April 16, 2000. Jan 2014. <http://news.bbc.co.uk/2/hi/health/713375.stm>

Appendix B:

1 Atkinson, Kaye Foster-Powell, and Jennie C. Brand-Miller. "Glycemic index (GI) and glycemic load (GL) values determined in subjects with normal glucose tolerance." *Diabetes Care, Vol. 31, number 12, pages 2281-2283.* Dec 2008. Feb 2014. <http://care.diabetesjournals.org/content/suppl/2008/09/18/dc08-1239.DC1/TableA1_1.pdf>

2 "Glycemic Index and Glycemic Load for 100+ Foods." *Harvard Health Publications, Harvard Medical School.* Publication date unknown. Feb 2014. <http://www.health.harvard.edu/newsweek/Glycemic_index_and_glycemic_load_for_100_foods.htm>

3 "Glycemic Index Food Chart." *South Beach Diet Plan For Beginners.* 2012. Feb 2014. <http://www.southbeach-diet-plan.com/glycemicfoodchart.htm>

4 "Self Nutrition Data." *NutritionData.* 2014. Feb 2014. <http://nutritiondata.self.com/>

Printed in the United States
By Bookmasters